Practical Law for Arts Administrators

Charles Arnold-Baker

ISBN 0 903931 58 3
ISSN 0142 5218

CITY ARTS SERIES
General Editor: John Pick

PRACTICAL LAW FOR ARTS ADMINISTRATORS
John Offord (Publications) Ltd.
P.O. Box 64, Eastbourne, East Sussex.

Printed by Cooper Harvey Ltd.

Introduction

The plan of this book (discernible from the Table of Main Subjects) is to outline the public institutions, and then the persons who use them, the documents and property with which those persons are concerned and the capital which they may have to manage or borrow. Next came the major sources of conflict, then the major means of agreement and finally the curious hybrid system of jurisprudence surrounding questions of employment. The last block of paragraphs is concerned with the restriction of the powers of Trustees to invest money.

A book for practical arts administrators cannot be comprehensive or it would be unusably long, and it cannot be very short without being misleading. I have, therefore, tried to amplify the substance by diagrams, and to distinguish imaginary examples in *italics* from the facts of decided cases. I have omitted almost all case names because lawyers will know them and lay arts administrators will not want them.

I am grateful to Dr. John Pick of The City University for the many improvements which he has suggested, and to Mrs. Jane Purkiss for typing a troublesome manuscript. Mistakes and omissions are mine.

Charles Arnold-Baker

Contents

Who Does What

Distinction between Civil and Criminal Law

1   Law, and consequently law courts, may be distinguished into civil and criminal. Civil law treats of the (relatively) peaceful relationships between persons (e.g. marriage, contracts, money, trusts), and private conflicts (e.g. trespass, nuisance, libel) and also relationships between persons and things (e.g. ownership, copyrights). Criminal law is concerned with those matters which the state forbids. In general, the rules, whether civil or criminal, are obeyed by most people most of the time; the courts are brought into action only when something goes wrong.

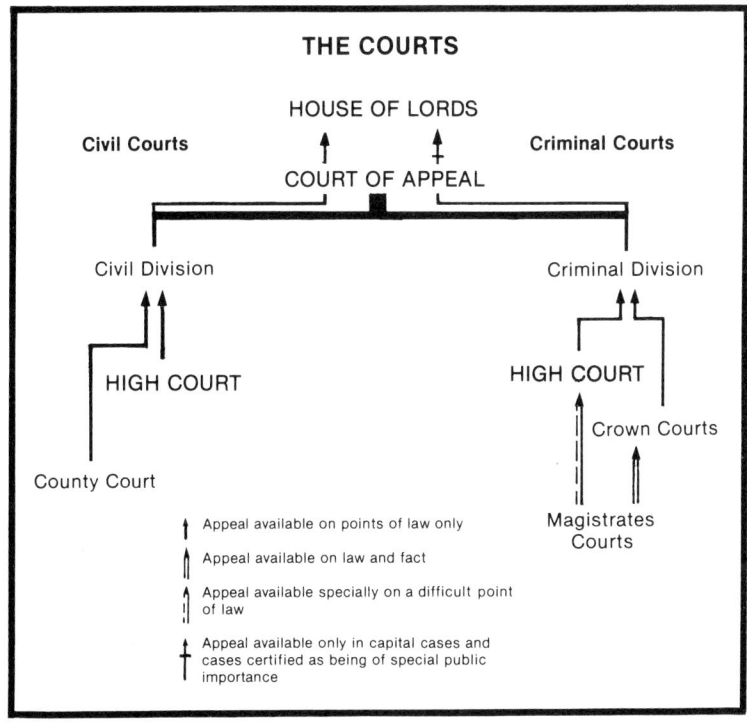

Peculiarities of Courts

2 English courts never take an initiative. They act only when called upon to act by somebody (called the plaintiff in civil proceedings or a prosecutor in criminal proceedings) outside themselves. Consistently with this, they do not act as investigators, but listen to evidence and argument brought by opposing sides. Their procedure is not inquisitorial but adversarial.

3 A civil court resolves a quarrel between party and party by awarding or refusing *compensation* (called damages) or by ordering or refusing to order a defendant to do or refrain from doing something (injunction). A criminal court, once a criminal act has been sufficiently proved, imposes *punishment* which may consist of a fine, imprisonment, community service order or other purely punitive measure.

4 It will be seen that the distinction between the two jurisdictions, is, as a matter of necessity, not clear cut. Some "anti-social" acts are both civil and criminal. A burglar may be sent to prison for stealing my silver (criminal) but I want my silver back (civil). A mugger may be put on probation for hitting me on the head (criminal), but I want compensation for the injury (civil). There are means for avoiding duplication of proceedings in many, but not all, cases.

5 Since a civil court is obliged to settle any quarrel brought before it, it must accept the parties' own definition of the nature of the quarrel between them and use the evidence made available by them, and it has to give judgement based upon the balance of that evidence. A criminal court uses the legal definition of a crime, requires the prosecutor to prove the commission of that crime beyond reasonable doubt, and is, therefore, always biased in favour of the defendant.

Law and Fact

6 In both jurisdictions there is a strong distinction between law and fact. Originally most courts consisted of a professional judge whose legal rulings were conclusive, and a jury of twelve amateurs, assembled for the occasion, whose factual findings were equally conclusive. To make sure that the twelve amateurs were not influenced by prejudice or irrelevance, rules of procedure and evidence were devised to ensure that they knew nothing about the case save what they ought to know. Even when, as in most modern cases, the same person or persons act as judge and jury this dis-

tinction is carefully maintained. It is of the highest practical importance because, save in the case of appeals from magistrates courts, an appeal from a lower court to a higher can only exceptionally raise a point of fact, and must be confined to points of law.

Legal Personnel

Solicitors

7 The general practitioners of the law are the *solicitors* and it is they with whom the ordinary person deals. There are about 30,000 of them, mostly organised in partnerships with their clerks, secretaries and typists. Their training consists partly of law and partly of accountancy, and a period of apprenticeship (called articles). The bulk of their work is conveyancing (the investigation and transfer of the possession of land) and company business, with, in the more disorderly big cities some minor criminal practice. Though solicitors appear as advocates in the many courts below High Court level, court work does not, speaking generally, bulk large in most solicitors' practices. They are paid by their clients mostly on the basis of scales reflecting a percentage of the value of a transaction.[1] An increasing number of solicitors' firms have foreign branches or correspondents.

8 Particulars of solicitors and their firms will be found in the annual "Calendar of the Law Society".

Commissioners for Oaths and Notaries

9 A few solicitors in any given area are *commissioners for oaths*, before whom persons have to make oath in any case where a document (e.g. an oath of allegiance or a statutory declaration)* has to be sworn. They charge a small fee per oath. A *notary public* is really a slightly grander and rarer commissioner for oaths who acts as a publicly recognised witness, especially in international transactions, such as protests to the condition of a ship's cargo or foreign powers of attorney. Until lately a dying species, the EEC is bringing the English notary public back into life.

Barristers

10 The specialists of the law are the 4000-odd *barristers* (otherwise called counsel), who are permitted to deal with lay clients only

---

[1] See, however, "Costs" paragraphs 38-40.

through a solicitor. They are not allowed to have partnerships with each other or with solicitors. Their five year training consists of theoretical and procedural law and includes practical exercises and a period of apprenticeship (called pupillage) after qualification. The bulk of a barrister's work, which is mostly related to court appearances, consists of legal research into any problem which a solicitor may put to him, and the drafting of opinions embodying such research. A junior barrister (i.e. one who is not a QC) also drafts most of the documents needed for civil proceedings in the High Court. Barristers alone may appear as advocates there and above. They may, and often do, appear at lower levels. In real life a junior spends more time on paper work and research than in court. A QC (Queen's Counsel) is forbidden to do some kinds of paper work, and spends more of his time in court where he commands higher fees than a junior. A QC must have been in practice for at least 10 years. Barristers charge fees varying with their reputation or rank, the nature of the work and the length of a case. These fees are negotiated through their clerks and paid by the solicitor, who charges the lay client for them as an expense. Particulars of all barristers are contained in the annual "Bar List".

Magistrates

11 In magistrates' courts, cases are heard before two or more part-time Justices of the Peace (JPs) or a single stipendiary magistrate. JPs are unpaid laymen appointed by the Lord Chancellor on the recommendation of the Lord Lieutenant. Stipendiaries are barristers or solicitors paid full-time, and are found only in large urban areas.

Judges

12 Recorders, circuit, and High Court judges must have been barristers. Solicitors may become County Court judges. It is rare for a judge below the High Court to be promoted to it, but promotion from the High Court upwards is normal. A High Court judge is known as Mr Justice So-and-so; after promotion to the Court of Appeal as Lord Justice So-and-so and on promotion to the Lords as Lord Something-or-other.

Masters and Registrars

13 Civil courts include an important body of "sub-judges" called Masters in the Queen's Bench and Chancery Divisions, and

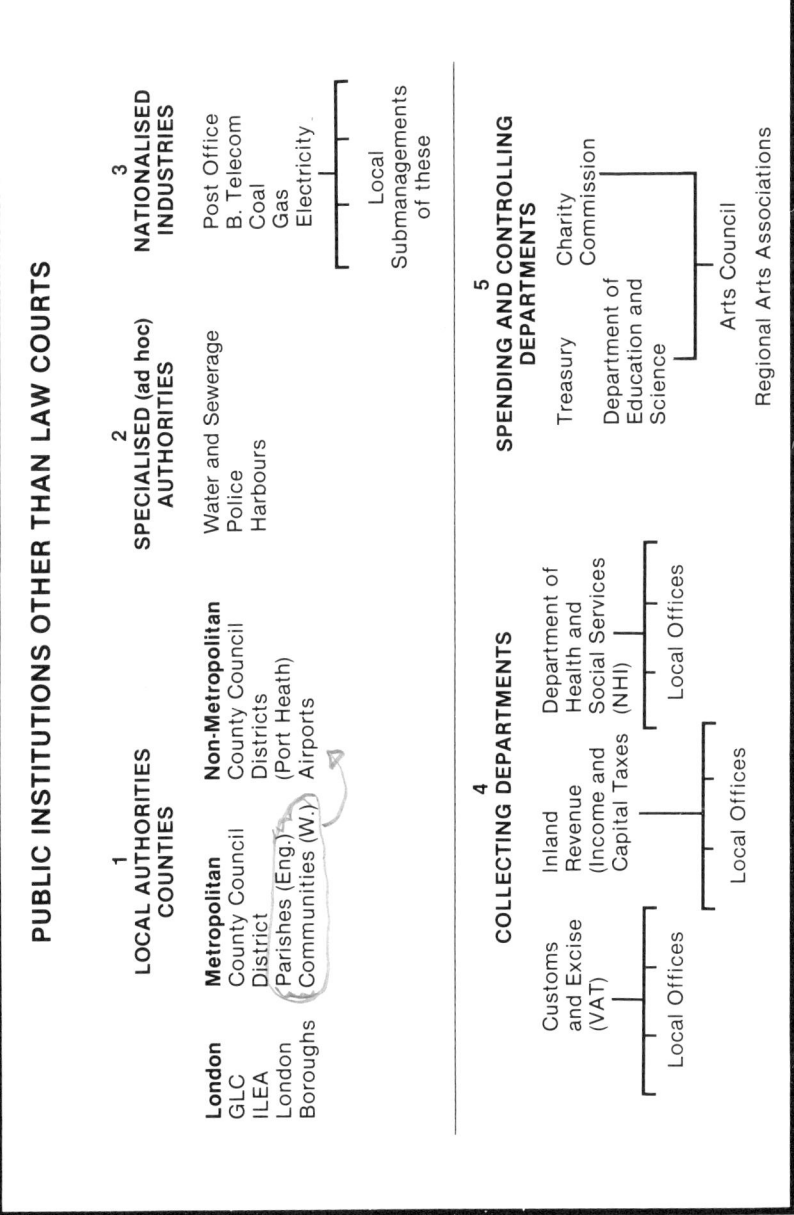

PUBLIC INSTITUTIONS OTHER THAN LAW COURTS

1
LOCAL AUTHORITIES COUNTIES

Metropolitan
County Council
District
Parishes (Eng.)
Communities (W.)

Non-Metropolitan
County Council
Districts
(Port Heath)
Airports

London
GLC
ILEA
London
Boroughs

2
SPECIALISED (ad hoc) AUTHORITIES

Water and Sewerage
Police
Harbours

3
NATIONALISED INDUSTRIES

Post Office
B. Telecom
Coal
Gas
Electricity

Local
Submanagements
of these

4
COLLECTING DEPARTMENTS

Customs
and Excise
(VAT)

Local Offices

Inland
Revenue
(Income and
Capital Taxes)

Local Offices

Department of
Health and
Social Services
(NHI)

Local Offices

5
SPENDING AND CONTROLLING DEPARTMENTS

Treasury

Charity
Commission

Department of
Education and
Science

Arts Council

Regional Arts Associations

Registrars in other courts. They decide the issues ancillary to the main business of a trial, such as (beforehand) where it is to take place, or (afterwards) what costs should be paid, or how much maintenance a divorced husband should pay.

Tribunals and Inquiries

14 There are said to be over 2000 specialist tribunals besides the courts, and in addition many fundamentally administrative functions are performed using a judicial or apparently judicial method. The most important cases are liquor licencing, where a committee of a local authority sits in public as a court; and planning appeals heard by an inspector of the Department of the Environment. Hearings before these bodies look deceptively like trials in court, but often, as in planning, the tribunal is eliciting facts to supplement information already known to the department which makes the decision; strict court procedure is seldom maintained, and the rules of evidence are significantly relaxed.

The Public Institutions

The Six Groups

15 English public institutions of interest to the arts may be considered in six groups, viz:-

i) LAW

The courts of law which state what the law is, enforce it and are responsible **to** the law. These have no discretion and no power of initiative (see paragraphs 1-14 above).

ii) LOCAL BODIES

The locally elected bodies which are governed **by** law, but are responsible to those who elected them, and are supervised by ministers. Within the limits (sometimes strict) of their legal powers, they may do, and take initiatives, as they please as long as they please their electors.

iii) NATIONAL BODIES WITH LOCAL OFFICES

Specialist authorities locally appointed, whose work is confined to a single complex of services, mostly of a routine character.

iv) NATIONALISED INDUSTRIES AND THEIR LOCAL
SUB-MANAGEMENTS
These are not, strictly speaking, locally responsible.

v) GOVERNMENT DEPARTMENTS
With local branch offices responsible to Headquarters.

vi) CENTRALISED NATIONAL BODIES
Government departments and agencies without local offices.

Numbers ii), iii) and iv) are influenced rather than controlled by, government departments through a government control of capital expenditure. The daily activities (as opposed to long term policies) of iii) and iv) cannot be questioned in partliament; those of v) and vi) can.

The Financial Nexus

16 From the point of view of the non-public arts administrator, the relationships are mostly (but not exclusively) concerned with the flow of money. *Rates* are collected to finance groups (ii) and (iii). *Charges* are made by group (iv) in return for services. *VAT* is paid to the Customs and Excise, *Income* and *Capital taxes* to the Inland Revenue, *National Health Insurance* to the Department of Health and Social Security. Conversely *Grants* may be paid out by the Arts Council, Regional Arts Associations, and all the local authorities; the Arts Council grants, though calculated and paid in advance, are meant to guarantee against losses, save in the case of the so-called Project Grants which, as pump-priming operations, may be calculated without initial reference to possible income. *Tax Exemptions* may be secured by Charities against the Inland Revenue, and *Exemptions* or *Zero Ratings* from the Customs and Excise. *Mandatory and Discretionary Rate Reductions* may sometimes be secured in respect of the activities of groups (i) and (ii).

The non-public administrator will, therefore, wish to arrange affairs so as to secure the greatest feasible share of public money, while rendering his employer liable for the least possible amount of rates and taxes. In practice the sum of the grants and concessions will seldom cover the long term cost of the operations, and it will be necessary to develop other resorts through patronage, appeals, voluntary help or commercial enterprise, sponsorship and good capital management.

Secondary Institutions

17 An already complex situation is rendered even more complex by the existence of public and quasi-public arts institutions. Some of these, like the British Museum, resemble nationalised industries in that they have special statutory managements and are influenced financially by the government. Others, such as the Fitzwilliam Museum at Cambridge or the Playhouse Theatre at Oxford, belong to Universities, and there are many, such as the Countryside Museum at Oakham, the Walker Art Gallery at Newcastle, the Belgrade Theatre at Coventry or the Royal Festival Hall in London, belonging to local authorities. Then there is a large miscellaneous group owned by public or charitable trusts. These vary from the modest Tolzey at Burford to Sir John Soane's curious Museum in Lincoln's Inn Fields. Lastly, there exist many bodies with some, not always marginal, interest in the arts. These are not easy to categorise, but they include arts and arts administration faculties at universities and polytechnics, City livery companies such as the Goldsmiths and the Clothworkers, the Textile Department at Bradford University, the British Film Institute, and foundations such as Carnegie, Gulbenkian and Leverhulme.

18 Most of these are important for their personnel, their contacts, their ideas or the, often valuable, advice which they can give; only a few disburse money.

Going to Law

Courts and their Expense

19 In a private dispute, the amount involved is obviously important. The cheapest form is the, so called, Small Claims Court, in the rare cases where there is one. This deals with money claims up to £350. It is really a form of arbitration*. Those concerned are volunteers and the court cannot operate unless the respondent (defendant) agrees in advance to be bound by the court's decision. The next cheapest, especially for a small monetary claim, is the County

Court (up to £5000).[1] Here judgement may be expeditious, but enforcing it (supposing the other side is reluctant to pay) can be elaborate and tiresome. As many arts organisations have a turnover of less than £5000 a year, this will usually be the court for them. The most expensive is the High Court (unlimited) but it is also the most reliable. Arbitration, save in some highly specialised issue, such as metal-fatigue or maritime salvage, is seldom as cheap as one hopes; the parties have to pay the arbitrator, as well as their own costs.

Has the Other Side any Money?

20 A vital early consideration is the financial status of the defendant. Is he, as lawyers say, worth powder and shot? It is useless to get judgement against a person with no money, for you cannot take money which is not there. A secondary consideration is whether (as in a motor accident) your injury is covered by his insurance.

When to Go to a Solicitor

21 A private individual is always entitled to conduct his *own* legal affairs including his *own* case in court. There is a negative side to this proposition. He cannot conduct anyone else's case, therefore he cannot act for trustees, even if they include himself, or for a corporation (such as a private company) which is a body different from himself. In routine matters, such as *selling* a house, it is possible, especially where the title is registered, to do it oneself, and some stationers sell kits of instructions on how to do it. Buying property is more dangerous and difficult, because of the searches required to ensure that the place can lawfully serve the purchaser's purpose.

22 Where court proceedings seem likely, the prospective litigant, having taken notice of the lawyer's proverb "he who is his own advocate has a fool for a client", should consider firstly whether the dispute is irreconcilable. Thus, if he is on the defending side, does his conscience or sense of logic tell him that the claim or charge is without foundation or bound to fail and should be resisted? If he is on the active side, does that *same* sense of logic tell him that he ought to win? If the answer in either case is "No", he should attempt a compromise or reconciliation. If, on the other

---

[1] There is a good HMSO pamphlet on *Small Claims in the County Court.*

hand, the anwers are "Yes", he may think it worth while to go to a solicitor to force a better settlement. Suppose, however, that, on those answers (either "yes" or "no") he decides not to go to a solicitor, he should next consider if he is feeling strongly emotional about the matter. If he is, he may be wise to change his mind and go nevertheless. Indignation always hinders argument.

Preparing to see and seeing a solicitor

23 The solicitor will wish to know whether his new client is serious. Initially, to test his story, he may seem slightly hostile. This is not a bad sign.

24 To save time and money (for all these things will be needed sooner or later), the client should

    a) think out his story beforehand; many people are otherwise incoherent;

    b) try to define what he wants; it is surprising how difficult angry people find this;

    c) bring with him the names and addresses of all possible witnesses;

    d) bring with him any documents or exhibits or photographs of exhibits which seem relevant. If he hands them over, he should ask for a detailed receipt, and, better still, obtain Xerox's, especially if they are formal documents such as leases or receipts.

Proof of Evidence

25 In a large firm, once the solicitor has accepted the case, the client will be handed over, with luck then and there, to a statement taker who will extract everything relevant to which the client can speak of his own knowledge. This will, in due course, be typed out and sent to the client. It is known as a "proof" and begins:

"Julian Snodgrass of 53 Acacia Settlement, Bloggsville, will say:"

It serves as the foundation upon which the solicitor will build the proceedings, and it will, with or without amendments, form part of the proceedings, and it will, with or without amendments, form part of a barrister's brief. When, or if, the case approaches a hearing it will also, quite often, throw up ideas about other witnesses and other documents which may be needed.

The Solicitor's Activities

26 There will now follow a period of some length during which the solicitor must go through all the motions necessary to bring the matter to trial. These may be divided into two, often overlapping, groups: preparation of one's own case, and dealings with the other side. The former will include tracing witnesses (who may be ill, on holiday, abroad or simply bad at answering letters), taking statements, finding and copying documents and bank statements, taking or obtaining photographs, having translations made, and so forth.

The Procedural Steps

27 The latter includes a series of procedural steps, whose ultimate purpose is to ensure that each side and the court know the issue or issues which will have to be tried, and that there are no practical obstacles to such trial. The total number of steps may be as high as forty before ever the hearing is reached. The plaintiff must serve on the defendant a Writ and Statement of Claim showing that he intends to move the court and why. The defendant will reply with a Defence and perhaps a Counter-claim. The plaintiff may then put in an Answer to the Defence and will wish to deliver a Reply to the Counter-claim. Each side may find that one of these documents is insufficiently precise and may demand Further and Better Particulars, which have to be drafted and handed over.

Discovery

28 The next stage is called Discovery. The parties' solicitors exchange lists of relevant documents known to them or in their possession, distinguishing between those which they will produce without question and those which they object to producing, and, if there is a dispute, it will be necessary to apply to the Master or Registrar for a decision. In certain (rare) instances, interrogatories may, with the Master's leave, also be administered. Interrogatories are designed to elicit information peculiarly within one side's knowledge, yet essential to the fair presentation of the other side's case.

The Evaded Timetable

29 The time between each step outlined above is regulated by a timetable, but solicitors can always ask their opposite numbers for

more time and, if refused, can apply to the Master. Correspondence about time often forms a large part of the papers in any action. The clients pay for such letters, about which they are never consulted, and the habitual allowance of more time is a major element in the law's delays. This may work injuctices; for witnesses die or forget; impecunious plaintiffs may be kept out of their money and lay clients may have their lives considerably disorganised. A client can, however, do something to help. He can make sure that his solicitor has all the material at the very beginning; he can, at the start, ask for a reasoned estimate of the time before a case is likely to be heard, and he can, without being too interfering, inquire after progress.

Summons for Directions

30 The papers exchanged between the parties are called the Pleadings, and the stage has now been reached when the Pleadings are said to be closed, and the issues to be tried defined. It now becomes necessary to settle the administration of the trial (or hearing) itself; that is to say, to decide where it is to be held (*London? Manchester?*), whether there is to be a jury (usually No, save in libel), how many expert witnesses are to be called, and so forth. This is done by a Summons for Directions, issued by the plaintiff's solicitors to all the other parties requiring them to appear before a Master, who makes agreed decisions, or decides himself if there is disagreement.

Counsel

31 It will be remembered that Junior Counsel's work is much concerned with drafting the papers and opinions required in the preparations so far. Once instructed by solicitors in the case, he will continue to be employed in it. He will probably be briefed to appear on the Summons for Directions - a proceeding which can last only a few minutes.

Setting Down

32 After Directions the solicitors will make sure that they are ready to go to trial, that all their witnesses are available, all the documents copied, etc. and the plaintiff's solicitors will then set down the case for hearing. This puts it, so to speak, in the queue and there is nothing to be done but wait till the cases ahead have been disposed of. The length of the waiting period is unpredictable: some of the

cases in the queue may take longer than expected, others may be settled out of court before or during the hearing, or something may go wrong like a judge falling ill or a witness being intimidated. In due course the case will appear in the Warned List and everybody gathers together for the great day.

Procedure at a trial

33 The plaintiff's counsel begins briefly by explaining the nature of the case. The plaintiff is then called into the witness box and sworn. He gives his evidence, called Evidence in Chief, in reply to questions from his counsel, but these questions (save on immaterial matters) must *not* lead him (or suggest the answer). When he has finished, counsel for other parties may cross-examine. They *may* ask leading questions, and their object is to test the evidence in chief for consistency, accuracy of recollection or good faith, and to put to him the general nature of the defence so that he has a fair opportunity to deal with it. Finally the plaintiff may be re-examined by his own counsel, but only to clear up ambiguities or misunderstandings which may have arisen during cross examination.

34 The plaintiff's other witnesses come next, are called in order, and treated in the same way.

35 As documents and exhibits must be sworn to, they will be produced by witnesses during their evidence in chief as appropriate.

36 When all the plaintiff's evidence has been given, it is the defendant's turn. His counsel may now submit that there is no case to answer - a proposition usually requiring a long analytical speech - or more likely, he may, in a complicated case, shortly summarise the nature of the defence in so far as cross examinations have not made it obvious. More likely still, he will, without delay, call his witnesses, beginning with the defendant; and they will be treated in the same way as the plaintiff and his witnesses.

37 Evidence for the defence having been completed, counsel make their final speeches. If there is a jury, the judge sums up and puts the points which the jury has to decide. The jury retires and, after a while, returns with its verdict. If, as is most probable, there is no

jury, the judge delivers a reasoned judgement showing how he reached his conclusions on the law and the facts. Judgement is finally entered for the plaintiff or for the defendant, as the case may be, with or without costs.

Costs and Payment into Court

38 As a matter of practice (but not law) the losing side will be ordered to pay the winner's costs, but the actual amount payable almost never covers the amount expended. There are three main reasons for this. Firstly, at any stage before the hearing, the defendant may pay a sum of money into court and tell the plaintiff. If the plaintiff takes it out of court, that is the end of the case, but if he decides to go on, he will be refused costs incurred after payment in, unless he not only wins but is awarded damages exceeding the payment. To prevent prejudice, the sum paid into court is not disclosed to the judge until after judgment. Secondly, a party normally awarded costs may be penalised if he has behaved unreasonably, for example by insisting that the obvious should be proved by witnesses when he could have admitted it without harm to his case. Thirdly, and most important, the loser can only be made to pay the amounts permitted "on taxation".

"Taxation"

39 Taxation (the word is used in the biblical sense of enumeration) takes place before a Master, or County Court Registrar, who has to make sure that the winner does not make unreasonable demands. In small claims before the County Court, the cost of a solicitor is seldom allowed at all. Otherwise, his solicitor produces his bills, the loser's solicitor objects to items and the Master decides. These bills, which may include witnesses' air fares, hotel bills, secretarial and copying, will usually be cut down on the basis of current market experience. A party who chooses to accommodate a motor mechanic witness at the Ritz will probably find that only the sums appropriate to a more ordinary hotel will be allowed.

The Expense of a Case

40 Inflation makes it impracticable to name, in a book, a figure which will become out of date since it was written. The foregoing description will, however, indicate the main headings in the expense of a case, viz:-

i.   Court Fees
ii. Solicitors Charges
iii Secretarial and Copying
iv. Witness Expenses
v.   Expert Witness Fees
vi. Barrister's Fees

In a case lasting a day, with only one counsel, items i to v will, generally, amount to about 75% of the total. If it lasts a week the expense will have doubled, items i to v constituting about 50%. In a county court one-day action expenses of both sides together may make proceedings uneconomic unless the sum at issue exceeds three months average salary, for they will amount to about two weeks-worth.

Enforcing Judgments

41 A successful plaintiff will want the relief (damages, or an injunction or whatever) which he claimed, plus his costs. A successful defendant will want his costs. Most parties will simply carry out the judgement, but a minority try to postpone or avoid their obligations. Some of these may be in genuine difficulties (e.g. a business which is in turn owed large sums by its customers) or genuinely too poor to pay (in which case they should not have been sued in the first place), but a noticeable and growing proportion are swindlers, and it is the duty of the solicitor to be sufficiently astute or ruthless to ensure that his client gets his award.

42 In theory, judgments are enforced in three ways.

43 In the case of a non-monetary judgment (e.g. an injunction or similar order to do, or to refrain from doing, something, like continuing to pirate his copyright), disobedience may lead to imprisonment for contempt, but only if the plaintiff's solicitor applies for a committal order. This may lead to a prolonged battle if the defendant denies his disobedience or alleges a mistake or leaves the country. The courts are, in any case, reluctant to deprive a person of liberty, and consequently the procedures for enforcing its own orders in this way tend to be dilatory and strewn with procedural obstacles.

44 In the case of the (much commoner) monetary judgments, disobedience may be overcome either by bankruptcy or liquidation

proceedings or by execution (much misused word!). In either event, the solicitor has to set the proceedings specially in motion.

45 Execution involves applying to the court for authority to seize and sell enough of the opponent's property to satisfy the judgment. It can be frustrating. Notice of the application has to be served on him. He may allege that he is too poor (having perhaps transferred his property to his wife or a dummy company) or he may simply disappear. Hence it may become necessary to establish fraudulent transfers, or to trace and sequestrate his property, and problems may arise if others have claims or if some of the property taken (e.g. a TV set) really belongs to someone else such as a hire purchase company. The lower the level of the enforcing court the more attention is paid to the defaulter's means, so that the 'successful'' party may end up with an instalment order for a not very useful periodical amount, upon which his opponent, in due course defaults; whereupon further proceedings may be needed. All these supplementary proceedings incur further costs which also have to be recovered.

46 Bankruptcy or liquidation (of a company) involves a different sort of application. Where the opponent is a commercial business, the mere threat often works wonders, because the proceedings bring the business to an abrupt stop, damage business standing, and put the employees out of work. The first proceedings are also remarkably expeditious. On the other hand, the process, if actually started, brings in all the opponent's other creditors (e.g. the Inland Revenue), who may be owed more money than or have priority over the claimant, with the result that, on the final division of the assets he may get less than he bargained for.

International Complications and Security for Costs[1]

47 Art is increasingly international in its habits: for example, there are travelling theatre companies, orchestras, and exhibitions, and international carriers such as hauliers, air and shipping lines which move them, and there are problems of international copyright and film distribution. The risk of interference by third parties (e.g. strikes and lockouts at ports and aerodromes or local revolutions) or by natural calamities (e.g. Caribbean hurricanes or

---

[1] For litigation insurance see paragraph 50.

Turkish earthquakes) increases. To engage in proceedings with a foreign element may involve special considerations not otherwise present. An intending plaintiff may have to consider whether to sue in England or in some foreign court, and he may, therefore, need to consult solicitors with the appropriate foreign contact. The strength of foreign judicial systems varies as much as their law, and methods of enforcing judgment (e.g. in some African countries) may be sketchy.[1] Secondly, the opponent may have no assets in England, if the proceedings are in England. A defendant can usually get round this difficulty by demanding that the foreign plaintiff shall pay money into court as security for the defendants costs, in case the defence is successful.

Legal Aid

48 The Legal Aid Fund is financed by the government and administered by local committees of the Law Society. An individual (but no one else) who is a party in proceedings (otherwise than for libel or slander) can obtain money to finance his case in the High Court. The amount paid depends on his means, which are assessed by the local office of the Supplementary Benefits Commission. If he has any capital above £2500, he will be expected to contribute it. His other means are called his disposable income, and consist of his earnings less necessary outgoings such as rent, allowances for food, dependents, travelling to work, and so forth. If the disposable income is above a maximum, he will get nothing. If below, the amount of legal aid will depend on the difference between the maximum and the actual disposable income. If the latter is very low, the Fund may pay the total cost. The Fund, conversely, is entitled to a first claim on any costs which he may recover as a result of the proceedings.[2]

49 It will be obvious that Legal Aid puts the very poor (who have the nation at their back) and the very rich (who can afford it) at an overwhelming advantage over individuals in the middle income levels, besides trusts and companies which have to depend on their own resources. Moreover, in cases where a legally aided party loses, the Fund has, unjustly, only a very limited liability for the winner's costs. A public authority, using public money, can

---

[1] An elderly acquaintance of the writer obtained judgement in a North African court against a burly local inhabitant, and learned that he was now authorised to take the money himself.

[2] The details are in the *Legal Aid Handbook*.

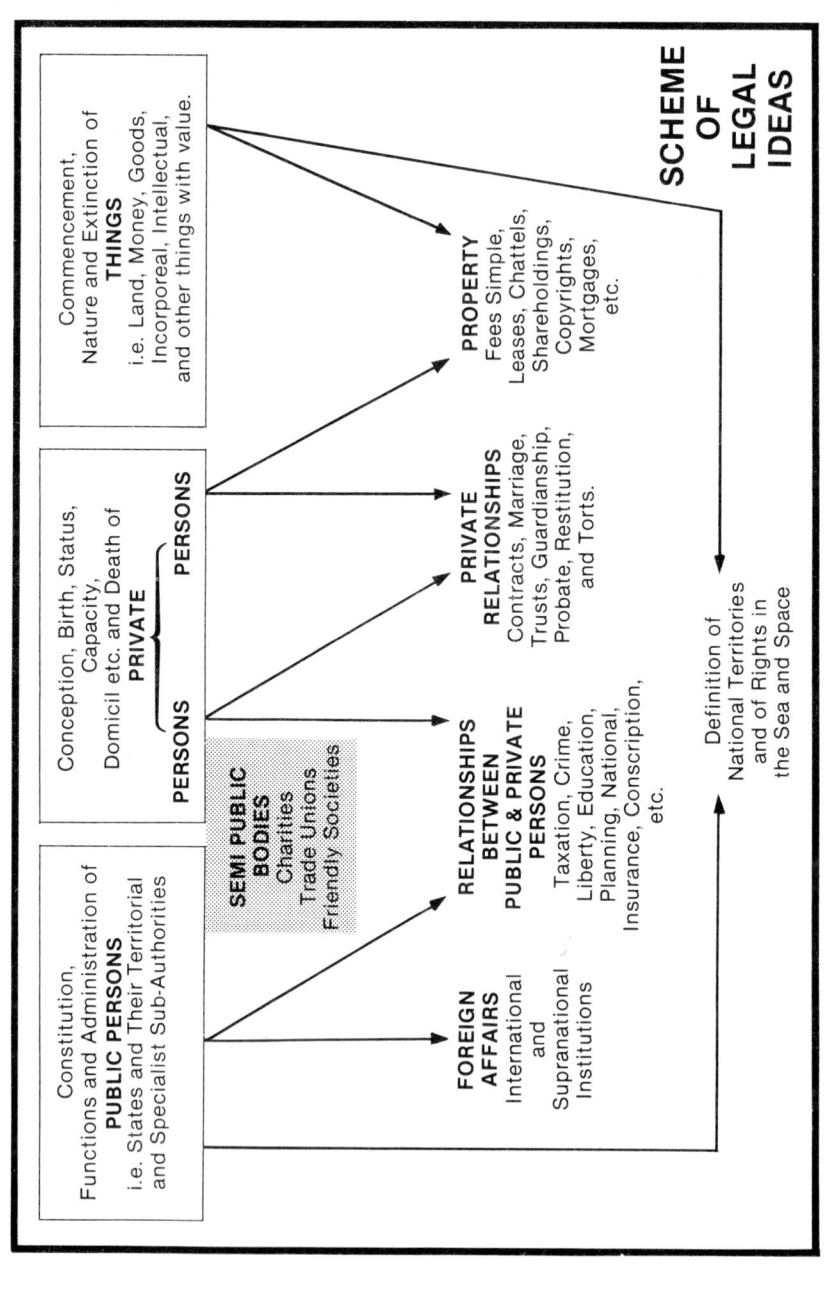

SCHEME
OF
LEGAL
IDEAS

Constitution,
Functions and Administration of
PUBLIC PERSONS
i.e. States and Their Territorial
and Specialist Sub-Authorities

Conception, Birth, Status,
Capacity,
Domicil etc. and Death of
PRIVATE

PERSONS

PERSONS

Commencement,
Nature and Extinction of
THINGS
i.e. Land, Money, Goods,
Incorporeal, Intellectual,
and other things with value.

**SEMI PUBLIC
BODIES**
Charities
Trade Unions
Friendly Societies

**FOREIGN
AFFAIRS**
International
and
Supranational
Institutions

**RELATIONSHIPS
BETWEEN
PUBLIC & PRIVATE
PERSONS**
Taxation, Crime,
Liberty, Education,
Planning, National,
Insurance, Conscription,
etc.

**PRIVATE
RELATIONSHIPS**
Contracts, Marriage,
Trusts, Guardianship,
Probate, Restitution,
and Torts.

PROPERTY
Fees Simple,
Leases, Chattels,
Shareholdings,
Copyrights,
Mortgages,
etc.

Definition of
National Territories
and of Rights in
the Sea and Space

resist a 100% aided plaintiff, also using public money. Har anyone else can.

Need for Insurance

50 It follows from this that anyone involved in activities likely to bring him into dispute, will be wise not only to insure in the usual way, but to make certain that he is well covered against the cost of legal proceedings. He may need cover against damage to instruments, musical scores, or pictures; against accidents on theatre staircases, or stages; against box-office thefts; and so forth.

Legal Persons and Trusts

Natural and Artificial Persons

51 The English Common Law of Personality was always defective. "Persons" are either natural or artificial and only persons can own things. A natural person begins when born alive, has limited rights, legal obligations and capacities which grow in number and importance until it becomes fully fledged on its 18th birthday; it can then do anything that an ordinary human can do, and it continues until abruptly terminated by death. An artificial person is invisible but is created for a purpose, either by the Crown (for example, a university created by charter) or under parliamentary authority (for example, a local authority or a limited company).[1] It can do only those things which serve its purpose, it exists as long as the law permits, even if it has no human members, and is ended by liquidation.

Death or Liquidation

52 This bald summary reveals the need for supplementary arrangements. Both types of person need them for winding up their affairs at extinction or death. The property must be got in, the debts paid, and then the balances passed to those entitled to them. Where the natural person has left a will, this is done by his *executors* who will, as far as possible, carry out the terms of the will. If he leaves no will, *an administrator* is appointed to distribute

---

[1] For company formation see paragraph 97.

the balances, in accordance with rules of law, to relatives, if any. These functions are carried out in the case of an artificial person (except a public authority) by a *liquidator*, who will distribute the balances in accordance with the charter, or the memorandum and articles of the company or otherwise as the law directs.

It is the duty of an executor, administrator, liquidator or trustee in bankruptcy to secure the best possible price for anything which he deems it necessary to sell.

Agents

53 Persons, however, wish during their life or existence to do many things for which this simple scheme is too restricted. It may be necessary to act at a distance from the office or without someone's personal presence (e.g. arranging a concert in Rio de Janeiro), or to have things done in which a specialist is needed (e.g. hiring Rajput miniatures for an English exhibition). In such cases the person wishing to act (*the principal*) may employ an *agent* who is endowed with such powers to act on the principal's behalf as the principal *can* and *may in fact*, confer. The agent is, so to speak, the principal's local other self, within the limits of his authority. It follows that, in general, he cannot have more authority than the principal possesses (a matter of importance where minors are concerned) nor must he depart outside the scope of his authority.[1] The importance of making the limits of an agent's - or indeed an employee's - authority clear is nowhere greater than in arts organisations, where business is habitually conducted on the telephone and anybody may answer a telephone caller.[2] In fact, an artificial person, being without bodily parts, always necessarily acts through agents.

Employees

54 Apart from agency, it is rare for work to be carried on in isolation. A person will need others (*employees or servants*) to do work for it, and under its close or at any rate regular supervision. Such persons work under a contract of service which states the nature of the work, the pay (if any), the hours and so forth. Employees are sometimes, if that is the nature of their work, also agents. This is

---

1 See paragraphs 472-9.

2 One important body was committed to public press statements by its office cleaner.

commonly the case with an executive of an arts (or indeed organization or company, who may be making contracts daily (behalf as its agent besides working in other ways, all at one regular salary.

Contractors

55 Thirdly, it is common for particular work (e.g. wiring, or transporting props) to be done by bringing in outside *contractors*. It may be common to speak of employing contractors, but in law there is a fundamental difference between an employee and a contractor. An employee works as part of the business of the employer who is liable to third parties for wrongful acts done in the course of the employment by the employee. A contractor carries out his contract in his own way, without direct supervision and is liable to third parties for his own acts. It is dangerous to interfere with a contractor, for interference may, from the point of view of an injured outsider, convert him into an employee.

Partners

56 Fourthly, there is the problem of *partnership*. People wish to do things together for a variety of reasons: because they separately have not enough capital, or because one has money and another skill, and so on. People are free to make such agreements and carry on their business jointly and arrange to share the profits. As between themselves, partners regulate their relationship by agreements which often take the form of a deed,[1] but the major feature of a partnership is that all the partners are equally liable for all its debts: a creditor may sue and recover the whole of a debt from any one of them, and leave him to settle up with the rest. This distinguishes a partnership from a limited company, whose share holders' liability to outsiders is limited to the amounts represented by their shares and no more, and which must give notice of that fact by including "Limited" or, as the case may be, PLC (Public Limited Company) in its name.

Trusts and Charities

General

57 The arrangements mentioned above do not exhaust the requirements of human nature. Persons often need to be in a position to

---

[1] See paragraphs 141-4 .

deal as owner with property (in the sense of any valuable thing) for a purpose other than their own advantage, or for someone else. Since the Common Law does not allow private persons to create artificial persons, the supplementary law called Equity has devised an ingenious substitute, which appears to be unknown in the laws of countries never subject to British rule. This is the Trust, which has been defined as "the relationship which arises whenever a person called the trustee is compelled in Equity to hold property ". . . . . for the benefit of some persons (of whom he may be one and who are termed *cestuis que trust*) or for some object permitted by law, in such a way that the real benefit of the property accrues, not to the trustee, but to the beneficiaries or other objects of the trust".[1]

58 *A primitive illustration may help to understand the concept. A crusader gives his land to a friend on the clear understanding that the friend will give it back when he returns from the Holy Land, and manage it for him meanwhile. He returns, but the friend refuses to give it back, and claims to be, as indeed he is, the owner at Common Law. The Crusader goes to the Lord Chancellor for equity ["fair dealing"]. The Lord Chancellor recognises the friend's ownership at Common Law but threatens to imprison him until he makes over his Common Law rights.* Equity, while professing not to deal with Common Law titles, acts *against the person*, who abuses undertakings upon which he has accepted the property.[2]

Formation

59 There is no set method for creating a trust. All that is necessary is that the ownership of something shall have been *actually* vested in someone for the clear and imperative purpose of using it for a defined end or for the benefit of some person. The constitution of trusts can be completely informal, so much so that many people would be surprised to discover that they are trustees. It is said that

---

1 Keeton *Law of Trusts*, 1968 page 5, "Cestui que trust" is pronounced "setty ke trust".

2 The boundaries of Pennsylvania were fixed by a decree of the Lord Chancellor in this way, not because he might have jurisdiction there, but because the defendant (Lord Baltimore) was in England and could, if necessary, be imprisoned until he executed the necessary deeds. In a very recent case, a property owner found himself in much the same position as the returning crusader, with the same result.

every third person is a trustee. The vicar who collects money in church becomes a trustee of each coin as it is put into the bag, simply because he has announced the purpose of the collection from the pulpit. Collectors at University Rags are in a similar position. The treasurer of a club is a trustee of its funds upon the trusts represented by the club's constitution or rules. An executor is a trustee of the deceased's property for the purposes laid down in the will. A local authority is trustee of its public money for the benefit of its inhabitants. Many trusts, such as family settlements, are constituted by a trust instrument in the form of a deed. Others, especially charitable trusts, may be constituted in the Memorandum of Association of a private company or in a formal declaration registered with the Charity Commission, or in a Scheme made by that body, or by the Chancery Division of the High Court. Some are even created by private or public Acts of Parliament.

Traceability

60 Just as the method of declaring the trusts is legally immaterial, so also is the personality of the trustee. The essentials are that property shall actually have been set aside and impressed with a clear trust. This corpus of property or "fund" can be traced into the hands of any person except a purchaser for *full* value who did not know, and might not reasonably have been expected to know, of the trust. This innocent, sometimes called the *darling of equity*, is very rare, but the operation of the system is clearly illustrated when he is encountered. He buys the property from a trustee. He cannot be brought into the trust system, but the purchase money paid to the trustee remains trust property and the trustee can be forced to disgorge it. A person can even be a trustee against his will; for example, where a person interferes with a trust fund, or mixes its money with his own (as happens in informally constituted bodies such as clubs or benefit societies), he may find that he has rendered himself liable to account for any dealings with its property, and replace any losses. Such a person is called *a trustee of his own wrong*.

No Trustee

61 It is, moreover, a principle of equity that a properly constituted trust shall not fail for lack of a trustee. In the last resort, the court will, on request, appoint one.

Private and Charitable (or Public) Trusts

62 A private trust, considered from the point of view of the beneficiaries, is a special form of property regulating perhaps the
simultaneous or successive rights of members of a family. For
example, someone may leave property on trust to pay the income
during life to a person, and then to divide the capital equally
between four other identified persons. Private trusts are, in
general, regulated by the ordinary laws on property, of which a
fundamental policy is that property cannot be indefinitely tied up.
This *policy against perpetuities* is not wholly applicable to charitable trusts, with the result that special arrangements exist for
dealing with the obsolescence of ancient charities. Secondly, since
taxes and rates serve public purposes and every charitable trust
must equally serve a public purpose, there is a general policy, for
the avoidance of duplication, to keep charities outside the scope of
taxation.[1] Thirdly, bodies, such as the Arts Council, empowered to
make grants from public funds, are often hindered by the law from
making grants to bodies which are not charitable, or may as a
matter of policy refuse to do so. Fourthly, where a trust is private
and, therefore, comparatively limited in purpose, the number of
trustees is limited to a maximum of four, but where a trust is
charitable and, therefore, public, there is no such limitation on
numbers. This may have inconvenient results, which, however,
can be avoided by careful drafting.

What is Charity?

63 The word "charity" has changed its meaning radically since it was
established in the law in the 16th Century, and it has to be treated
nowadays as a purely technical term. It is, and for good reason,
remarkably imprecise. Its meaning is founded upon the preamble
to the long repealed Act 43, Elizabeth I Chapter 4 of 1601 (often
simply called the Statute of Elizabeth) and this preamble took
note, by way of a list of examples, of the existence of a variety of
public-spirited activities, for which the rest of the repealed act leg-
islated. The courts have not used the preamble as a hard and fast
definition, but have worked from it by analogy as times have
changed: it is indeed not very easy to find a common denominator
among the examples or the extensive case law descended from
them. This is hardly surprising, for an activity might not be
charitable in one era, yet thought highly charitable in another or

---

[1] See paragraphs 81-2.

unnecessary in yet other changed social and legal circumstances some generations later. The policy of the courts has been, within fair limits, to retain a degree of adaptability to the changing human condition.

64 Greatly daring, and subject to every imaginable safeguard and probably many exceptions, a charitable trust may perhaps be considered as a fund not directed towards the benefit of a closed group of private persons, but intended to help persons or lawful causes which are, or may be, in difficulties.

Classification of Charities

65 As a result, however, of a partly misleading attempt in 1891[1] to classify charities, and the passage of the Recreational Charities Act 1958, it is usual to bundle up charities into five parcels which by now are battered and bursting at the seams. The reader should understand that the five groups, with their examples, are mentioned below as an aid to understanding. The subject can never be tidy.

Relief of Poverty

66 Poverty does not mean destitution, but a person is not necessarily poor merely because he cannot afford the advantages provided by the trust. Thus encouragement of poor emigrants is charitable, encouragement of emigration generally is not.

Furtherance of Education

67 This must include an element of instruction or improvement. The mere increase of public knowledge, even by research, or the acquisition of experience is probably not enough. The following have been held educationally charitable: choral singing in London (1943); the spread of knowledge and appreciation of the words of the composer Delius (1957); the endowment of the Shakespeare Memorial Theatre at Stratford upon Avon to perform Shakespeare's plays, revive English classical drama, and stimulate the art of acting (1923); school prizes for sports (1915) or an educational game such as chess (1945). The following have been held not charitable: preserving a useless collection of pictures and furniture as a museum (1965); political propaganda masquerading as education (Conservative 1933, Labour 1949).

---

[1] *Pemsel's Case* (1891) AC 531.

Advancement of Religion

68 This includes any religion, the maintenance of a church or part of one, and even the objects of a morally respectable Ethical Society not concerned with religion at all.

Public Recreation

69 This heading, created by statute in 1958, makes it charitable to provide or help to provide facilities for recreation or other leisure time occupation, if the facilities are provided in the interests of social welfare. They must be designed to improve the conditions of life of those who need them on grounds of age, youth, infirmity, poverty or social or economic circumstances, or they must be available to the public, or the female (but not exclusively the male) members of the public at large. The act covers village halls, community centres, women's institutes, and has been applied to an indoor swimming pool (1966), and it extends to the provision of the facilities by organising any activity.

Trusts Beneficial to the Community

70 This is the most difficult of the headings, for the benefit to the community is not to be assessed by subjective criteria but must come within the general spirit and intendment of the law of charity. Thus the following have been held charitable: public works such as a bridge (1601); prizes for best kept cottages and gardens (1923); a grove of trees in Israel (1970); the welfare of animals generally (1915).

71 Even if a trust appears to fall under one of the five headings, it must still satisfy two other criteria. It must promote a _public_ benefit and it must be _exclusively_ charitable. A trust for purposes which in the opinion of the trustees are charitable, would not be charitable because they might be wrong. A trust to promote some beneficial cause by securing legislation is not charitable because nobody can know till after the legislation has been passed whether it will be charitable or not.

Official Machinery concerned with Charities

72 Trustees are, in general, left to administer their charitable trust as best they may, and their duties do not in most respects differ from those of any other trustee. They must be businesslike in preserving and maintaining the property, in investing the funds,[1] in getting in the debts, and they must keep proper accounts. They must see that the property really is used for the purposes of the trust, and must not divert it to some other purpose, however praiseworthy. In a private trust, the trustees are under the eye of those personally interested, and problems of supervision only seldom arise. In the case of a charity, that close personal interest is lacking and, in theory, the supervisor is the Crown acting by the Attorney-General in the Chancery Division of the High Court. Actually, court proceedings are very rare, for the routine business (i.E, 99.5% of it) is delegated to the *Charity Commission.*

Charity Commission

73 The supervisory function is, in practice, limited because the Commission has no active inspection apparatus. It acts solely on application or complaint. Thus there is power to remove a trustee but only if someone asks for it, and though trustees must make up annual accounts and preserve them for seven years, they need send them to the commission only on request, and such requests will not be made unless somebody has raised a suspicion. There is no set form for such accounts. There is power to conduct an inquiry into the affairs of a trust, but it is very seldom used. In the preservation of the property the law is very slightly more active, for trustees cannot mortgage the trust property, or take legal proceedings at the trust's expense without the Commission's sanction. Moreover, they are bound to register[2] their trust with the Commission. Registration, once accepted, is conclusive proof that the trust is entitled to the rate and tax advantages of a charity, but failure to register does not deprive the trust of its charitable character: it merely makes it harder to prove.

Official Trustee and Charities Investment Trust

74 In addition, two devices exist for simplifying administration and investment. These are the *Official Trustee* and the *Charities Investment Trust* (C.I.T.). The Official Trustee simply holds the legal title to property on behalf of a trust and he exists to get round the difficulty that whenever trustees change, it otherwise becomes necessary to re-execute all the documents of title. What is not always understood is that he has no managerial functions what-

---

[1] See paragraphs 74-5 and 593 el seq .

[2] See paragraph 79 .

ever. He must simply and only do what the trustees tell him. He never manages the investments. Failure to realise this has often led to serious losses of trust funds.

75 C.I.T., on the other hand, is a properly managed investment fund with which any charity may voluntarily place its money if or when it wishes, in the assurance that in so doing it is obeying the law which governs the investment of trust money. C.I.T. since its inception has been very successful and has kept the value of the funds entrusted to it a step or two ahead of inflation. Failing investment with C.I.T., trustees must manage their investments themselves, in accordance with the Trustee Investments Act 1961, which contains important limitations on their powers.[1] This may require more vigilance, activity, consultation and correspondence than a small fund may really support.

Obsolete Charities, Schemes and Cy Près

76 It is a basic feature of trust law that the terms and constitution of any trust cannot be altered without the consent of those interested. In the law of charity the right to give this consent is part of the Crown's supervisory jurisdiction and is mostly exercised by the Charity Commission. As usual somebody (generally the trustees) has to apply to the Commission before it will act, and lack of such applications is probably the main reason why there are always *some* unsatisfactory charities. There are hundreds of thousands of charities. The relatively small number of unsatisfactory charities get undue publicity.

77 The document which embodies an alteration to a charity is called a *Scheme*. In real life most schemes deal with ancillary matters of convenience rather than the objects of a charity itself. It may be thought desirable to alter the number of trustees or add to the bodies entitled to appoint them, or to change the accounting period. Such schemes will generally be uncontroversial and unopposed, but the Commissioners will, all the same, go to some lengths to find out if this is really so, mainly by advertising, and they will take their time. They have, indeed, a dilatory reputation which has had some justification, but they proceed upon the principle that, as far as possible, changes shall be agreed, not controversial.

---

[1] See paragraph 593 et seq .

78 Applications to alter the objects of a trust, being fundamental, are, as may be expected, treated with even greater caution, and in accordance with the principle known as *Cy Près* (Norman French = near to the present case). This assumes that a founder's purpose must be honoured as far as possible because if the intentions of founders are too easily disregarded, people may be discouraged from giving money for public purposes. Hence, if, but only if, a trust becomes impossible to perform (e.g. if the area of benefit ceases to exist) or unnecessary (e.g. because a service such as maintaining bridges is *now* provided by public authorities) or undesirable (e.g. because the original deed prescribed a religious test) a scheme will be made setting out new purposes as close as may be to the old ones.

Registration

79 A charity must be registered with the Charity Commissioners unless it is exempt by statute, or excepted by regulations (these two classes consist of national bodies like the British Museum, universities, the armed forces, the churches and the Boy Scouts). In addition a charity need not register if it has no permanent endowment, nor income from property exceeding £15 a year nor the use and occupation of land. Once registered, the fact of registration is conclusive that the trust is charitable. It is given a number which should be quoted to rate and taxation authorities when claiming rate or tax exemptions.

Property Dealings

80 A charity cannot sell, mortgage or charge any land forming part of its endowment without the Charity Commissioner's consent, nor grant a lease for a fine (premium), nor for more than 22 years without a fine, unless any such transaction is permitted by a scheme.

Taxation

81 Charities are exempt from income tax, corporation tax and both capital gains taxes upon most of their investments, and, in certain circumstances, also upon trading profits, and where somebody covenants (by deed) to pay income to a charity for at least four years, the charity recovers the income tax at the standard rate (for which he is no longer liable) from the Inland Revenue, and the charity may persuade him to promise to pay over any tax above that rate for which he has also ceased to be liable.

Rates

82   If written notice is given to the rating authority (the district or metropolitan borough council) that a property is occupied by a charity and wholly or mainly used for charitable purposes, the charity becomes entitled to a 50% reduction in the rates which would otherwise be levied on the property and the authority may (but is not bound to) remit the rest. The authority can also make remissions to non profit making bodies whose main objects are concerned with education, social welfare, literature, the fine arts or recreation.

Forming Arts Organisations

Classification

83   Local arts organizations come in all sorts and sizes. They may conveniently be classified into "public", "voluntary", and "hybrid". The "hybrid" is a consortium of "public" and "voluntary" bodies.

Public Organizations

84   By a public organization is here meant an emanation of a statutory authority and notably (by whatever name known) a local council committee or a joint committee of several councils responsible for a picture gallery, art museum, civic theatre, concert hall, arts complex or other similar institution. Such a committee may be small (say five members) or very large. It will be composed of councillors with, sometimes, co-opted outsiders whose number is restricted to one third of the membership.

Advisory Committees

85   An unusual but perfectly legal method of attaining a similar result is for the council to arrange for one of its officers (e.g. the Director of Arts and Recreation) to make all the decisions but to require him to work with a consultative committee. The advantage of this is that there is no restriction on the number of outsiders who may be members of a consultative committee. The disadvantage is that it can only make recommendations: it cannot enforce its views. Since the director will always in practice consult somebody, this advantage is probably more theoretical than real, and the com-

mittee's experience and public status means that the identity of the advisers is known.

Inherent Agency

86 The important legal feature of either arrangement is that it creates at most an agent or delegate of the parent council or councils. However much the committee or officer may be in practical control, their authority, property and funds are not their own but that of their principal, which may change the authority or constitution, alter the budget, or even abolish the arrangement altogether, subject, however, to binding obligations assumed towards other parties. The reason for this exception is that if the committee or officer has made a contract, they have, as agent, made the principal liable upon it. Thus the contract stands even thugh the arrangement vanishes. Similarly thê employees, from the highest to the night watchman, to whom such a committee or officer gives instructions, are not employed by them but by the council (or councils) which they represent, and the council is ultimately responsible to outsiders for anything which goes wrong, and which attracts a legal liability.

Obligatory Budgeting

87 All such arrangements have two particular financial features. Only the full council as such may levy a rate or issue a precept* (which for this purpose amounts to the same thing) or borrow money. It can never delegate these powers. It will no doubt pay close attention to any recommendations made to it, but it must make the decision itself and can ignore the recommendations. The practical consequence is that it has to lay down an annual budget within which the committee or officer must work. The arrangement, however, presupposes that they, having the day-to-day management, will know more about it than the council at large. They will, therefore, be expected to draft (in the form of a recommendation) their own budget for the council's approval. Since other spending departments will be doing the same, there will have to be discussions with them and the Treasurer's department beforehand to ensure that, as far as possible, the competing demands neither exceed the money known to be available nor lead to excessive friction between the departments or, at a later stage, between councillors.

Administrative Timetable

88 The reader will perceive that this creates a time table problem. A

local authority financial year runs from 1st April to 31st March. Annual precepts must reach the rating authority by the previous 10th March, and the government makes known the grants it will pay to county, district and London borough councils in the previous autumn. Since these grants are themselves related to forecasts of expected expenditure, including the arts expenditure, the drafting of a year's budget recommendations has to begin about 18 months ahead of the year concerned. In September 1984 is the time to start work on the budget for April 1986 to March 1987. It is obviously desirable that financial administration should be conducted with foresight, but these requirements introduce an element of rigidity which can be only partially cured by provision for contingencies.

Voluntary Organisations

Declaration of Trust

89 A voluntary organization has to be operated through the medium of a trust, that is to say it needs a clear statement of its objects, and its property has to be vested in a trustee or trustees so that it will be used to further those objects[1] and no others. Since a body of trust property can be traced into the hands of anyone (except the darling of equity*) to whom it comes, and that person can be forced to act as a trustee of it upon the original trusts, it follows that a proper statement of the trust objects is paramount. The methods by which a statement can be made (The Declaration of Trust) are infinite but for the avoidance of doubts and future disputes it is wise to use the most formal, that is to say a deed, and to have it professionally drafted by lawyers.

Area of Benefit

90 The lawyers must, accordingly, be instructed, and for this purpose it is important for the promoters of the scheme to be clear on certain points. The first is the *area of benefit*, and this must be sufficiently defined. Is it to consist of a particular village or town? or a group of adjacent ones? or one or more local government districts? or one or more counties? or all England or the United Kingdom, or the World at Large? Whatever it is, the lawyer should be told,

---

[1] See paragraphs 57-82.

bearing in mind that a very wide area may be so vague in terms of definition as to abort the whole scheme.

Charity or Not?

91 Secondly, some thought must be given to the question of charitable status. A charity has rate and tax advantages and can attract grants from other charitable foundations; it is more likely than a private trust to secure financial support from public funds and companies. On the other hand, the law limits the type of objects which are regarded as charitable. Accordingly, the lawyer must know clearly whether a charitable trust is desired or not, bearing in mind that if charitable status is desired, it may be necessary to restrict or abandon some of the original purposes contemplated. Once a charity has been accepted for registration by the Charity Commissioners the fact of registration is, for most purposes, conclusive of its charitable status. It is, therefore, helpful to base consideration of the problems upon a copy of a trust instrument of a similar organisation already registered.

Art Union?

92 Thirdly, it may be desirable to consider the Art Unions Act 1846. This legalised the formation of associations for the purpose of buying paintings, drawings and other works of art to be distributed by chance or otherwise among members, subscribers and contributors forming part of such associations, or for raising sums to be distributed by chance or otherwise among such persons on condition that the money is spent entirely on works of art. Members are exempt from prosecution for being concerned in "illegal lotteries, little goes or unlawful games" in consequence of any such distributions, if the association is either incorporated by royal charter or approved, originally by the Privy Council then by The Board of Trade and now by the Department of Trade (and Industry) but the charter or deed can be revoked if the association is perverted from its original purpose. Rules and regulations require, among other matters, that the rules as well as the instrument constituting a proposed association must be submitted for approval, that the first committee of management must have, at least, nine members, and that the method of election and the filling of vacancies must be approved by the Department. The names of prize winners must be advertised in a local newspaper

---

1 See paragraphs 81-2.

and the Department notified. After the payment of expenses, all the proceeds of a lottery must be distributed by way of prizes. No prize may be a work of art by an acting member of the committee of the union.

The Trustees

93 Fourthly, once the objects or purposes have been settled, it is necessary to identify and establish the trustee or trustees, and arrange to vest the property in them. There are many possible permutations but it conduces to clarity of thought to distinguish, at least in one's mind, between *holding the property* and *managing it*. The same people can do both, but this is usually convenient only in the case of a very small trust. Usually the property will be vested in a *holding trustee or trustees* who must take orders from a *managing body*. This latter body may have a variety of names such as "board of directors" or "managing trustees".

Holding Trusteeship

94 The mere function of holding can be performed by individuals in whom the property is jointly vested. There must in practice be more than one, because a receipt for money can be validly given only by two or more. A private trust may not have more than four trustees: a charity may have any number. There must be an arrangement for appointing new trustees. The disadvantage of a group of individuals is that every time its membership changes through death, resignation or other contingency, all the documents of title have to be re-executed in the names of the new membership and all the shares have to be reregistered. This can be laborious or controversial. Outgoing trustees or their executors may have to be traced and consents obtained, and such people, especially if very old, may be dilatory correspondents.

95 These worries can be avoided by vesting the property in a holding trustee who never dies, namely in the Official Trustee of Charitable Property or in a company specially incorporated for the purpose. Many charities make use of the Official Trustee satisfactorily, but some organizations feel that he is impersonal and far away (with consequent postal delays) and, in addition, he does nothing whatever to manage the property or to watch and manage investments. That is the business of the managing body who have to instruct him on purchases and disposals.

Private Company as Trustee

96 It has, therefore, since World War II become a common practice to create a private limited company for the sole purpose, stated in its Memorandum of Association, of holding all the property, shares, and securities and to deal with them solely on the instructions of the managing body. Such a company will probably have 100 shares of £1 each, only two of which will be issued, one to the chairman and one to the secretary of the company. This satisfies the rule that a private company must have at least two shareholders. Its registered office will be at the office of the organisation, and these two officers will conveniently be the organization's treasurer and secretary; they will pass the shares to their successors by a simple transaction whenever they themselves change. In this way, though holding and management will be kept legally separate, they will in fact be associated in a practically inseparable embrace.

97 A private company can be formed by direct application to the Registrar of Companies, but it is important that its objects should be clearly stated in its Memorandum of Association. This is a matter of technical draughtsmanship and can best be handled by the solicitor responsible for drafting the trust instrument. There are also two other ways of setting up such a company. One is to buy a dormant company ''off the shelf'' from a firm specialising in the sale of such companies, and then to change its Memorandum of Association to suit the trust. The other is to employ a Company Agent to form a Company for the purpose. The latter course has advantages, for a well established company agent is very experienced in such matters.

98 The creation of a private company will always cost *some* money, partly in Companies Registration fees and partly in professional fees. In 1983 the cost was about £140.

"Pipeline" Arrangements

99 The formation of a holding company may be attended by some delay partly of a procedural nature and partly, perhaps, if the cash for the formation expenses is not instantly available. It may, however, be desired to start operations quickly. If this is the case, it is possible to vest the trust property temporarily in individual holding trustees upon the trusts already drawn up, and then for the Managing Body to instruct those trustees to pass the ownership of the assets to the company after it has been formed.

The Managing Body - General

100 Unlike the Holding Trustees, which are little more than legal machinery, the Managing Body is the powerhouse of the organization, for its decisions, within the limits of the Trust itself, bind the Holding Trustees. The Managing Body is itself a body of trustees. Its constitution will be set out in the Trust Instrument or a Supplementary Trust Instrument, and careful thought should be given to four groups of points. The first is its immediate and the second its long term composition; the third is the means of altering or renewing its membership, and the fourth its powers. If these matters are not satisfactorily settled in advance, it becomes very difficult to do so later. In fact, in the case of a private trust it can be virtually impossible, and in the case of a charity, a scheme will have to be obtained from the Charity Commissioners, and this can take a period measured in years.

Immediate and Long Term Composition

101 The long term composition should be considered first. What sort of organization is this to be? Is it to be a group representing a wider homogeneous assembly of *people* such as all the painters of Yorkshire, or is it a group each of whose members represent a particular *organization?* And if the latter, are the eligible organizations to be of uniform type such as the drama clubs of East Anglia, or of differing character so as to admit not only the sketching clubs of Gwent but the Welsh National Eisteddfod and local authorities and banks? To some extent the choice of basic membership will be governed by the objects, because some organizations will be more interested in particular objects than others. Hence, it may be desirable to have the "target" organizations in mind when the objects are being drafted.

Further "Pipeline" Arrangements

102 Where a managing body is to consist of representatives of other existing organizations, much time can be consumed in obtaining their consent and the appointment of their representative. It may be necessary for them to go through lengthy or disputed formalities. They may have to alter their own constitutions, or they may have difficulty in finding a suitable or willing appointee. To avoid a lengthy hiatus while enthusiasms cool, it is generally wise to provide in the trust deed that certain named persons shall constitute the immediate Managing Body and to name a date or set a

time limit (say two years) by which its new membership shall come into office. Very often some or many of those named persons will, in fact, have the confidence of the organizations whose formal participation is to be secured, and it is very desirable that this should be so, lest the decisions of the immediate Body commit the organization to policies which the long term Body may wish to change.

Periodical Elections

103 Managing Bodies composed wholly of representatives of other organizations often manage very well without fixing a term of office, but rely upon their constituents to fill vacancies when they arise, using the procedures suitable to themselves. The case is otherwise with a Body representing a large, perhaps scattered, membership of individuals. Somehow the members must be able to elect their representatives and fill their vacancies. The practical problems do, however, have to be thought out. For reasons which will appear[1] it is desirable to have an institution such as a General Meeting which has to be convened at least once a year, and at first sight it seems sensible to use the opportunity of such a meeting to elect the Managing Body. But this is less simple than it looks. In very small and local organizations it can be done without notice by resolutions proposed in favour of particular persons (present or absent) who will be known to everyone; but where the organization is less local or larger, members will want notice of the names of candidates, and this, in its turn means that the candidates consent to nomination will have to be secured before agendas are posted.

104 With increasing size, a further difficulty arises. The wider the area, the smaller the proportion of people likely to attend a general meeting, which can, indeed, become little bigger than the Managing Body itself. When this happens the Managing Body's ability to reflect the wishes or needs of the membership may imperceptibly but steadily darken. It can be helpful in such circumstances to allow non-attending members to give proxies (sent out in blank with the agenda) to those attending. A proxy form should state the name of the person who is to vote with it, and in addition it should specify whether he may vote as he pleases or whether he is to vote

---

[1] See paragraphs 106-7.

for particular persons, and it must be signed by the person giving it.

Postal Ballots

105 The last resort is the postal ballot. This is time consuming, for it is necessary, having got candidates names and consents, to draft and print the ballot paper (with or without suitable descriptions and potted biographies), allow periods for postal transmission, for marking (bearing in mind that a member may be away when it arrives), further periods for postal return and counting. If return stamped and addressed envelopes are not included, many members will simply not bother, and since the counting will be done at the office it may be desirable (to avoid unseemly wrangles) to have independent witnesses to it, or to have the ballot conducted by an independent body like the Electoral Reform Society. The total expense per vote and diversion of energy is considerable, and experience shows that it is difficult to hold a postal ballot in less than two months. The obvious conclusion is that only a very rich body can afford habitual postal ballots. For lesser ones, they should be reserved for fundamental questions such as a proposal to apply for an alteration of objects or winding up, and then only upon a strongly supported written demand.

Need for General Meetings

106 Companies must by law hold general meetings of all shareholders for certain purposes, and one at least must be held annually, at which the year's audited accounts are presented and officers elected. The holding company mentioned above[1] will have only two shareholders but they still have, as shareholders, to pass the accounts and elect themselves respectively as company chairman and secretary.

107 Trusts do not have to hold such meetings as a matter of law, but most charitable trust deeds provide for them, because it is a sensible thing to do and because the members or interested parties will, if so minded, call meetings anyway.

Constitution of General Meetings

108 In an organization of individuals, the membership of the general

---

[1] See paragraphs 96-8 .

meeting is not hard to define. It will generally consist of all those who have the requisite qualifications described in the Instrument, and who have paid their subscriptions by a certain date. The latter point can lead to inconvenience if the Secretary has to check with a receipt list at the door. The difficulty can be overcome by fixing a definite subscription date, sending agendas only to those who have paid by that date, and treating the agenda as the entrance ticket.

109 Different principles apply in the membership of an organization of organizations. To confine the general meeting to ordinary representatives would make it virtually identical with the Managing Body. To let in all the individual members of the participating bodies could have bizarre results: the Albert Hall might not contain them, or there could be identification problems. Do you really want the whole of the T.U.C., or all the directors of Barclays Bank? And there could be dangerous problems of weighting and packing. The Barset Fife players may outnumber all the rest, simply because the meeting is being held at Barchester.

110 Hence in the constitution of this type of general meeting it is necessary to distinguish between voting members and those invited only to participate. The Instrument should lay down the number of voting members per organization; it can conveniently be a multiple of the number of its representatives on the Managing Board, and they should receive distinctive looking agendas (printed, say, on pink paper). The co-operation of the constituent bodies should be sought in rounding up their other participants, who will be entitled to do anything except vote. In real life this means that an attractive programme must be framed to overcome natural inertia.

General Meetings - Arrangements

111 *Every user of this book will have experienced at least one of those awful AGM's where somebody reads the notice convening the meeting (as if one did not know how one got there), and then somebody else reads an endless narrative of the discussions and speeches at a meeting a long year ago, which the unrecognisable chairman then asks permission to sign.*

Next come the accounts, read, in the absence of the Treasurer, by the Secretary in a low grey sound full of pence and halfpennies. "A very satisfactory result", says the Chairman. "Does the meeting accept the accounts? Can I have a proposer and seconder, please?" Somebody holds up a hand - perhaps, gentle reader, you do for the sake of doing something. You are at the back and haven't heard a word. "Any other business?", the Chairman says, threateningly. The audience shifts in the hot and sleepy atmosphere. "Very well. I declare the meeting closed." And everybody thankfully leaves.

112 There must be at least one such meeting in Britain every hour of the working year, and they give voluntary activity, in particular, a bad name. The main defect is that the organizers, the chairman and all others responsible regard them as distasteful formalities and make no secret of their view, and this mood not only communicates itself on the day, but tinges the character or repute of the body concerned. Yet, since formalities are inevitable, one may as well enjoy them.

113 The commonest soporific is a bad seating plan. If chairs are arranged thus:

Plan A

90% of those present see nothing except the backs of each others' heads, and those at the back hear nothing. If the same room is arranged thus:

Plan B

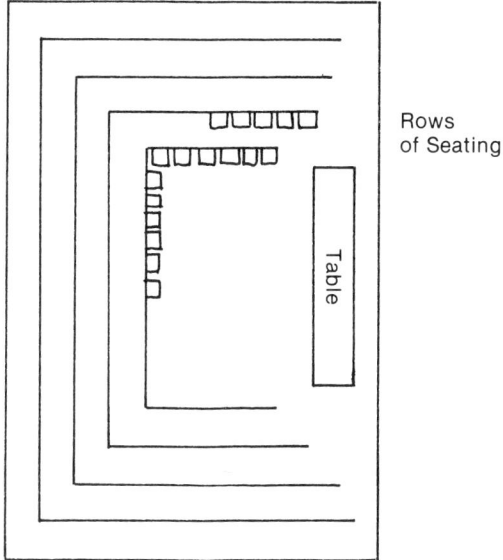

Rows
of Seating

everyone is closer to the focus of business and nearly everyone will see faces and appreciate character.

Business

114 At an Annual General Meeting, the presiding officer will initially be the President and, if his term of office is about to expire, his first duty after signing the minutes[1] is to supervise the election of his successor. If he is proposed for a further term he may preside over his own election and may, indeed vote for himself. There is, however, a well established custom that where he is opposed, he should call for the election of a temporary presiding officer to conduct the election. Some Instruments provide for this specifically.

[1] See paragraphs 120-1.

Casting Vote

115 At Common Law every member entitled to vote has one vote and no more. It follows that the presiding officer has only one vote himself. The Instrument can, however, confer on him a *second or casting vote* for use only in a tie, but it must do so specifically. Where a presiding officer has only one vote he customarily does not vote save to break a tie. Where he has two votes he must, if he wishes to vote at all, use his first vote at the same time as everyone else. There is a practical custom designed to prevent the Chair from being involved in controversy, that the presiding officer votes, if possible, so that the issue can be reopened. For example, if the issue is whether a building should be sold, his vote in favour makes it impossible to raise the matter again: his vote against does not.

116 Once the President is elected, he must conduct the election of the other officers. There may be vice-presidents. There will certainly be a Treasurer and Auditors, and there will be the Managing Body or Committee; the latter usually but not always elects its own chairman.

Presentation and Circulation of Accounts

117 The next, and technically important, business is the presentation of the accounts, which should have been circulated with the agenda, and can, therefore be assumed to be within the knowledge of those present. Points of finance are the Treasurer's affair and he should deal with any matters or questions raised upon them, but it is always desirable to have the Auditor available. The accounts represent the organization's activities in a mathematical form, and it is generally helpful to circulate a written report of those activities with them. The public presentation of such reports is a matter requiring some skill, and it is usually the province of the Chairman of the Managing Body, or sometimes the Secretary or Chief Executive (by whatever title known). Fortunately an arts organisation generally has something to exhibit. A picture exhibition, or a concert, will say more about those activities than any verbal report; they will attract attendances and they are perfectly legal as long as they do not elbow out the formal business required by the trust instrument. A general meeting ought to be a public relations exercise.

Questions and Resolutions

118 Besides the reports and elections, there may be a variety of items arising, mostly, from thoughts in the minds of casual participants. These, broadly fall into three groups: viz, requests for information, resolutions, and matters arising on previous business. It is convenient to set aside a time for questions *before* the other matters, because the answers may be helpful in later discussion. Resolutions should be taken in the order in which notice of them was received, and in some organizations written notice is required well in advance. This has the effect of shutting out an idea which somebody has just had on the spur of the moment.

Amendments

119 An amendment to a resolution must not negative it, and should always be written down before it is discussed. As the effect is to substitute new words in the original, an amended resolution must be voted as amended, for it to become effective. It is quite common for an amendment to secure a majority, but for the resolution, as so amended, to be lost.

Previous Business

120 Matters can be raised on previous business at any time, but the better the presentations and conduct at a meeting the fewer such matters will be. The commonest and most often mismanaged occasion is in connection with the signing of the minutes at the very start. Signature of the minutes means that those present at *this* meeting agree only that the minutes accurately recount what happened at the *previous* meeting. The only questions which can be in order on a motion to sign the minutes relate to their accuracy. The merits of what the minutes recount cannot then be discussed. It may be, after signature however, that someone wishes to inquire what action was taken on a particular matter described in those minutes, or raise some other such point. In 95% of such cases, it will be found that the question is due to be answered at a later stage in the meeting (e.g. by the person presenting the annual report), and it should be postponed to that stage. Otherwise the meeting may become confused, or repetitious.

121 Nature of Minutes

The purpose of minutes is to record *events*. These events are the fact of the meeting recorded, together with its time and place, and the decisions which were made. These should be described as shortly as possible consistently with accuracy. It is not necessary to state reasons unless accuracy is impossible without them. Speeches and members' observations should never be recorded in the minutes themselves, but may (for example, an address by an invited speaker) be recorded in an appendix.

122 If votes on any question are counted, the figures should be minuted.

Attendance Records

123 At large meetings it is useful to get members to sign an attendance register at the door. At small meetings attendances are sometimes recorded in the minutes.

Voting

124 The Instrument may lay down methods of voting, but this is not necessary because if it does not, the law gives the presiding officer a discretion to use any method which will achieve an accurate result. Elaborate voting systems can waste much time. The following is a summary of the best compromise; it enables obvious votes to be taken in seconds, while reserving the doubtful for more formal procedures.

125 Firstly, on every issue the chairman calls for those in favour to say "Aye" and then for those against to say "No". If the result is obvious he declares it. Secondly, if he is in doubt, or if somebody else claims a count, he calls for those in favour to show one hand (holding a voters agenda paper or ticket) and these are counted, and then similarly for those against. It is desirable, before the meeting begins, to appoint tellers to count votes, and in a large meeting it is essential to divide it beforehand into blocks with a teller for each block. The tellers as they conclude their count must *themselves write down the result*. Failure to observe this precaution can lead to great difficulties. At the end of the counts, the tellers' slips are handed to the presiding officer who adds them up and announces the result. This procedure is carried out within sight of the meeting itself and is thus sufficiently guaranteed against mistake or fraud. Thirdly, however, a secret ballot (i.e. in writing) may be claimed. This has the effect (desirable or un-

desirable) of concealing voters' opinions. It is also the method in which the most precautions against mistake or fraud have to be taken. The reason is that even if votes are counted in the meetings' presence, few, if any, can see what is being done. Hence, before the ballot papers are distributed the meeting should be invited to appoint some of its own (say three) members as tellers to supervise the counting, which will usually be done by the Secretary or his staff. These supervising tellers agree the figures before they are passed to the Presiding Officer.[1]

Honorary Officers

126 Many organizations have honorary, virtually honorific, officers, e.g. a President, Vice President, etc., who do not take part in day to day business. Before including provision for them in the Instrument, it is important to give some thought to their function. The present writer believes that their numbers should be small and confined to persons who are able and willing sometimes to intervene powerfully for the organization's benefit, with relevant outside bodies, or whose advice is in some way likely to be exceptionally wise or who can add lustre to the organization's reputation. A world famous violinist as president will obviously be an asset to a musical body, but so will a Lord Lieutenant who is on good terms with the County Council. Conversely, it is a mistake to clutter up the notepaper with the names of persons of secondary distinction whose interest is merely polite. They cost money and are usually a broken reed.

Treasurer and Book Keepers

127 Since one of the major duties of trustees is to keep accounts, it is desirable to start at the very first moment: otherwise there will be unrecognizable items which take a disproportionate effort to explain. Somebody capable of book keeping should be found at once and if the Secretary has such knowledge so much the better. The function of the Treasurer, commonly an honorary officer, is to oversee the book keeping (usually at some distance), to watch the

---

[1] In parliaments of English origin, formal voting is by division, i.e. by walking through different doors for "Aye" and "No". This can be expeditious if well organized. In most continental legislatures and at Strasbourg, they use a very time consuming method of vote by roll call.

general financial position, and to be ultimately responsible for the Annual Accounts and Balance Sheet. He is thus a person who has to be easily available, especially as he normally signs the cheques. As the organization's finances may be expected to expand, it will be helpful to have a treasurer who can give good advice on investments,[1] and banking.

The Secretary or Executive

128 In practice all the threads of administration have, to avoid confusion and duplication, to pass through one point, and at that point there has to be a secretary or executive. He need not be an expert in the field where the organization operates, but he does need to have a temperamental sympathy for the subject matter. His essential character is a talent for administrative action and a willingness to learn. The occupant of his job will have to be paid in the end, if not immediately.[2]

Documents and Part Performance

Distinction between Ownership and Contract

129 Oddly enough English law does not trouble its head much about ownership, for if someone had to prove his ownership of something before he could recover it or protect it, the cost and trouble in terms of justice and litigation expenses would be very burdensome. The law is more interested in protecting lawful possession. Thus, in proceedings related to property, the court does not ask who owns it, but which of the disputants has the better right to possession, and it tends to presume that the man in possession ought to be left in possession, unless somebody can show a good reason otherwise.

---

[1] For investments and requirements of professional advice, see paragraph 593, et seq.

[2] For contracts of employment, see paragraphs 499-591.

130 A contract on the other hand, is an agreement whereby ﹐
bind themselves to do something for each other and, where
contract is concerned with property, its eventual purpose is oft،
to transfer the legal possession in return for money. The distinction between the contract which confers a right to have possession
transferred and the actual transfer of the possession is very
important, especially in relation to strangers or third parties. *I
agree to sell you my car for £2000 which you pay. Before I hand it
over, George offers me £2500. I accept his money and hand it over
to him. However maddening this may be for you, you have no right
to make George hand it over to you, because when I sold it to him I
was still in possession and had something to sell for which he paid.
Your redress is against me. I have broken the contract with you
and you are entitled to be put, by financial means, back as far as
possible into the position in which you would now be if the contract
had not been made.*

Transfer of "Ownership"

Moveables

131 *Moveable* things are transferred by physical hand-over or by
distinctly setting aside to the transferees' order. When I buy
a picture it becomes mine at the moment when it passes from the
dealer's hand into my suitcase. (A door becomes a part of a house
when the carpenter has hung it.) I buy a piano, one of several
identical ones now in your warehouse and to remain stored there
until I call for it. It becomes mine only when you have somehow
physically distinguished it from the others. If you borrow money on
the security of the instruments in that warehouse, the creditor may
recover his money by seizing them. Whether he may include my
piano in the seizure depends upon whether it has been set aside for
me.

Things not moveable

132 There are, however, two classes of property which cannot be transferred by a primitive physical process. These are interests in
immovables such as land or buildings, and *abstract property* such

as shares and copyrights which have value but not physical substance. For these the method of transfer involves a process in writing. Unfortunately, the law on this is a collection of bits and pieces of which the following has to be a selective summary.

Land

133 *Land*, includes anything adhering to or firmly rooted in it such as a house or a tree (but not a Dutch barn or a rose bush), and also certain invisible rights (called easements) such as a private right of way or (so called) way leaves for water pipes, electric cables and so forth. Interests in these must be transferred, or (as the case may require) created by deed, save in the case of a lease for less than three years.[1] In the steadily expanding registration areas, the deed will be followed by a registration of the title in the local land registry. Declarations of trust affecting land must be made in writing.

Securities

134 Legal mortgages and charges on land, and bills of sale secured on moveables must be created or, as the case may be, transferred by deed.[2]

Shares

135 *Shares* of any description in a limited company, whether public or private, are legally owned by the person who is registered as the owner in the company's register of shareholders. Hence shares are transferred by reregistration. Your share certificate is not a document of title: it is merely evidence that on the date when it was issued, your name appeared in the register. If I buy and pay for your shares, your failure to hand over the certificate (perhaps because you have lost it) makes no difference to me, for the company will, in due course, issue me with one of my own. On the other hand, the company will want a written indemnity in case you, on the strength of your now invalid certificate, try to sell the shares which you no longer own. Similarly, if, after sale of the shares but before I can get my rights registered, the company goes into liquidation, you remain the shareholder involved in the liquidation.

---

[1] See paragraphs 150-54.

[2] See paragraphs 290-341.

Copyrights

136 *Copyrights* come into existence by the author's act of creation in writing down or otherwise recording the work. They spring fully armed from his mind, and nothing more is needed to give him the ownership, unless the work was of a pictorial character and commissioned or unless the author made the work in the course of his employment to do so, in which cases the commissioner or employer becomes the owner without further formality. If, however, the copyright is to be assigned, the first and all later assignments must be made in writing signed by, or on behalf of, the assignor.[1] Such an assignment can be made prospectively, that is to say before the copyright comes into existence.

Contracts in General

137 Of the millions of contracts made every day, nearly all are made by word of mouth, and business would come to an abrupt stop if this were not so. Housewives out shopping may make twenty a day. Many contracts (e.g. ordering a taxi) are made by telephone. International contracts are often made by telex. There are special customs about concluding bargains, in particular trades or markets such as the stock exchange[2] or in auctions. Apart from the cases already mentioned, and bills of exchange, hire purchase agreements regulated under the Consumer Credit Act 1974, all of which must be in writing, the law lets people make their contract by whatever means they please. In some walks of life (e.g. acting) standard contracts are much in use. Whatever the practices or social or financial compulsions, these standard contracts have *in law* no special sanctity. They are a mere convenience. Among artists of all kinds, informality is normal and can sometimes create great difficulties. There may be different recollections of the content of a telephone call, or an over-expansive conversation in a theatre bar. In strictly contractual arrangements, a certain formality is no bad thing.

---

[1] See paragraphs 53 and 427 for the difficulties which may arise in connection with young "pop" composers.

[2] English is full of expressions reflecting this, e.g. "to pay on the nail" was a method of making a contract at Bristol; "to shake (hands) on it" an agreement to sell farm produce; "to be had for a mug" (of ale) a method of settling a towage contract on the Severn.

Exceptional Contracts

138 Two types of contract are, however, required to be evidenced in writing. These are *contracts for the sale of land* [1] and *contracts of guarantee*, that is to say, contracts to answer for the debt, default or miscarriage of another. Usually such a contract will be a formal written document which each party will sign, or two identical documents, each party signing the one to be kept by the other. Convenience may dictate this degree of formality but the law does not. The requirement is that the contract be *evidenced* in a writing signed by the party to be charged, i.e. made liable upon it. The writing is simply a special form of evidence of the parties' intention to be bound, and of the nature of the obligations to which they were bound. Letters are adequate for this purpose and, indeed, common. A letter which set out the terms but repudiated them has been held to be sufficient evidence. The common printed formula on business notepaper "nothing in this letter constitutes a contract" is thus not necessarily waterproof, for it will not prevent the letter being used as *evidence* of the contract's terms, though other evidence may have to be adduced to show that the contracting parties meant to be bound by them. The requirement of a signature can, however, have one-sided effects. If you write and sign a letter to me and I only reply by telephone, I may be able to hold you liable on the letter but you cannot do the same to me. This is usually less unfair than it looks, because the circumstances may be such that you will have another cause of action*

Part Performance

139 Where the law requires that a contract shall be merely *evidenced* in writing, a person will not be allowed to use that requirement to cheat another out of his due. Thus, if, on the faith of an oral agreement for a long lease, I enter your land and spend money converting a building into a practice room, the law will not allow you to take the benefit of my outlay simply because of the absence of a signed writing. I shall be allowed to prove the contract by other means. This doctrine of part performance has limitations: it applies, firstly, only where the acts of the parties are such that they necessarily reflect or are clearly attributable to, the nature of the original agreement between them. Hence, a payment of

---

[1] For definition of land see paragraph 151.

money, being always ambiguous, is not by itself an adequate act of part performance. Secondly, the acts of part performance must be such as would prejudice the performer if the agreement is held void. Thirdly, the plaintiff must, somehow, prove the terms of the contract.

Release or Replacement of Contracts

140 Obviously a party to a contract cannot release himself or change it unilaterally, but there is nothing to stop the original parties doing so by a mutual agreement which is, in fact, a new contract. Such a new contract must, as to form, follow the rules of contracts generally.

Deeds - Description

141 A deed is a solemn written and dated statement made in formal language, usually engrossed on good paper, signed and sealed by the person or persons executing it in the presence of at least one witness, (whose name, address and profession must be stated and who signs it himself as a witness), and delivered. Any mark will do as a signature so long as it is made with the intention of signing. The seal, nowadays, is usually a red wafer gummed to the paper opposite the signature. Delivery is the act of bringing it into force. This is done formally by the executant putting his finger on his seal and saying, "I deliver this as my act and deed", but it can equally be done informally by giving or sending it to the person to be benefitted or his solicitor. An undelivered deed is called an *escrow* and remains in limbo until delivered. Escrows appear to be commoner in the U.S.A. than in England, for English law presumes delivery unless the contrary is proved.

Effect of a Deed

142 The peculiarity of a deed is that it derives its force from its solemnity, and one who executes it is not allowed, as against some other party to it, to deny any statement of fact or any promise which he made in it.[1] The court will enforce the deed exactly, on the demand of someone entitled under it. The only defence (known as *non est factum*) is that the apparent executant never executed it. In other words, that the document is a forgery or that it was

---

[1] The full significance of this will become apparent in paragraphs 392-436 on contracts.

made under overwhelming physical threat or, perhaps, under the influence of drugs not administered by himself, or as a result of a mistake not due to his own carelessness. Deeds have many different names depending upon the immense and growing variety of purpose which they serve.[1]

143 The extreme flexibility of deeds is such that they can (and often are) used to incorporate contracts, and even (though rarely) wills. There are also some relatively unusual cases where a deed *must* be executed: these include the conferment of a power of attorney, and the transfer of a patent.

Release and Cancellation

144 It is in the nature of a valid deed that the executant cannot revoke it. On the other hand, others can create a situation in which it cannot be enforced. This is done by a deed of release made by a beneficiary under the original deed, whereby, in effect, he binds himself not to pursue his rights. If there are several beneficiaries, a deed of release by one of them will not affect the *rights* of the others. Total cancellation by all or the only beneficiary is effected by tearing out the seals. Where several people have jointly made a deed of suretyship or guarantee, the release of one of them from his *obligations* automatically releases the others, for otherwise their liability might be increased without their consent.

Wills

145 People commonly make artistic provision in their wills. They leave pictures to galleries, or money for musical prizes, or money or property to arts associations, or, like the late George Bernard Shaw, an endowment for a museum.

146 Any person of full age can make a will. Wills are called ordinary or privileged. Ordinary wills must be in writing, signed by the testator in the simultaneous presence of at least two witnesses who must also sign in his presence. A privileged will may be made by an airman, soldier or seaman on, or under orders for, active service. No particular form or witnessing is required: words scrawled on an eggshell, and words spoken from a train window on Victoria Station have been proved as a privileged will. In practice

---

[1] See glossary.

most privileged wills are made on a form included in the back of the individual's personal record book.

147 A witness may be a beneficiary under an ordinary will only if there are at least two other witnesses who are not. A will speaks from death i.e. it affects the situation at the testator's death, (not at the date when it was made) and is carried out by one or more executors either named in it or appointed by the court. They pay (in order) the deceased's debts, then the legacies and finally transfer the residue to those entitled by law or named in the will.

148 A trust (charitable or otherwise) may be, and often is, created by a will, and its provisions count as a legacy.

Revocation of Wills

149 A will is revoked by marriage, destruction by the testator with an intention to cancel, or by another will. No other methods are possible. Those parts of a will but not necessarily the whole of it, in favour of a spouse are revoked by a divorce. In the case of marriage, the cancellation of any previous will is automatic and without formality. Destruction is best effected in the presence of a witness, or the testator can leave a note to say that he destroyed the will in order to revoke it. Otherwise it may later be argued that it was destroyed by mistake. From an executor's point of view, it is helpful to begin every will with the words, "I hereby revoke my previous wills", even if no previous will ever existed, because the executor then knows that he need not look back beyond the date of the will which he has in his hand.

Property

General

150 Property is a relationship between a person and a thing, but things vary in quality, and the relationship must vary to suit the person and the thing. It is convenient to think of things, with the Romans, as being either immovable such as land, or movable such as a piano, or abstract such as copyright, but English law has habitually used classifications which only approximate to this, namely, into real property, comprising those things in which a legal estate

can exist, and personal property or chattels, in which it cannot. This division puts land, and certain abstractions such as easements* into the class of real property, while leaseholds and all other things are personal. Another method of classification represented the means whereby the right of property could be demonstrated. Here *choses** *in possession* were things which were physically possessed, and included all things at somebody's disposal; *choses in action* were things not at his disposal, but to which he might have to assert a right by bringing an action in court. The sitting tenant of a house has a chose in possession; his landlord's right to the house after the lease has expired is a chose in action.

Definition of Land in English Law

151 "'Land' includes land of any tenure, and mines and minerals whether or not held apart from the surface, buildings or parts of buildings (whether the division is horizontal, vertical or made in any other way) and other corporeal hereditaments*; also a manor, an advowson, and a rent or other incorporeal hereditaments*, and an easement*, right, privilege or benefit in, over or derived from land; but not an undivided share in land . . ."[1]

Of the "other corporeal hereditaments" the most important are trees and fixtures. The latter are things which would be chattels were it not that they had been annexed to or incorporated in the land or building. Thus, for example, doors, windows, mantelpieces, electric wiring and switches, affixed, however lightly to the 'land', for the convenient use of the land, are part of it, but things, however large, not affixed to the land such as a Dutch barn or a five ton printing machine are not. Even strong attachment, if it is for the more convenient use of the thing not the land, may not result in annexation.

Length of Interest and Content of Ownership

152 Once I know what sort of property I have in contemplation, the two practically interesting questions are, "how long do I have possession of it?" and "what may I do with it?" The answer to the second question will vary to a certain extent with the answer to the

---

[1] Law of Property Act 1925 s205 (ix).

first. It is proposed to pursue these two questions initially in relation to land.

The Duration of the Interest

153 The longest possible legal interest in land, technically called a legal estate in the land, is called the *Fee Simple*; it continues for ever unless interrupted by some lawful means (e.g. sale). It is said to be *Absolute* if there is no event or condition which will bring it to an end; it may be *In Possession* if the owner is actually in control of it, or *In Reversion* if his right to take control depends upon some event such as the expiry of a lease to a tenant; and it may be *Encumbered* if someone else has a right in or over it, for example, if it is mortgaged or if there is a private right of way across it, or *Free of Encumbrances* if no such burdens exist. The highest and, therefore, the most valuable possible right in a piece of land is thus known as the *Fee Simple Absolute in Possession Free of Encumbrances*. A fee simple is transferred by a *Conveyance*.

Freehold

154 The second type of legal estate in land is called the *Term of Years Absolute*. This is, as its name implies, a right of possession for a period of time, with a definite or ascertainable beginning and end, which is, therefore, less than infinity. The period must amount to at least one day, and cannot apparently exceed 3000 years. It is created by a *lease* or an agreement for a lease, transferred by an *assignment** and extinguished either, automatically by exhaustion of the term, or by *surrender**, *re-entry**, or *notice**. The possessor of the term is called the tenant, the grantor the *landlord*. Unless there is a stipulation to the contrary in the lease, a tenant may himself create a term of years absolute by means of a so-called, sub-lease in favour of a tenant of his own, commonly called a *sub-tenant*. As a person cannot give more than he has, such a "sub term" must begin at least one day after, and end at least one day before his own term. Such arrangements are common, especially where developers have taken a long lease of a substantial area and are then sub-letting it in small parcels for building. Equally, unless forbidden by his sub-lease, a sub-tenant can create a term of years, which must, of course, be shorter at each end than his own sub-term and so on. The law in general permits such arrangements, even if practical, economic or contractual factors may make them unusual. Thus, a Term of Years may itself be In Possession or Reversion and it too may be Encumbered or Free of Encumbrances.

155 The commonest way of paying for a term of years is by way of rent, but a single lump sum is lawful, if rare. Sometimes there is a lump sum (called a *fine* or *premium*) in addition to the rent.

156 Thirdly, from the point of view of the owner, an encumbrance is not a legal estate in his land, but it is an interest owned by or created for someone else's benefit and capable of subsisting as a burden upon and for periods comparable with the duration of the owner's estate. For purposes of the diagram opposite two only have been used, viz, the *mortgage* and the *estate contract*. Their essential feature is that they "run with" the land; they adhere to it abstractly as much as a house adheres physically, and when a new owner comes into possession, he takes them too for good or ill.

The Content of Ownership

157 In theory, the possession of land originally included possession "up to heaven and down to hell" and the liberty to do what one liked within the cubic space so described. This liberty included the right to exclude anyone else at will. This primitive freedom was never, in fact, complete and has, especially in recent times, been much eroded, but it remains true that, where the law does not forbid, there is still a residual right to do as you like.

Rights of Others in Your Land

Support

158 Every landowner is entitled to have his land supported at the boundary by the neighbouring land in the manner so far accustomed. Thus, where a deep excavation on my land, for foundations of a new building, causes your land to subside, I am liable to you. This is a regular urban problem.

---

[1] For more details on various types of encumbrance see paragraphs 94-204, 290 et seq.

SAMPLE INTERESTS IN PROPERTY

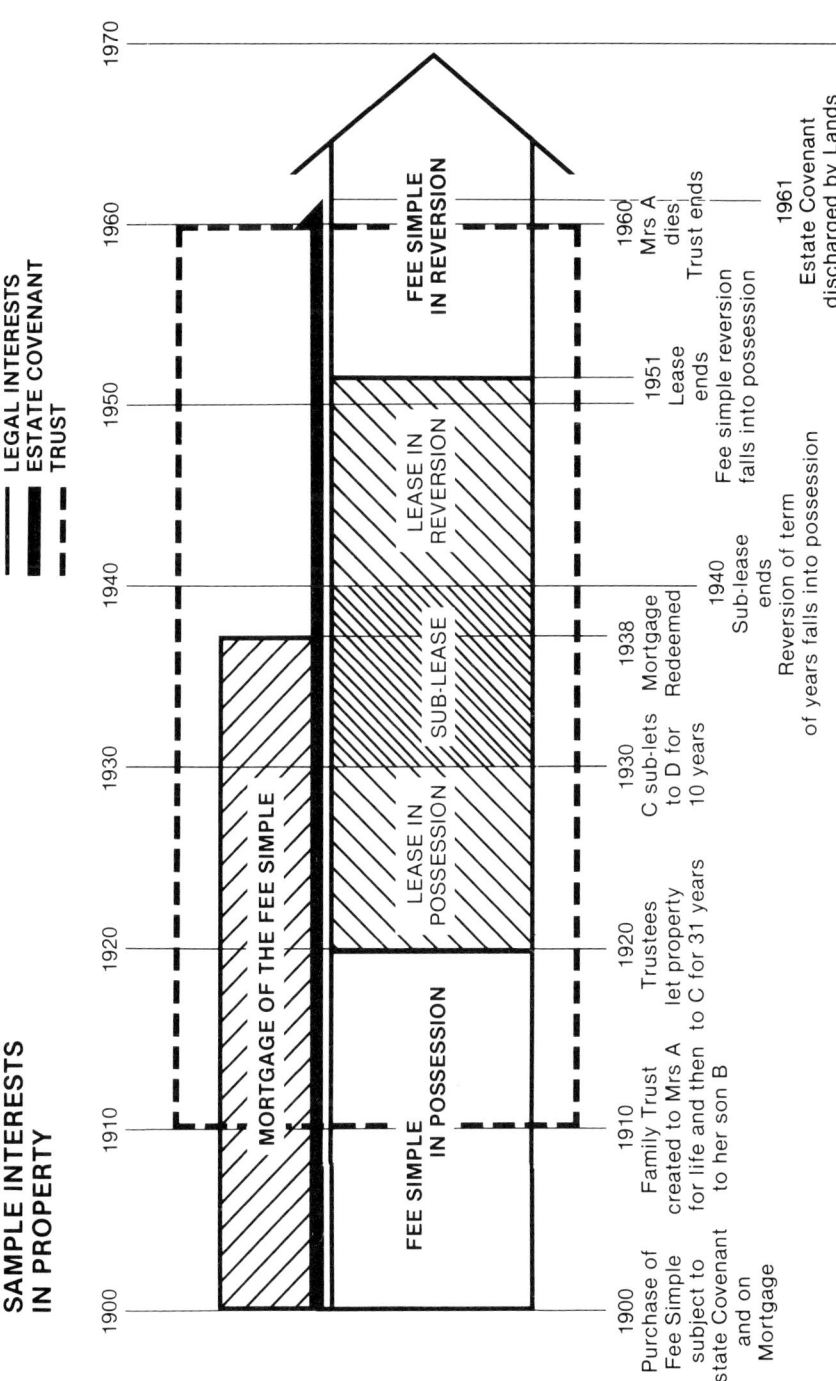

LEGEND:
- ——— LEGAL INTERESTS
- ▬▬▬ ESTATE COVENANT
- – – – TRUST

MORTGAGE OF THE FEE SIMPLE

FEE SIMPLE IN POSSESSION

LEASE IN POSSESSION

SUB-LEASE

LEASE IN REVERSION

FEE SIMPLE IN REVERSION

Timeline: 1900 — 1910 — 1920 — 1930 — 1940 — 1950 — 1960 — 1970

1900
Purchase of Fee Simple subject to Estate Covenant and on Mortgage

1910
Family Trust created to Mrs A for life and then to her son B

1920
Trustees let property to C for 31 years

1930
C sub-lets to D for 10 years

1938
Mortgage Redeemed

1940
Sub-lease ends
Reversion of term of years falls into possession

1951
Lease ends
Fee simple reversion falls into possession

1960
Mrs A dies
Trust ends

1961
Estate Covenant discharged by Lands Tribunal

Easements and Wayleaves

159 Easements are rights which exist for the benefit of one piece of land (the dominant tenement), for the benefit of another (the servient tenement) in different ownership. The law will protect rights of this kind from disturbance by an occupier by injunction* and, if necessary, damages.

Leases

160 Tenants and landlords have to respect each others rights in the land as set out in the lease made between them, or as settled by law where the lease is silent.

Planning and Development Control

161 Development control represents the most far reaching and pervasive invasion of the liberty of any owner of property to do what he wishes with his own. The following represents a bare outline of the planning system and of the development control administered within it.

The Authorities

162 There are seven types of authorities which exercise planning functions or have powers closely related to them. In principle, county councils are county planning authorities responsible for *overall strategic planning*, whilst district councils are district planning authorities responsible for *planning control*. In certain cases, however, the Secretary of State will have set up joint county or district planning boards. In a national park, however, in principle *all* planning functions are exercisable by the county planning *authority*, but in some few cases there may be either a National Park Joint Planning Board or a National Park Special Planning Board. Both types of board have county planning status. Finally, in national parks which have no board, the county council or councils concerned must set up a National Park Committee to exercise certain special functions.

Structure Plans Procedure

163 A county planning authority surveys its area, draws up and

publishes a report, publicises it and gives those who might be expected to do so an opportunity to make representations. In the light of the report and representations it then draws up a structure plan, copies of which it must make available for public inspection. This consists of a generalised diagrammatic map with a written statement, and it must be submitted to the Secretary of State of the Environment for confirmation. Objections to the plan may be made to him, and each public copy of it has to be accompanied by a statement of the date by which such objections have to be made. There is provision for ensuring that the public has opportunities for criticism or objection, and in due course the plan is either confirmed with or without modifications, or rejected. If rejected, the county planning authority must go through the whole procedure again. Structure plans may be altered after confirmation. The procedural requirements for alterations are similar to those for the plans themselves.

Nature of Structure Plans

164 Structure plans are not meant to deal with details, but are concerned with the general solutions to problems which confront planning authorities in attempting to forecast such major matters as population and traffic movements, changes in employment habits and land uses following market or technical developments.

These plans guide (but do not bind) district planning authorities in the way that planning applications should be handled, and contain, either explicitly or less frankly, clues to the intended or expected future of each locality. A structure plan will not, for example, indicate the probable site of a housing estate: but it will probably indicate whether a village is to be expanded or allowed to die, or whether a town is to have a new suburb. It may thus be useful for forecasting the population in the catchment area of a projected theatre or other arts institution.

Development Plan Schemes

165 Though, in principle, local plans are made by district planning authorities, a county planning authority may, in consultation with the district authorities, establish a development plan scheme. This sets out which authority in a given locality (outside a national park) is to draw up the local plan. By this means, the county authority can ensure that certain local plans are drawn up by itself.

Local Plans

166 A local plan (like a structure plan) is based upon a survey and report, and must eventually conform to the structure plan, but the authority responsible for it need not wait until the structure plan has been confirmed. It consists of a map and a fairly detailed statement showing proposed developments, land uses, and proposed improvements to the environment and traffic management. There may be more than one local plan (each for a different purpose) for the same area, and the plan usually includes diagrams, illustrations and other descriptive matter which are designed to explain it, and which form part of it.

Local Plan Procedure

167 The procedure for preparation and adoption of local plans resembles that for structure plans, except that, instead of the plan having to be confirmed by the Secretary of State, it is adopted by the responsible authority unless he objects to it within three weeks of submission to him.

168 Since a local plan has detailed effects upon the uses to which land may be put, and limits the discretion of the planning authority in dealing with planning applications, the authority may and, where certain kinds of objections are made, must hold a local public inquiry before adopting the plan.

169 Adopted local plans may be altered or repealed. The procedure is similar to the preparation and adoption procedure.

Action Areas

170 A structure plan may indicate an action area. This is an area which in the county planning authority's view should be developed or re-developed as a whole. The authority responsible for making the local plan is bound to draw one up for an action area as soon as possible.

Development Control

171 Plans are given effect by a variety of means, of which development control is the most detailed.

What is Development? The Principle

172 In principle, development is the "carrying out of any building,

engineering, mining or other operations, in, on, over or under land or the making of any material change in the use of any buildings or other land", [1] and it is necessary for an intending developer to seek permission for his proposed development. Since, however, the full rigour of the rule would rapidly bring everything to a halt, there are a number of far-reaching exceptions and general permissions.

Exceptions Defined by The Act

173 Certain acts and activities are treated as not involving development. These are, firstly, maintenance, improvement or alteration of a building affecting only its interior or not materially affecting its external appearance; secondly, road works and works on sewers, mains, pipes, cables and other apparatus by local authorities or statutory undertakers*; thirdly, uses incidental to the enjoyment of a dwelling-house and within its curtilage; and, fourthly, agriculture, horticulture, fruit and seed growing, the keeping of any creature for the production of food; forestry, and the use of buildings for agriculture and forestry.

Exceptions Defined by Use Class

174 A further important relaxation arises from classifications of uses in the so-called Use Classes orders. The principle is that if land is being used for a purpose in a particular class, a change of use to any other purpose in the same class is considered not to be a development.

175 There are 18 classes of which the following are the most relevant:
Use as
Class I   a shop except to sell hot food, tripe, pets, cats' meat or motor vehicles.
Class II   an office;
III   a light industrial building;
IV   a general industrial building.
Uses as:
Class X   Warehouses and Repositories;
XI   Hotels, boarding and guest houses;
XII   Residential schools and colleges;

---

[1] Town and County Planning Act 1971 s 22 (1)

XIII   Churches, chapels, etc.

Class XIV   Hospitals, Sanatoria, and homes for children, old people, handicapped persons, and convalescents, and nursing homes.

Class XV   Non-residential health centres, clinics, nurseries, creches, surgeries and dispensaries.

Class XVI   Art Galleries, museums, and public libraries and halls.

Class XVII   Theatres, cinemas, music and concert halls.

Class XVIII   Dance halls, skating rinks, swimming, Turkish, vapour or foam baths, gymnasiums and sports halls.

Permitted Development and Enterprise Zones

176 Many developments, in some cases subject to condition, are permitted by the Secretary of State by General Development Order. There are 23 classes of these but only the following are likely to affect arts administration:

Class I   Within the curtilage of a dwelling-house.

Class II   Minor operations such as gates and fences under 2 metres high, access to roads, and painting of buildings.

Class III   Change of use from a general to a light industrial building, and from a shop selling hot food, tripe, pets, cats, meat or motor vehicles to a shop included in Use Class I.[1]

Class IX   Repairs to unadopted streets.

Class X   Repairs to services such as sewers and cables.

Class XI   Replacement of war damaged buildings.

Class XII   Development under local or private Acts.

In addition an Enterprise Zone Order may permit any development or class of development in advance within the Zone. These Zones exist in mostly run down, central urban areas and, in addition to enjoying significant relaxations of the planning law, they are temporary rate - and tax-havens.

Application for Planning Permission

177 If a proposed operation falls within none of the exceptions or permissions sketched above, it is a development for which permission is required, and for which the intending developer must apply to the district planning authority or, as the case may be, to the national park planning board. The authority to which he applies may pass it to a different authority. In any case, his application will

---

[1] See paragraph 175 above.

not fail because it was made to the wrong one, and the district planning authority must tell him the name of the authority to which the application has been passed.

178 The application is made on a form supplied by the authority or board, and must be accompanied by appropriate plans and specifications. Three copies may be required. It has long been a practice to ask for a fourth copy for the English parish or Welsh community council (which is entitled to notice) if one exits.

179 Applications may initially be for *outline planning permission*, for the erection of a building, followed by a further application for *detailed planning permission* for such matters as have been reserved by the authority for further approval under the outline planning permission.

Time Factor

180 If an application is not granted within two months, or such longer time as may be agreed between the applicant and the authority dealing with it, it is deemed to have been refused, and the applicant may, therefore, appeal against the refusal. In practice, extended periods are so readily agreed, that the average processing time for all but trivial cases is five months.

"Nasty Neighbours"

181 Applications for certain kinds of development have to be given special publicity. The applicant must advertise in a local newspaper, and, in addition must post up, reliably, a notice on the land, advertising his intention, for at least seven days in the month preceding the application, unless he has no right of access to the land. The advertisement and notice must name a place in the locality where the application and accompanying plans and documents are available for public inspection, and the authority cannot determine the application for at least three weeks after it has been issued.

182 These rules govern applications for:

Public Conveniences
Refuse Disposal
Scrap and Coal Yards

Mines and Quarries
Retention, Treatment or Disposal of Sewage, Trade Waste or
Sludge
Buildings Higher than 20 Metres
Slaughter Houses
Knackers Yards
Poultry Plucking or Killing
Casinos
Fun Fairs
Bingo Halls
Theatres
Cinemas
Music or Dance Halls
Skating Rinks
Swimming Baths or Gymnasiums (not part of a school, college or
university)
Turkish, Vapour or Foam Baths
Zoos
Dog or Cat Breeding or Boarding
Motor or Motor Cycle Race Tracks
Cemeteries

Outdoor Advertisements

183 A form of planning consent is required for any outdoor advertisement even if its display does not involve development. Advertisements displayed before 1 July 1948, may remain in use but the
local planning authority can challenge any such advertisement by
requiring the persons responsible for its display to apply for its
retention. There are also areas of special control[1] where only
defined classes of advertising are permitted, and where the
planning authority cannot grant consent for anything outside these
classes.

Advertisements Defined
184 The definition of advertisement for these purposes is extremely

---

[1] See paragraph below.

wide and includes:

"any word, letter, model, sign, placard, board, notice, device or representation, whether illuminated or not, in the nature of, and employed wholly or partly for the purposes of, advertisement, announcement or direction, and (without prejudice to the preceding provisions of this definition) includes any hoarding or similar structure used, or adapted for use, for the display of advertisements."

Thus the words "Theatre Box Office" on a shop fascia, or "Bloggs Art Gallery Upstairs" on a door plate will be advertisements as well as the large poster advertising a forthcoming attraction. Control does not apply, however, to:
i) advertisements on enclosed land not readily visible from outside or from any part of the enclosure to which there is public right of access;
ii) advertisements inside a building unless they are illuminated and visible from outside, or unless the building is one used principally for the display of advertisements;
iii) advertisements on vehicles;
iv) advertisements incorporated in and forming part of the fabric of the building, other than a building used principally for the display of advertisements or a hoarding;
v) advertisements displayed on articles for sale, or pumps or dispensing machines if the advertisement relating to the article for sale is not illuminated, and does not exceed 0.1 square metres in area.

Purposes of Control

185 These powers of control are powers of site control and must be exercised only in the interest of amenity and public safety.

In considering questions of amenity, the local planning authority must take into account the general characteristics of the locality, especially features of historic, architectural, cultural or similar interest. Under questions of public safety, it must consider the safety of those using any road, railway, canal, harbour or airfield likely to obscure or hinder the interpretation of traffic signs.

186 The authority may not impose any condition amounting to censor-

ship of the subject matter of any advertisement, nor may it consider such questions as the economic value or social desirability of advertisements, nor the revenue from rates which it may derive from commercial advertisements.

Deemed Consent

187 All advertisements covered by the regulations, require consent but, as with development control, the full rigour of the rule would be intolerable and so certain advertisements are *deemed* to have received consent. Apart from advertisements displayed on 1 August 1948 until challenged by the local planning authority, advertisements are deemed to have consent if they fall within any of the so called *specified classes*. These may be challenged by the local planning authority; and, conversely, the Secretary of State may direct that the classes are not in force in a particular area or in a particular case.

188 Arts institutions may find themselves within any or many of these six classes. They include:

CLASS I - *Functional advertisements* of local authorities, statutory undertakers and public transport undertakers;
CLASS II - Miscellaneous advertisements *relating to premises on which they are displayed*, viz :
a) for the purpose of identification, direction or warning not exceeding 0.2 square metre each;
b) relating to any person, partnership or company separately carrying on a profession, business or trade at the premises; limited to one advertisement, not exceeding 0.3 square metre in area, in respect of each such person, partnership or company, or, in the case of premises with entrances on different road frontages, one such advertisement at each of two such entrances;
c) relating to any institution of a religious, educational, cultural, recreational or medical or similar character . . . . on the land; limited to one advertisement, not exceeding 1.2 square metres in area, in respect of each such premises or, in the case of premises with entrances on different road frontages, two such advertisements displayed on different road frontages of the premises.
CLASS III - Certain *temporary* advertisements. This includes advertisements announcing any non-commercial local event of a religious, educational, cultural, political, social or recreational

character, or relating to any temporary matter in connection with such an event or local activity and limited to a display of advertisements occupying an area not exceeding a total of 0.6 square metre on any premises.

CLASS IV - Advertisements on *business premises*, (e.g. a commercial theatre) displayed wholly with reference to all or any of the following: the business or other activity carried on, the goods sold or services provided, and the name and qualifications of the person carrying on such business or activity or supplying such goods or services, on those premises, provided that:

a) no such advertisement may be displayed on the wall of a shop, unless the wall contains a shop window;

b) no such advertisement may be displayed so that the highest part of the advertisement is above the level of the bottom of any first-floor window in the wall on which it is displayed;

c) the space which may be occupied by such advertisements on any external face of a building in an area of special control must not exceed 0.1 of the overall area of that face up to a height of 3.6 metres from ground level; and the area occupied by any such advertisement is, notwithstanding that it is displayed in some other manner, computed as if the advertisement as a whole were displayed flat against the face of the building.

CLASS V - Advertisements on the *forecourts* of business premises wholly with reference to matters specified in Class IV above; limited as respects the aggregate area of the advertisements displayed under this class on any such forecourt to 4.5 square metres; but a building with a forecourt on two or more frontages is treated as having a eparate forecourt on each of those frontages.

CLASS VI - *Flag* advertisements.

3) Advertisements for which the period of express consent has expired unless the planning authority imposed a condition, when granting consent, that the advertisement may not continue to be displayed at the expiry date.

4) Advertisements relating to travelling circuses and fairs - subject to certain conditions these may be displayed on unspecified sites for a limited period.

Express Consent

189 Unless an advertisement has deemed consent, express consent must be obtained. The authority may refuse consent or may grant it subject to standard conditions and to any other conditions it

thinks fit. The standard conditions require advertisements to be kept clean, tidy and safe. Consent cannot be given for a period longer than five years without the approval of the Secretary of State; the authority may grant consent for a shorter period, but it must state its reasons for doing so.

Appeal

190 If the local planning authority refuses consent or attaches conditions, the applicant may appeal to the Secretary of State.

Development and Advertising Consent Combined

191 Though a proposed display may involve development, it is not necessary to apply for planning permission, for this is deemed to be granted by a consent.

Offences

192 It is an offence punishable by a fine to display an advertisement in contravention of the regulations. The persons displaying an advertisement are deemed to include not only he who puts it up, but also the person on whose land it is displayed and the person whose goods or business are advertised; but, in the latter two cases, it is a defence to show that the advertisement was displayed without his knowledge or consent.

Special Control Areas

193 In areas of special control, only the following classes of advertisement may be displayed:

Without express consent
advertisements in the specified classes;
advertisements inside buildings;
advertisements as to travelling circuses and fairs.

With express consent
structures for exhibiting notices of local activities;
announcements or directions relating to nearby buildings and land, e.g. hotels and garages;
advertisements required for public safety;
advertisements which would fall within one of the specified classes but for infringing the conditions as to height, number or illumination.

Easements and Estate Contracts

Definitions

194 An easement is a right (a) annexed to a plot of land (called the dominant tenement), (b) to utilise other land, (c) of a different owner (called the servient tenement), (d) in a particular manner, (e) not (as in a *profit a prendre*) involving the taking of anything from it, or (f) preventing the owner of the servient tenement from using his land. Easements, must actually benefit or accomodate the dominant tenement as such. There cannot be a right of way across servient land in Kent for a dominant tenement in Northumberland. Though, in a sense, invisible, easements are legally land,[1] and contracts and grants for them must follow rules relating to land.

195 An estate contract is made between a vendor of a large property and each purchaser of a smaller plot within it (as in a building estate), and is expressed to be for the benefit of purchasers of other plots. It is designed to maintain the character and value of the respective plots and commonly provides that purchasers shall, for example, fence their land properly, not build within a certain distance of their boundary, or allow their plot to be used for particular noxious or immoral purposes. In so far as such contracts are enforceable by (as well as against) other plot owners, they resemble easements.

Examples of Easements

196 Easements are either positive (i.e. to do something) or negative (i.e. to prevent something) or enable the dominant owner to create nuisances. The commonest *positive* easements are rights of way; rights of fixture (e.g. signs, hoardings, name plates, fascias, telephone wires); storage; the passage of air, gas, effluent or water through defined channels; the conveyance of electricity through specified cables. The commonest *negative* easements are the

---

[1] See paragraph 151.

rights to support and to light.[1] The commonest easements, *to create nuisances*, arise out of industrial or trading activities such as discharging smoke, emitting vibrations or noises.

Manner of Creation of Easements

197 Apart from those created by Act of Parliament, (e.g. in a railway act) an easement must be created, in principle, by a specific grant made by somebody qualified by age and by ownership of the fee simple of the servient tenement to make it. In fact, vast numbers enjoy no such ascertainable origin and are acquired by prescription*. There is no substance in the belief that a right of way is created by carrying a corpse along it.

198 Prescription is a succession of rules under which, if an easement has been exercised, without the use of force or concealment or with the servient owner's permission, for a long time, the law will presume the existence of a proper grant. The long term originally started with the coronation of Richard I (3rd September, 1189) but then, if the dominant owner showed very long continuous use, the court was ready to presume a grant made before that date, but since lost. The disadvantage of the rule is that such a claim is necessarily defeated if it can be shown that the right could not, or did not, exist at even one brief moment (e.g. by common ownership) since 1189. Hence, the courts developed the idea of the lost *modern* grant, and now presume such a grant if the right has been exercised for twenty years. This doctrine is sometimes vulnerable too, for a grant cannot be inferred if it would have been illegal at the time, or if it contravened a statute or custom, or if the supposed grantee or grantor was disqualified (e.g. a minor, or a statutory body without power to grant easements).

Hence, the Prescription Act, 1832, provides that the Lost Modern Grant doctrine applies after twenty years, but that after 40 years continuous use a claim can be defeated only by an express agreement by deed or in writing.

Limitation of Character of Easements

199 As easements abridge the enjoyment of the servient tenement, the

---

[1] For "ancient lights", see paragraphs 203-4 below.

law tends to construe them narrowly. Thus, if I am entitled to walk across your land, it does not follow that I may ride a horse, bicycle or other vehicle across it; a right to make one sort of noise will not entitle me to emit another which is louder or of a different, more strident, quality; and I must exercise my easement only for the benefit of my dominant tenement, not for some other (which I may have acquired) beyond it, and so, for example, increase the volume of the traffic across your land.

Extinction

200 Easements are extinguished (apart from statute) by deed, or by part performance, [1] or by presumption of a lost modern release after many years of non-use. The period so required tends to be longer than that required for a lost modern grant. It is a fallacy to suppose that rights of way have to be walked annually. In addition, easements are destroyed if the fee simple of the dominant and servient tenements fall into common ownership, but this destruction is suspended during the currency of any lease of the dominant tenement (otherwise the tenant might not be able to reach his own front door).An obsolete estate contract can sometimes be discharged, on application, by the Lands Tribunal.

Enforcement, Abatement and Resistance to Abuse

201 Where there is a wrongful interference with an easement, the dominant owner is entitled not only to sue for damages and an injunction, but he may instead abate the nuisance himself, that is, he may take physical action to put the matter right. If this does not involve entering the servient tenement, he may act at once. If it does, he should give notice to avoid a fight, unless of course there is an emergency. He must behave reasonably, doing no more than is essential to remove the interference and, though he may, if unavoidable, interfere with the servient owner's rights, he renders himself liable if he interferes with the rights or property of a third party.

202 The same rules in reverse apply to a servient owner who finds that the easement is being excessively used or abused; indeed, if the abuse cannot be abated without stopping the whole use, he may do

---

[1] See paragraph 139.

so, but he cannot obstruct lawful use by others (e.g. he cannot turn off a watermain to a whole block of flats because one tenant is using more than he should).

"Ancient Lights"

203 An easement of light (sometimes called "ancient light") can exist only for the benefit of a building and in respect of an aperture in it. It can be created in the same ways as other easements, and in three other ways as well. These are an informal assurance by the servient owner upon the faith of which the building with the necessary apertures is erected; an implied grant by a land owner who has reclaimed part of his land, and granted away another adjacent part, and thirdly, and most commonly of all, 20 years actual enjoyment of light accessible across the servient land. This last arises under the Prescription Act 1832: it cannot be claimed against the widespread properties of the Crown, and discontinuance of enjoyment (but not outside interruption) stops time running.

204 The right to light is not a right to a view but, to be successful a person who complains of an interference must show that according to the current notions of mankind his building (e.g. his picture gallery) must, to a sensible degree, be less fit for its purpose than it was before.[1]

Licences and Tickets to Use Land

General

205 In law, a licence is merely a permission to do something which would otherwise be unlawful. It creates no right of property and, therefore, it gives the licensee nothing which he can transfer to

---

[1] The management of the nineteenth century Gaiety Theatre encountered such a problem. They met with opposition from the *Morning Post*, a newspaper whose office windows overlooked a yard beside the site of their projected new theatre. Unwilling to be held up by legal processes, they solved their problem by building the offending portions of the theatre during a weekend when the staff of the *Morning Post* was away. The *Morning Post* gave in. A legal writer can hardly be expected to advise such a course, even if the resources of the modern building trade make it feasible.

somebody else. [1] You have no right to enter my theatre, conce hall, picture gallery or other place save with my leave even if you are with somebody who has my leave, and I am, in general, entitled to exact such conditions as I think fit for granting it.

Bare Licence

206 *A free or bare licence*, granted without consideration*, (e.g. the admission to a picture gallery simply by opening the doors) or admission to the areas of common access to the various parts of an arts centre can be withdrawn at any time, without notice and without reason given. I may lawfully expel you because I dislike your hairstyle. In practice, I do not behave like that because it creates trouble and gets into the newspapers. J put up notices forbidding certain things ("NO SMOKING"; "NO FOOD OR DRINK TO BE CONSUMED ON THE PREMISES"; or "STICKS AND UMBRELLAS TO BE HANDED IN TO THE CLOAKROOM".) and contravention of the notices then represents (without limiting my discretion) moments when I, certainly, will withdraw the licence. Such notices merely add to the occasions upon which all the world knows that this will happen: there are, indeed, others, and these are represented by the purpose, express or implied, for which you enter the premises. If you enter my picture gallery, you do so to look at the pictures, not to slash them, or molest other art lovers, or go to sleep on a bench or make a political speech. In such instances, the general nature of the permissible limits is fairly obvious and , in any case, I have an absolute right to determine them precisely. If I withdraw the licence, I say so or otherwise make the matter clear. If you do not leave within a reasonable time (which might be one minute if you are standing by the door), you are a trespasser as much as if you had broken in when the building was closed, and you may be dealt with accordingly.

Licence for Value

207 In the case of an *ordinary licence for value* (e.g. a theatre ticket), the situation is different. Such a licence is a contract whereby, in consideration of the payment, the licensee is admitted to the premises for a specific purpose (e.g. to view, from the numbered seat allotted to him, the play about to be performed) subject to

---

[1] But see paragraphs 210-211.

specific conditions, of which he must be informed in advance. He is, therefore, entitled, under the contract, to remain until the purpose has been accomplished, or get his money back. It may contain express stipulations printed on the ticket or it may incorporate stipulations by reference. This is done by printing on the ticket words such as: "issued subject to conditions incorporated in notices exhibited on the premises", and then having clear notices, (e.g. "No Smoking in the Auditorium") in large letters legible at a distance, put up at places where they will obviously be seen, especially before or at the time when the ticket is bought. Otherwise, there might be a dispute about offer and acceptance.[1] By this contractual means, the intending licensor can minimise the difference between a licence for value and a bare licence almost, but not quite, to a point of disappearance. The limit is that the conditions which he seeks to impose must not conflict with the purpose for which the licence (e.g. the ticket) is sold. This is most often an academic point, because if it does, the customer will not buy it, or will loudly demand his money back, but it can, however, arise in cases of more prolonged admission such as a licence to use a studio during a period of six months.

Implied Obligation of Licensor

208 If the licence for value has no express stipulations, its terms will be implied by the intention of the parties as inferred from the circumstances, and the customs of the particular activity. Admission to a concert implies not only the exclusive right to use a particular seat, but to use those parts (e.g. bars, restaurants, W.C.s) of the building in which members of the audience move or do things in common.

Implied Obligations of Licensee

209 The licensee, obviously, has correlative obligations. He must not do anything inconsistent with the purpose for which he is admitted, and the limitations on his behaviour are the same as if the licence were a bare one. If he persistently barracks the performance, for example, he can be asked to leave and compelled to do so if he refuses or fails to do so. If, strictly speaking, he is entitled to his money back, he is also, as a trespasser (which he

---

1 See paragraphs 395-406.

will have become) liable in damages for a good deal more, and will be glad to get away with it. Where a substantial sum is involved, as with a theatre box or a group booking, it is wise to take the names and addresses of those concerned and put off further argument to a later time. This will enable you to threaten (with some plausibility) counter proceedings if any claims are made.

Licensed Coupled with an Interest

210 There is a third type of licence which, whether for value or not, is irrevocable. This is known as a *licence coupled with an interest or grant*. This arises, commonly by implication, where the licence is ancillary to some acquired right of property which would be infringed or frustrated without it. If I sell you a picture in my gallery, or the gravel in my land or the right to put up posters on my hoarding, I must, if I am not to make delivery myself, not obstruct your access, and the licence is thus irrevocable as long as it is needed.

Assignment to Third Parties

211 A licence coupled with an interest can be assigned to someone else along with the interest. But otherwise, a bare licence cannot be assigned without the licensor's consent, and a licence for value is a contract to which the ordinary rules of contract apply. [1] Hence, it may stipulate (as often happens by the use of the words, "NOT TRANSFERABLE") that it is not to be assigned.

Enforceability against Third Parties

212 Neither bare licences nor licences for value (if not coupled with an interest) can be enforced by the licencee against a third party. If I grant a concession (short of a lease) to a caterer to sell food and drink in my theatre bar, and then sell the theatre, he cannot insist, against the wishes to the new owner, on continuing his previous activity. He may, of course, have a case against me for breach of contract.

Enforcing a licence coupled with an interest against a third party, may be more complicated. If the ownership of the interest has passed to the licensee (you have bought and paid for the gravel or

---

[1] See paragraphs 392-439 especially 438-9.

the picture) the licence is enforceable against the person to whom I have meanwhile sold the land or (very probably) the gallery. If, however, there is only a contract to pass the interest, and the interest has not yet passed, perhaps because it stipulates for a future date or because you have not yet paid, then, in the case of land, the licence will be enforceable against the person to whom I have sold it, only if the licence is registered in the Land Charges Register* as an estate contract. There is no similar arrangement for registering agreements about chattels*: hence it seems that in this case, you would not be able to fetch the picture from the gallery which I have sold.

Borderline between Licences, Leases and Easements

213 Whatever a grant is called in the document by which it is made, the courts will pay attention to the realities. An easement exists for the benefit of a dominant tenement, that is, for a piece of land. A licence exists only for the benefit of a person. Similarly, it will usually be easy to tell whether a grant is really a lease or a licence, because a lease (even if called a licence) gives exclusive possession of the land, whereas a licence (by whatever name known) usually gives only a right to do something or some particular things on it. All the same, it is possible to grant a licence which entitles the licencee to exclude all others and, in such a case, the distinction between a lease and a licence will depend upon whether the conduct of the parties shows that it was intended to pass an interest in the property (which is good against all the world) or merely to confer a personal privilege (which is not), as most often happens where there is "a family arrangement, an act of friendship or generosity or such like to negative any intention to create a tenancy"[1]. All the same, the law tends to presume a lease in cases of exclusive possession and, therefore, if a licence is intended, the intention should be enunciated clearly. This is particularly important where people are admitted regularly to premises or rooms, such as studios or practice rooms, for intensive and sometimes prolonged daily use and who then get into the convenient habit of leaving music scores, books, instruments, artist's materials, equipment or clothes there, and then, after a while, begin to assert that the place is "theirs".

---

[1] Per Denning LJ in *Fucchini* v *Bryson*, 1952, 1 TLR 1386.

OWNERS OR OCCUPIERS OBLIGATIONS IN PREMISES

DESIGN SPECIFICATION CONSTRUCTION

MANAGEMENT SUPERVISION

BUILDING REGULATIONS (formerly Byelaws)
—Materials
—Site Preparation
—Stability
—Conservation of Fuel & Power
—Sound Insulation
—Crowd and Vehicle Control
—Refuse
—Ventilation etc.
—Chimney and Flues
—Heating and Incinerators
—Drainage and Sanitation

FIRE PRECAUTIONS Fire Certificates
—Means of Escape
—Fire Fighting Equipment
—Warning Apparatus
—Limitation on Numbers on the Premises

HEALTH AND SAFETY AT WORK
—Plant
—Systems of Work
—Handling and Storage
—Ease of Access and Egress
—Working Environment
—Training
—Information
—Policy Statement
—Safety Representative
—Safety Committee

Mostly enforced by Criminal Sanctions

LICENSING by Justices or Other Authorities
—Liquor
—Theatre
—Cinema
—Music and Dancing
—Sundays
—Billiards
—Betting and Gaming
—Gaming Machines

OCCUPIERS LIABILITY
—Common Duty of Care
—Lawful Visitors
—Trespassers

TORT
—Negligence
—Breach of Statutory Duty

Condition of Premises

General

214 The laws on the condition of premises have different origins and purposes, and compliance with one group of laws, particularly on safety, will not necessarily protect the owner against proceedings brought by somebody who has suffered an injury: their purpose is to prevent trouble, in particular cases, but, in general, they can be completely effective only at the moment when they are enforced; the occupier remains liable to anyone who gets hurt, even in those cases, unless he can show that there was a hidden defect of which he could not have been aware, but which should have been observed by a diligent building inspector at the time. This can happen in the case of foundations or other parts of a building liable to be covered up after inspection. A second purchaser, whose house fell down, has successfully sued the district council for the negligence of its inspectors, for the defects were unknown to the preceding owners.

Building Regulations

215 If I wish to erect a building, or alter it structurally, or execute works or install appliances (such as a W.C. or gas boiler) in it or make a material change in its use, I must comply with the Building Regulations 1976. These are voluminous and full of technical tables, and their purpose is to ensure that the substance of which a building is composed and its arrangement is such that it will, so far as the substance is concerned, be safe for its purpose. For reasons which will appear, a detailed understanding of these regulations is unnecessary (and probably unattainable) for a layman, but their general purport should be more widely known than it is.

The regulations, then, lay down standards for (Part B) materials, (C) preparation of site and resistance to moisture (D) structural stability (E) safety in fire [1] (F) thermal insulation of dwellings (FF) conservation of fuel and power in buildings other than dwellings (G) sound insulation (H) stairways, ramps, balustrades and vehicle barriers (J) refuse disposal (K) open space, ventilation and height of rooms (L) chimneys, flues, hearths and fireplace recesses (M) heat producing appliances and incinerators (N) drainage, private sewers and cesspools and (P) sanitary conveniences.

Notice of Intention to Build

216 The authority whose business it is to enforce the regulations is the London borough or district council, each of which employs expert building inspectors for the purpose. If I wish to do any of the things governed by the regulations I must give notice of my intention in accordance with Schedule 3 to them, and this notice must include various plans, sections and specifications in writing. The subject matter of these will depend upon whether I am erecting a partially exempt building (e.g. a potting shed or separate machine house), or any other building, or making alterations or extensions or undertaking works and installing fittings. The authority's inspectors can also require detailed drawings and calculations. The practical effect is to force people to employ an architect in all substantial operations, or an experienced builder with a drawing office, in the others.

Later Notices

217 Secondly, assuming that the building inspectorate has passed the plans (upon which, of course, it may raise inquiries), "the builder", that is to say I or my contractor, must give notice to the authority in writing on certain occasions. The nature of these is such that in practice it is most convenient for the contractor to give it. The occasion and length of notice is as follows:

---

[1] See also paragraphs 220-223.

(i)	Date and time of commencement of the operation	
(ii)	Before covering up excavations for foundation, damp course, or any concrete or other material laid over the site:	twenty four hours
(iii)	Before haunching or covering any drain or private sewer:	
(iv)	Before executing works or installing "fittings":	seven days

218 Though in general the authority must enforce the standards centrally laid down, it has power (save in Inner London), on application, to dispense with or relax any of them, except those in Part D on structural stability; and there is a right of appeal, against a refusal, to the Secretary of State.[1]

219 While in real life my participation in these procedural matters is nominal rather than actual, my architect and my contractor will in every case be acting as my agent and may thereby be fastening a liability to third parties upon me if something goes wrong. Of course if something does go wrong, I may (sometimes) be able to sue them, or the authority, for negligence, but this is often an uncertain and expensive consolation.

Fire Precautions

220 Building Regulations Part E and their predecessors the Building Byelaws have long imposed standards of fire precautions, but the Fire Precautions Act 1971 has introduced a system which will slowly but inexorably impose standards regulated by fire experts. The Secretary of State[1] can designate particular classes of buildings so long as they are used for entertainment, recreation, instruction or for purposes of any club, society or organisation,

---

[1] For the Environment.

or for use involving public access or as a place of work, and he may make regulations about fire precautions respecting them. It then becomes an offence to use a building for a designated purpose without a fire certificate. This is issued by the fire authority (the county council or a combination of them) and specifies the means of escape and the ways in which they are to be kept clear, the type, number and location of fire fighting equipment and warning apparatus, and it may lay down requirements about their maintenance, about training and about limiting the number of people allowed on the premises at one time.

221 The Fire Authority's powers are so peremptory that it may require alterations to buildings before it will issue a certificate. Hence the 1971 Act contains co-ordinating provisions. The building regulations authority must consult the fire authority before passing certain plans or dispensing with or relaxing requirements under the building regulations, and the fire authority must consult the building regulations authority before requiring alterations.

222 There is a right of appeal to a magistrate's court within 21 days against a refusal of a fire certificate or against an onerous provision in one. Apart from these provisions, which apply only in designated cases, a fire authority may apply on the ground of serious fire risk to persons, to a magistrates court to close or restrict the use of any building which can be designated (whether designated or not).

All arts institutions fall within the definition of places which can be designated, therefore the threat of closure by magistrate's order hangs over them all. This and the provisions for co-ordination make it highly desirable to consult the fire authority at all appropriate stages, whether or not a fire certificate is legally needed at the time, for otherwise the authority may later have to take enforcement action when, as a result of a further designation order, a fire certificate becomes compulsory.

223 Local authorities may make loans on mortgage to enable alterations to be made, in cases where a fire certificate might otherwise be refused. The problem with such loans is the high rates of interest reigning in the 1980's. Any local authority, including the

lending authority, however, has power [1] to incur expenditure which is in its opinion for the benefit of its area or its inhabitants, or in contributions to the funds of a charity, and this power might be used to reduce the weight of interest charges so long as the loan exists.

Health and Safety at Work

224 We have now reached the stage where a suitable and legally safe building exists. It is now necessary to anticipate things which may go wrong because of the way in which circumstances within it affect people working there, - and some others. The 1974 Act was passed to secure the health, safety and welfare of persons at work and of persons who might be affected by their activities, and to control or prevent the use of or acquisition of explosive, flammable or dangerous substances and the emission of noxious or offensive substances into the atmosphere from relevant premises. This is done by imposing a long series of obligations on employers and self-employed people, a very few on employees, and the creation of a Health & Safety at Work Commission and Executive with an inspectorate. It should be observed, however, that nearly all the provisions of the act, in so far as they are enforceable, are enforced by criminal sanctions and, except for some breaches of health and safety regulations causing damage, never give rise to civil liability. The act thus leaves the common law on this subject (for example, on negligence) virtually untouched).

Employer's Duties

225 The employers' duties are to ensure, so far as is reasonably prac-ticable, the health, safety and welfare at work of all his employees, in particular in plant and systems of work, and in the use, handling, transport and storage of articles and substances; by providing necessary information, training, instruction and super-vision; by maintaining places of work so as to be safe, healthy and easy to enter and leave; and by providing a working environment

---

[1] Under Section 137 of the Local Government Act 1972.

which is safe, without health risks and adequate for the employees' welfare at work. He must in prescribed cases make and periodically revise a statement of policy on these matters and bring it to his employees' notice, and he must consult a safety representative (if any) appointed from his employees (but representatives appointed by Equity and the Musician's Union need not be in his employ), by a trade union which he has recognised, or which has been recommended for recognition by ACAS* and must, if required to do so by two such representatives, set up a safety committee.

Safety Representative

226 The safety representative is entitled in his employer's time and at his expense, but is under no duty, to investigate hazards, dangerous occurrences and complaints relating to employees' health, safety or welfare at work, to make representations to the employer about them or general relevant matters, to inspect premises and relevant documents, to represent the employees at meetings with inspectors and enforcement officers at the work place, and to receive information from them and to attend meetings of the safety committee if any. The regulations [1] also contain a code of practice in six paragraphs and a set of guidance notes for representatives (in 27 paragraphs) and for safety committees (in 25 paragraphs).

Duty to Persons who are Not Employees

227 To persons other than employees there is a duty to provide information. To persons working on the premises who are not employees (e.g. artists in a public studio) the person controlling the premises has a duty to ensure that the premises, its entrances and egresses and any plant or substance there, are safe and without risks to health.

Regulations and Codes of Practice

228 The Executive has a very extensive power to make regulations and codes of practice. Regulations are enforceable criminally, and, as we have seen, may occasionally give rise to civil liability. Codes of

---

[1] SI 1977 No 500.

practice are not enforceable directly in either sense, but failure to observe a code is evidence in criminal proceedings under other health and safety regulations, and may create a presumption against a defendant. Regulations on Cinematograph Films[1] contain all the law on this subject and there are Code of Practice on Industrial Safety Belts, Harnesses and Safety Lanyards,[2] General Purpose Industrial Safety Helmets,[3] Workwear,[4] Rubber Gloves for Electrical Purposes[5] and Safety Footwear.[6]

Notifiable Accidents and Occurrences

229 Employers are obliged to notify certain types of accidents and dangerous occurrences to the enforcing authority, in practice represented by the inspectors. The *notifiable accidents* are those involving a major injury (a fracture of the skull, spine, pelvis, arm or leg bones other than in the wrist, hand, ankle or foot; the loss of a hand, foot or eye; and any injury involving 24 hours admission to hospital for treatment as an in-patient). The many *dangerous occurrences* include the collapse or overturning of any lift, hoist or crane, or failure of any load-bearing part of it which might have caused a major injury; boiler explosions; short circuits stopping work for 24 hours or likely to have caused a major injury; collapse of scaffolds more than 12 metres high; uncontrolled releases of substances likely to injure health.

Inspectors' Powers

230 An inspector has very extensive powers. He can enter relevant premises at all reasonable hours, accompanied if necessary by the police, and bringing with him necessary testing, sample testing and photographic equipment for use on or off the premises. If he finds dangerous things or substances he can require them to be dismantled or treated, and can impound them for examination or as evidence; and he is entitled to inspect books. If he concludes that a relevant statutory provision is being contravened or that such a contravention is likely to be continued or repeated, he can serve an *improvement notice* setting out the provisions concerned, the reasons why he thinks that they are being contravened and requiring the contravention to be remedied within a defined time.

---

[1] SI 1974 No 1841   [2] BS 1397:1979.   [3] BS 524:1975.   [4] BS 5426:1976.
[5] BS697:1977.   [6] BS 1870:1979.

Where activities are being or are about to be carried on which involve a risk of serious personal injury he may serve a *prohibition notice* to stop it at once. There are rights of appeal to an Industrial Tribunal against both types of notice. Where an inspector finds an article or substance which is in imminent danger of causing serious injury he may seize it and render it harmless.

Licensing (Liquor etc)

General

231 Assuming safe buildings and a healthy and safe working environment, there still remain a number of things which must not be done without a licence from a competent authority. These, and the competent authority concerned are as follows:-

Activity	Competent Authority
Sale of Liquor	In most cases the Licencing Justices for the local Petty Sessional area.
Theatre	Royal Letters Patent or in London the GLC and elsewhere the district council.
Cinema	In London the GLC, elsewhere the district council.
Music and Dancing	In London the GLC. In Essex, Hertfordshire, and in other areas within 20 miles from the City of London or Westminster, the district council. Elsewhere, if the legislation has been adopted by the district council, the Licencing Justices. Otherwise, no licence is required.
Sunday Public Entertainments	Ditto.
Billiards (including bar billiards, bagatelle and anything similar)	Licencing Justices.

Betting and Gaming	After certification by the Gaming Board, the Betting Licencing Committee of the Justices for the local Petty Sessional Area.
Gaming Machines	On on-licenced premises the Licencing Justices, elsewhere the district council.

Liquor Licensing (Privileged Cases)

232 If you wish to sell liquor by retail no Justices Licence is required if it is to sell wine only *and* it is licenced by Cambridge University or you are a member of the Worshipful Company of Vintners and the bar or shop in or within 3 miles of the City of London, in 30 so-called "porte towns", in 8 "thoroughfare towns" in the Dover Road or 34 such towns on the Great North Road. In addition, no theatre bar needs a licence to sell any type of liquor, if the theatre itself is licenced under the Theatres Act 1968 or byRoyal Letters Patent.

Justices Licences

233 If you are not in one of these privileged categories, you must obtain a Justices Licence. This is granted by the Licensing Justices who are a committee of JPs sitting at specially appointed licensing sessions. The licensing year runs from 5th April until 4th April next following. The Licensing Justices are required to hold an Annual Session (often called Brewster Sessions) during the first fortnight of February, and must fix and publicly notify the date and place at least 21 days beforehand. This means in practice that an application should be properly prepared before Christmas and have been submitted by the first week in January. The Brewster Sessions can be, and in busy areas habitually are, continued by adjournment, and it is usual to deal with routine unopposed applications first and with opposed or doubtful cases later. Since adjournments can last weeks, the advantages of making properly prepared and uncontroversial applications are obvious.

In addition to the Annual Sessions the magistrates must hold four or up to eight Transfer sessions each year.

Types of Licences

234 *On-licences** are either
    A *Ordinary* i.e. for consumption by non-residents
    B *Restaurant* i.e. for consumption with a sit-down meal
    C *Residential* i.e. for consumption by residents only,
and any of these three may authorise the sale of
    i Intoxicating liquor of all descriptions
    ii Beer, cider and wine only
    iii Beer and cider only
    iv Cider only
    v Wine only.
This gives 15 possible types.
Off-licences* permit sales for consumption off the premises of either
    i Intoxicating liquor of all descriptions
    or
    ii Beer, cider and wine only.

Applications

235 The most elaborate form of application is an application for a New Licence. In this the applicant must state:
    a His full name
    b His full address
    c His trade or occupation or all of them during the six months ending with the date of application
    d The type of licence desired
    e The situation of the premises to which the licence is to apply
and, in addition,
    f He must deposit a plan of the premises drawn, marked and coloured in accordance with the magistrates' requirements.

In most places, forms of application are obtainable from the Clerk to the Licencing Justices. Besides the application and plan themselves, the application has to be advertised by a notice at the premises for at least eight days before the hearing, and by an advertisement in a newspaper circulating in the vicinity. Moreover, the applicant must give notice to the police, the district council, and, where there is one, to the parish council in England or its Welsh equivalent, the Community Council, and also to the Fire Authority.

236 Other sorts of applications follow this pattern with or without notifications as under. LJJ = Licensing Justices.

Table of Notices of Application

Nature	Period of Notice	To Whom	Advertisements	Notice on Premises	Plans
New Licence Removal of Licence: Special Ordinary Hours Extended Loans for restaurant with music or entertainment Billiards	21 days	Clerk of LJJ Police Proper local authorities Fire Authority	Yes	Yes	Yes
Renewal of Licence	None, but applicant must appear in person on the day				
Occasional	24 hours	Clerk of LJJ Police (1)	No	No	No
Special Hours for Music and Dancing	7 days (2)	Clerk of LJJ Police	No	No	Yes
Table Meal Extension	7 days (2)	Clerk of LJJ Police (3)	No	No	No
Transfer of Licence	21 days	Clerk of LJJ Police Proper local authorities	No	No	No

(1) but if **two** notices are served on the Clerk he must pass one to the police.

(2) but 14 days notice must be given to the police before the extension or special hours are put into practice on the premises. The two periods can be combined in a single 14 days.

(3) In the case of a registered club, this application is made to the Magistrates' Court.

237 Appeals

Appeals are made to the Crown Court. In addition to the cases marked on the table there is a right of appeal against (1) any condition imposed on an on-licence and (2) any refusal to make a provisional grant final, to affirm a provisional grant or to consent to modifications of deposited plans (3) an order requiring a structural alteration or refusing consent to one (4) extinguishment of a suspended licence or refusal to postpone extinguishment.

238

Notice of appeal has to be given to the Clerk of the Licencing Justices (and others) within 21 days and the grounds of the appeal must be stated in the notice. Such notices and the appeal procedure tend to be technical and are generally best put into professional hands.

239 Restrictive Covenants

Covenants, however expressed, forbidding or restricting the sale of liquor upon or the use as a bar of particular premises are quite common and often of long standing. This complicated subject is unsuitable for treatment here, but it is important to know of the existence and nature of such covenants, if any, before acquiring premises. Such a covenant has occasionally been held to have lapsed where the person entitled to enforce it has failed to do so for several years, and the Lands Tribunal has power to discharge a covenant in whole or part, but it has to be satisfied of one of three matters, viz:

(i) that changes in the character of the property or neighbourhood or other material circumstances have rendered the covenant obsolete, or that its continuance in its existing form will impede the reasonable use of the property without securing corresponding benefit to others; or
(ii) that those entitled for the time being to the benefit of the covenant are of full age and capacity and have agreed to the change; or

(iii) that those entitled under the covenant will not be injured by the change.

Occupiers Liability

240 If I enter premises belonging to someone else, and there suffer an injury, who, if anyone, is liable to me, in what circumstances and to what extent?

The Responsible Occupier

241 The person who must make premises safe is not necessarily the owner or tenant as such, but the person who "has a sufficient degree of control over the premises that he ought to realise that any failure on his part to use care may result in injury to a person coming lawfully there". There may be several such people each under a duty in different circumstances. *My tenant's lodger breaks his neck at the foot of the stairs in the dark. If he fell because the stairs collapsed, I might be liable because structural defects are usually repaired by landlords. If a missing stair rod caused the carpet to trip him, my tenant might be liable since the maintenance and arrangement of furnishings is usually the business of a tenant. If he was tripped up by a wire left by an electrician called in to rewire the staircase lighting, the electrician, though an outside contractor, might be liable.* Each in his sphere "has a sufficient degree of control over the premises that he ought to realise . . . ". Each, then, is an occupier for the purpose of this branch of the law.

The Lawful Visitor

242 The occupier owes a duty of care to a lawful visitor, that is to say, first to someone entering the premises in the exercise of a right conferred by law (eg, firemen, police with search warrants, gas and electricity meter readers, health and safety inspectors) or, secondly, to any other sort of visitor who is not a trespasser. The occupier, however, can vary his liability to this other sort of visitor by contract.

The Premises

243 The definition of the premises within which an occupier can be liable to a lawful visitor, is as singular as the general definition of land in the law of property. It includes land so defined, and, in addition, structures not necessarily attached to the land such as grandstands, scaffolding and staging and even moveable structures such as ships, aircraft, railway trains, (in a Canadian case) a car, and a large tunnel digging machine. The liability in all these cases arises out of the condition of the premises, not their operation. *I am hurt by falling through a hole in the floor of the bus. The occupier is liable to me. I am injured on a bus journey through a collision. The person liable, if anyone, is the driver or some other driver.*

The Common Duty of Care

244 The duty which is owed to a lawful visitor upon the premises is called the *Common Duty of Care*. It is "a duty to take such care as in all the circumstances of the case is reasonable, to see that the visitor will be reasonably safe in using the premises for the purposes for which he is invited or permitted by the occupier to be there".

245 Reasonable care in all the circumstances does not make the occupier into an insurer. A foreseeable hazard (e.g. *a trained ballerina being thrown seven feet by her partner, or an acrobat's moll being swung beyond the safety net*) is not necessarily probable. "Reasonable care involves consideration of the nature of the danger, the length of time that the danger was in existence, the steps necessary to remove it and the likelihood or otherwise of an injury being caused." An occupier must, however, be prepared for children to be less careful than adults, but, on the other hand, may expect an expert to guard against special risks in his field. *I am too old and fat to get through your balustrade, but little Willy aged four may do so; if the local council grows delicious looking but poisonous plants in its park, and little Willy eats his fill and dies, the council will be liable. Conversely, the electrician, whom I engage to mend a defective circuit, may be expected to appreciate the dangers inherent in the defect and cannot expect me to protect him against them, but, of course, I must keep him safe against other hazards.*

246 As little Willy's adventures show, premises which are perfectly safe to one sort of person may be a trap for another. The Common Duty of Care is to render the particular lawful *visitor* safe. It is no defence for the occupier to prove, in the abstract, that he did everything reasonable to render the premises safe and that he complied with all the building Regulations and the Health and Safety legislation, though naturally these things will be helpful in practice. He still owes the Common Duty of Care to the particular lawful visitor. This is why a guard dog can be a mixed blessing: he does not always appreciate the legal difference between a lawful visit and a trespass.

Duty to Trespassers

247 It should, however, be observed that the Common Duty is not owed to an unlawful visitor, that is to say a trespasser. A person who comes in without permission or who is allowed or invited in for one purpose and then abuses his position to do something else, or someone whose permission to be there is withdrawn (e.g. when the museum closes) is a trespasser, though in some cases it may not be easy to prove the moment he became one. An occupier is bound to take reasonable precautions of the sort of humanitarian kind which will avoid serious injury (e.g. by preventing children from playing with electrical apparatus or by ensuring that the guard dog is not mortally ferocious) but subject to this a trespasser takes the premises as he finds them. It is otherwise where a trespasser is complaining of injury on the premises but at the hands of someone who is not the occupier (*e.g. where a plaintiff without a cinema ticket who is tripped up in the cinema by someone with a ticket*). Here the occupier is not liable, but the ticket holder cannot plead that his victim is a trespasser because the trespass is not against him.

Injuries

248 The injuries for which the occupier can be made liable to a lawful visitor are physical personal injuries, including infection and nervous shock; material damage incidental or ancillary to the personal injury (e.g. to clothes); to property (whether his own or someone else's) which he has brought on to the premises for the purpose for which he entered (e.g. to a contractor's apparatus),

---

[1] See paragraphs 345-7.

and to property placed on the premises with the occupier's consent and damaged, even though the plaintiff was not present. The liability includes liability for economic loss as a result of the injury. On the other hand liability for thefts by third parties cannot be implied in this way, though it can be created by contract.

Copyright[1]

General

249 The law of copyright is a statutory body of rules for protecting the economic interest of creators of works of art in the products of their own creativity. The rules do not protect an idea[2] until it has been reduced into a physical form; the form may be literary, dramatic, pictorial or sculptured, musical, or photographic in type but the rules are not wholly uniform in relation to the type, or to the country concerned or to the historical period when a given protected work was created. The subject has a strong international element because in the Western World four languages, viz, English, Spanish, Arabic and French account for over 60% of the literary output, with English well ahead of the others. World wide codification and uniformity is being slowly achieved through two international conventions, namely, the higher standard Berne Convention of 1886 and the lower standard Universal Copyright Convention of 1952: these were revised together at Paris in 1971. The international scene was until July 1982 dominated by the divergent policies of, on the one hand, British Commonwealth countries and, on the other, of USA, but between 1978 and July 1982 US law abandoned some of its predatory features and was approximated to those of the 1952 convention. The possession of English copyright protection does not, however, necessarily provide the same protection in the USA or elsewhere.

---

[1] This is a necessarily brief summary. The reader is invited to consult "Performance" by Leslie E Cotterell and published by John Offord (Publications) Ltd in 1977.

[2] See paragraphs 254-6.

Creation and Limited Duration after Publication

250 All western systems have two common features. Protection is never accorded to published works in perpetuity but only for a period of time, and, secondly, a copyright comes into existence simply by the author's [1] act of creation even though the author may not in fact be its owner. When the work is turned into a physical form the copyright automatically attaches to it; in the Commonwealth systems this is enough to enable the owner to enforce his rights, but in the USA three formalities are required beforehand. The published copies must show the copyright statement, consisting of the word "copyright", or the symbol©, with the year and his name; two copies must be deposited with the Library of Congress; and the work must be registered with the Congressional Copyright Office. As a matter of convenience most modern English books (including this one) carry the © symbol, but this is required by American not English law. Some other countries (e.g. France) have domestic formalities before action to enforce a copyright can be taken, but whatever the formalities are, only the copyright owner (or his agent) can operate them.

The First Owner

251 The first owner of a copyright is the author (or other creator) unless someone else commissions him to make it, or he is employed in the service of a newspaper or periodical to produce work for publication in it, or he makes the work in the course of his employment. In such cases the commissioner or the employer owns the copyright unless there is an agreement between him and the author making some other arrangement.

Copyright Owner's Remedies

252 The essence of copyright is that the owner may, with certain limited exceptions, prevent (by injunction) anyone else from publishing or performing the contents of a copyright work; he can require the customs to stop the importation of infringing copies; he can force the infringer to account for and surrender his profits, and he can treat infringing copies as if they were his own and had been

---

[1] For publisher's secondary copyright see paragraph 256.

converted [1] by the infringer. Alternatively, he is entitled to damages unless the infringer did not know and could not reasonably have known of the copyright, and conversely he may be awarded additional damages if the infringement is flagrant or highly profitable to the infringer. If, however, the infringement consists in the construction of a building in accordance with a copyright plan, he cannot obtain an injunction once construction has begun, but must content himself with the other remedies.

The General Rules on Duration

253 There is no limit on the duration of a copyright in an **unpublished** work but apart from a now small and dwindling number of cases where copyright (e.g. most of the Savoy Operas, and Kenneth Graham's *Wind in the Willows*) arose before 1912, copyright in a **published** work endures for the lifetime of the creator plus the remaining period of the year in which he died plus the next 50 whole years; if, however, it is first published, performed, broadcast or offered for public sale after his death, such event is treated as if it were his death. In the case of a work published in the lifetime of joint authors, the death of the last of them counts as the death. In the case of anonymous or pseudonymous works, however, the author or authors are treated as already dead unless their identity can be established by reasonable inquiry within the 50 years after first publication, by anyone without previous knowledge of the facts.

254 For *sound recordings, films and sound or television broadcasts,* the period is fifty years from first publication, but certain 35 mm films, other than newsreels and commercials, have to be registered before they are shown, and for these registrable films the period runs from registration.

255 *Artistic* copyrights endure, with one, photographic, exception, for the same periods. Artistic works for this purpose include (irrespective of artistic quality) paintings, sculptures, drawings, engravings, photographs, buildings and models of them, and also works of artistic craftsmanship having some artistic quality. In contrast with the rules in defamation, publication, so as to start time running, is not considered to have occurred merely because a

---

[1] See paragraphs 349-351.

work has been exhibited or performed; copies must have been made available for sale to the public. Photographs, however, are protected for 50 years after the year of publication whether the creator is alive or dead.

Publishers Secondary Copyright

256 A copyright also exists for 25 years in any typographical arrangement from the end of the year in which it was published. This, of course, includes a book and belongs, in the absence of other agreement, to the publisher. This secondary copyright is designed to protect him against photographic reproduction of work whose printing he has financed, even though the main copyright has since been licenced to someone else. A separate copyright of this class subsists in each edition of a work.

Quality of Copyrighted Material - Originality

257 Apart from typographical copyright, material, which can be protected, must be "original". This does not mean "unique" or even necessarily "unprecedented". The work must have been the product of its creator's mind, and (though he may find his case hard to prove) he will have a copyright even though someone else has created an identical work. On the other hand, mere copying, or the assemblage of trite phrases, or meaningless compilations cannot be protected.

Quality of Copyrighted Material - Aesthetic Quality

258 A literary work is simply a work in words reduced to a permanent material condition. No aesthetic merit is necessary. Copyright has been upheld in a business letter, an abridgment, and a railway timetable. The issue is unlikely to arise in this form in the case of dramatic and musical works because they must have *some* merit to be worth copying. No artistic quality is required for paintings, drawings, sculptures, engravings or photographs, but the exclusion is not maintained for works of architecture, and, in the case of works of craftsmanship, some artistic quality above a mere appeal to the eye is positively required. A plaintiff whose furniture (according to him) was "horrible, vulgar and brash" was refused protection because it did not deserve the statutory epithet "artistic".

Form of Copyrighted Material

259 Oddly enough, there seems to be no direct authority on the question whether a work can be copyrighted if it is not reduced to its customary material form. This question is nowadays important. A material form there must be, (which probably excludes a comedian's special gestures or "business") but suppose that an author dictates the first draft of his novel into a tape recorder, or a pop singer bawls a song for the first time into a microphone and recorder at a public concert, or a design is recorded as a computer program held in a memory bank, or somebody tape-records the recitation of an impromptu poem or a comedian's jokes or catch phrases? As long ago as the 6th Century, Justinian distinguished between the work of an artist and the paint and the wood or canvas of which it was composed, and there seems to be no obstacle to a similarly sensitive interpretation of the Copyright Act 1956.

Protection of Ideas

260 Since an idea is not, as such, a work (whether literary, dramatic, musical or artistic) there obviously cannot be copyright in it; on the other hand, it is going too far to say that the law of copyright protects only the form to which it is reduced. A reproduction in picture form of a novel has been held an infringement, and so has a stage version even though no line of dialogue was similar to any sentence in the novel. There is a dividing line between a general idea or single fact underlying a work, and, on the other hand, a detailed assemblage of ideas, facts, incidents or reasoning, necessarily expressed as a work, in a physical form, and bearing the imprint of its creator's mental personality and style. The former will not be protected, the latter may be. Whether a given defendent has overstepped the mark is a question of fact, to be teased out at a trial.

Ideas and Confidence

261 Somebody with an idea may or may not be able to protect it through copyright against all the world, but there are two circumstances in which he may protect it against one or more particular persons. The first is an express agreement, enforceable as a contract, whereby he will not disclose ideas to someone in consideration, usually, of commercial negotiations. The second, much

commoner situation, is known as the *equitable doctrine of confidence*, which is distantly related to the doctrine of the trust. Business people habitually tell each other things which are confidences necessary to keep business going, and they seldom consult their lawyers before lifting the telephone. Such disclosures are seldom protected by a contract, but they can be protected without one, provided that three conditions are satisfied.

262 These are, firstly, that the information is in its nature confidential, and not, for example, already in the public domain (e.g. that it can be found in an encyclopedia or that a supposedly secret object is in fact readily purchaseable, or that the secret has been publicly announced in an after dinner speech). Secondly, that the circumstances in which it was communicated imported such an obligation of confidence as any reasonable man would recognise, for example, where the information is "given on a businesslike basis and with come avowed common purpose in mind.[1] Thirdly, there must have been an unauthorised use of the information detrimental to the person who originally imparted it, (e.g. where a publisher's reader uses the ideas in a given manuscript to write and publish a book on the same subject himself). In such a case the injured party can proceed, usually by way of injunction, against anyone to whom the confidence has been disclosed without his permission. He must, however, be able to trace the connection or channel of communication.

What is Infringement of Copyright? - Direct

263 It is an infringement of any copyright, without permission to reproduce the work in any material form or to publish it by making copies available to the public. In addition, in the case of an artistic copyright, it is an infringement without permission to include it in a television programme whether broadcast or diffused, and in the case of a literary, dramatic or musical work to perform it in public, broadcast it or transmit it on a diffusion service, or to make an adaptation of it. Moreover, for purposes of protection, such an adaptation is treated as if its copyright belonged to the copyright owner of the original.

---

[1] *Coco v A N Clark* 1906 RPC at p48.

Indirect Infringement

264 It is just as much an infringement to effect the above infringements by importation, or by knowingly exposing for sale or hiring out things which constitute infringement by someone else, or by knowingly or for gain permitting a place of public entertainment to be used for an infringing performance.

Study, Fair Dealing and Quotation

265 To these sweeping rules there exists a major exception concerned with musical performing rights and records and a number of limited exceptions in favour mainly of the use of works in libraries for purposes of study, and the group of activities called "fair dealing". This covers quotations in periodicals, recitations and anthologies, provided that they are properly acknowledged.

Special Rules on Records of Musical Works

266 Musical works may, subject to exact compliance with four conditions, be recorded in the UK (but not imported), without the copyright owner's permission. The four conditions are:

Firstly, that recordings shall already, for purposes of retail sale, have been made or imported with the copyright owner's consent. A recording not made for retail sale such as for studio archives or as a film sound track does not satisfy this condition.

267 Secondly, that recordings do not contain any part of the work not already so recorded or imported with the copyright owner's consent nor constitute an adaptation of it (for example a rearrangement or a version for a different instrument) nor infringe a non-musical copyright or some other right not purely a musical copyright.

268 Thirdly, that the recording must be made for retail sale only.

269 Fourthly, that the recordist pays to the copyright owner or owners a royalty, the amount of which is laid down by law. In 1982 this was 6¼% of the ordinary selling price of each record.

270 An intending recordist is entitled to presume that a work has been recorded or imported if he gets no reply within seven days of

inquiry from a copyright owner with a known address in the UK. If there is no such known address he may advertise in the *London Gazette* and wait seven days. In either event he must next give or, as the case may be, advertise his intention to record, 15 days before he actually makes the recording.

Performing Rights

Collecting Societies

271 Musical copyright owners cannot hope to keep track of all public performances, and sponsors of such performances cannot hope to trace the copyright owners of all works which they may wish to present. The practical difficulty is overcome by the formation of voluntary collecting societies, which exist in 41 countries and also act on each others behalf in their own country. In the UK there are two: the Performing Right Society Ltd (PRS) and Phonographic Performance Ltd (PPL). PRS is open to composers and musical publishers; PPL to recording companies. Both are non-profit making bodies, and the principle is that a copyright owner-member assigns his right for its longest duration under the two international conventions on trust to the society, but only so far as is necessary for it to licence and collect royalties for public performance, broadcasting, diffusion and film synchronisation. The royalties thus collected are paid over to him.

272 In practice the societies seldom licence particular performances, but operate blanket licensing schemes for classes of premises in which music is performed, and these schemes each contain their own tariff. In 1979 there were 44 such schemes, including schemes relating to bands, bingo clubs, cinemas, commercial dance halls, non commercial halls, holiday camps, clubs, concerts and recitals, pop festivals, municipal and educational premises, open spaces, pubs, theatres and universty colleges, and juke boxes.

Performing Right Tribunal

273 As the two societies control almost all public performances in music and sound recordings in the UK, the law imposes, in certain cases, control by a Performing Right Tribunal. This deals only with two types of dispute between a music user or users and one or both

of the Societies; namely, a dispute involving a licensing scheme *as a whole,* and one in which a prospective music user requires a licence under a scheme or in circumstances not covered by a scheme.

Warranty of Originality

274 As there is no copyright registration and search system, a person who wishes to deal (lawfully) in someone else's copyright work must rely upon that someone else for the certainty that the work does not infringe any third party's rights. To some extent this difficulty can be circumvented by inserting a clause in the contract that the seller or creator warrants that the work is an original work. This enables the buyer, if attacked in copyright proceedings to recover his losses from the seller - if, unlike most authors, the seller has any money.

Transfer of Copyright

Death

I appointed XYZ to be my executors

275 When a copyright owner dies, the copyright passes automatically to executors named in his will; these may be special literary executors; but if none are named or if there is no will, it passes to his administrators only but by virtue of the Letters of Administration. Hence executors can act at once to protect a copyright (even before probate is granted) but administrators cannot until the Letters have been issued. This may take a considerable time (a year or more) because the Letters cannot be issued until the estate (including the copyrights) has been valued and the proper taxes assessed and paid on the value. The Letters, once issued, relate back to the moment of death, and therefore enable administrators to sue for breaches of copyright committed in the interval, but this may not always be as helpful as it seems, for old infringements may be hard to trace or prove.

court will issue to main beneficiary of will

276 The entitlement of a beneficiary to a copyright depends on the will if any, or otherwise upon the rules of intestacy. The executors or administrators are trustees on his behalf and transfer the ownership to him. It is not legally essential that this transfer should be in writing, but it is practically desirable that it should be.

dying with out a will

If a manuscript is left to you in a will -you get copyrights as in the copyright Act has a provision

Bankruptcy

277 A bankrupt's unsold copyrights pass to his trustee, who steps into his shoes, but where a bankrupt copyright owner is not the author, the trustee must not deal with or manage the copyright so as to deprive the author of his proper royalties or share of profits.

Company Liquidation

278 The protection accorded to an author under an individual bankruptcy does not apply if the copyright owner is a company. Hence on liquidation he can only prove for his money along with the other creditors.[1]

279 If a company in liquidation holds any copyrights as trustee, the liquidator must by means of a written vesting assent, pass them to their true owners. Other copyrights, not disposed of, will pass to the crown.

Assignment

280 It is possible *to agree to assign* a copyright by any means, but the actual assignment (i.e. transfer of the ownership) save as described above must be a written document signed by or on behalf of the assignor. Such a document can be in any form (e.g. a letter) and it need not mention copyrights specifically if the intention to transfer them can be inferred. A written and signed agreement to assign a future copyright, is effective to transfer the copyright when it comes into existence, provided that there is consideration and that there are no prior rights or unfulfilled conditions.

281 Assignments are of varying kinds. A *total assignment* transfers all the rights comprehended in the copyright for its entire duration in every country where the copyright subsists. A *partial assignment* may be limited to particular whole countries, or to a defined period of time, or to particular rights or any combination of these. Thus, for example, a copyright in a play might be assigned for five years in respect of stage performances only in Nigeria. The assignable rights are thus capable of as much subdivision as a business man thinks expedient.

---

[1] Could he have protected himself by means of a debenture or floating charge agreed with the company? I have never heard of this being tried.

Some of the possibilities are set out below:

literary, dramatic and musical works	reproduction; publication in serial form or in hard, limp or paper-back; performance in public; filmed performance; broadcasting; transmission through a diffusion service; adaptation for a different art form; translation; making a strip cartoon version; similar dealings with an adaptation.
artistic works	reproduction; publication; inclusion in a TV broadcast; transmitting them in a TV programme through a diffusion service.
sound recordings	making a record, performing in public; broadcasting.
films	making a copy; performing in public; broadcasting; transmission through a diffusion service.
TV and sound broadcasts	making a copy for non-private purposes; performing in public before a paying audience; re-broadcasting.
typographical arrangements	making photographic, xerox or other copies.

Assignments and (more importantly) licences of public performing rights of television broadcasts, must be obtained from the BBC or, as the case may be, from the Independent Broadcasting Authority.

Licences and Publishing Agreements

282 Few creators have the money, time or knowhow to undertake the many financial, technical and public relations activities required to make their work available to a public. This is done by publishers who act as financiers, production agents and wholesalers - and, occasionally, as printers. A publisher cannot publish a copyright

work without the copyright owner's permission and such permissions are commonly given by licence. A publishing agreement between an author and a publisher is thus normally a licensing agreement in which the author retains the copyright, but agrees to licence the publisher to publish the work subject to the conditions in the agreement.

283 The fundamental rules are that a licence requires no formalities (it can even be created by word of mouth) and that it confers no right of property in the copyright, but merely makes an action lawful which would have been unlawful without it. Hence, though the licence binds future copyright owners, it is not transmissible from one licensee to another, and the licensee cannot by himself take legal proceedings against infringements. *Exclusive** licences, however, have a special status. They must be in writing signed by or on behalf of the grantor and they confer upon the licencee the right to sue for infringements.

Common Expressed Conditions in Publishing Agreements

284 In 1982 there was no standard form of contract between copyright owners and publishers which had been agreed by representative bodies of both sides. The following is an account only of the most usual clauses in such agreements:

> a) A clause granting the licence.
> b) An undertaking by the author to deliver a complete manuscript fit for use by a printer, and to correct and return printer's proofs within an agreed or reasonable time.
> c) A provision requiring the author to pay for the cost of changes in the printed text (apart from corrections of printer's errors) exceeding an agreed amount (commonly 10% or 15% of the cost of composition).
> d) A royalty clause. By this the publisher undertakes to pay to the author a royalty calculated upon the published retail price of the work. In the case of books, this is commonly in two stages - a lower rate (say 10 %) on the first batch (say 3000 copies) and a higher rate (say 12½%) thereafter. Different rates are sometimes offered for hardback and for paperback editions: paperback percentages being usually lower (say 5% and 7½%). Paperback income per copy is,

therefore, apt to be much lower than hardback .

e) Usually the publisher agrees to pay an advance of royalties on delivery of the completed manuscript, or sometimes on signature of the agreement (or both). It is often non-returnable, but if it is not expressly non-returnable the author is liable to repay such part of it as is not covered by his royalties.

f) Usually the publisher reserves the sole control of production, advertising, price, sale and terms of sale and undertakes to publish within a reasonable time.

g) If the author dies or is otherwise prevented from completing the work (if it is of a learned character) the publishers sometimes have an option to purchase the copyright and the uncompleted manuscript and to commission someone else to finish it.

h) The author sometimes indemnifies the publisher against legal proceedings for anything in the work which is pirated, libellous, seditious, obscene or otherwise unlawful.

i) The author commonly has a right to inspect the publisher's relevant accounts at his own expense.

j) There is a great variety of termination clauses. Usually the publisher has a right to terminate the agreement on (say) three months notice, whereupon the author becomes entitled to buy at cost price any remaining unsold copies. Conversely, if the work is out of print, the author is entitled to give notice requiring the publisher to issue a reprint of a minimum number of copies within a certain time, and to terminate the agreement if the publisher fails to do so.

Implied Conditions in Publishers' Agreements

285 In addition to the express clauses, the following principles are implied in such an agreement unless excluded by its terms

i) The publisher is responsible for the custody of the manuscript or other master copy.

ii) Though the agreement is personal to the parties, the publisher can employ servants and agents to carry if out and can pass the burden of doing so to another publishing firm which he effectively controls, but this process of transmission cannot go further than this, without the licensor's consent.

iii) The publisher of a written work may make alterations of an insubstantial character, but not such as to change the nature of the work.

iv) The licensor can revoke the licence only in accordance with the terms of the agreement, or if there are no such terms, only if either the licence is a bare licence given free, or the licensee has broken the agreement in some fundamental way such as failing to publish within a reasonable time or failing to pay the agreed royalties. Reasonable notice is in any event required.

v) The licensor must not create a competing work and offer it elsewhere.

Performers Protection

286 There is no copyright in a live performance, but it is a criminal offence punishable with heavy fines or imprisonment knowingly to record, broadcast or film one without the performer's written consent, or to sell, let or distribute by way of trade or expose or offer for sale any such record or film or use it for a public performance or for exhibition to the public. Ordinarily a criminal prosecution is the only remedy, but if an aggrieved person can show that he suffered a special injury such as a reduction in his profits he may take civil proceedings to recover his losses.

Industrial Designs and Patents

Definitions

287 A *patent* describes a new and hitherto obscure idea susceptible of industrial application, and confers on the inventor a twenty year monopoly in it. The patentee can take action against any infringement of the principle described in the patent, even if it is accidental or is quite different in appearance. A *registered design*, is a new design which is registered at the Patent Office, and the monopoly so conferred lasts for 15 years. Registration protects not

the principle of construction, but features of the thing registered which, in the finished article, appeal solely to the eye of the customer and are applied by an industrial process.

288 Patents and registrations differ from copyright in several important respects. Unlike copyrights, their formalities (conducted at the Patent Office) create the protected right. They are enrolled, and a search can reveal their existence, nature, owner and date of expiry. They can be challenged on the ground that they are not new, and they confer a full monopoly in the sense that independent conception is no defence to proceedings in support of them.

289 Some but not all industrial designs (whether registered or not) necessarily fall within the protection of copyright, namely those which are traceable to an artistic work.[1] Drawings and patterns are the commonest roots of such protection. It is by this means that piracy of dress designs is prevented. Piracy of toy models, dolls and plaques has, however, been stopped as sculpture, and of jewellery as artistic craftsmanship.

Borrowing on Security

General

290 *The Blind Art Gallery [BAG] wishes to borrow a substantial sum from Leslie the Lender to reconstruct a wing suffering from dry -rot. Leslie, despite his knowledge of BAG's solvency and belief in the management's good faith, may wish to be certain of getting his money back. BAG, after all may lose its assets, through no fault of its own, by fire or storm, or its financial director may be disabled by a stroke and its affairs fall into confusion, or, as Leslie and everyone else hopes, a cure may suddenly be found for blindness, or a wealthy American might set up a rival and rich institution.*

The Five Types

291 To avoid such dangers it is common to bolster the borrower's obligation of repayment by means of security. This consists in giving the lender a second recourse or reserve resource to which

---

[1] See paragraph 255 above.

he can turn if the borrower fails to pay up. There are many forms of such security but they fall into five broad classes:

i) Personal *guarantee* or *suretyship*;
ii) Detention of a thing by *lien*;
iii) The attachment of the lender's right to be repaid to a moveable thing by *pawn* or *bill of sale*;
iv) A similar attachment to land or certain other assets by *mortgage*; and
v) A similar attachment to the assets of a business by *debenture* or *floating charge*.

No Uncovenanted Profit

292 It is an axiom of this branch of the law that such securities exist to enable a lender to recover only what is properly due to him. He cannot make an uncovenanted profit from the fact that the security happens to be worth more than the debt.[1]

Lender's Priority

293 An important feature of securities other than guarantees and liens is that insofar as the property burdened with his security is concerned, the creditor has priority over all other unsecured creditors. They must make do with the residue after he has been paid in full.

Guarantee or Suretyship

294 A person guarantees another (the debtor) by making himself liable to answer to the debtor's creditor for the debtor's debt, default or miscarriage. A guarantee must be in writing and signed by the guarantor or his agent. Since it is a form of contract, it requires consideration unless it is under seal, and as many trusts and arts organisations will not be able to provide a commercially viable consideration, the guarantee will often have to be under seal. Guarantees have an advantage in the case of charitable trusts because, as they are not mortgages, they do not require the Charity Commission's consent.

---

[1] Note the analogy with insurance. See paragraph 467.

295 A guarantee obliges the person who seeks it to be frank about his relevant affairs, for unless the guarantor is willing, free from undue pressure, and able to exercise his judgment with knowledge of the facts, he may be able to repudiate his guarantee.

Joint Sureties

296 Where there is a scheme to borrow funds under the guarantee of several, or sometimes even a large number, of sureties each for a proportion, it is important to remember that in the case of a debt owed to any given creditor, the discharge of one surety to that creditor automatically discharges all the others to the same creditor.

297 Guarantee is one of the oldest of commercial devices and a great deal of jurisprudence has grown up around it. For this reason, it is wise to have any guarantee drafted professionally.

Common Law Lien

298 In the common law *ordinary* or *particular lien*, a thing such as a motor car or suit of clothes is already in the creditor's hands because he is to mend or make it, or otherwise do something in relation to it for which he is entitled to be paid. When the time for payment is past he may retain possession until he is paid. This simple idea has been extended. A *general lien*, i.e. a lien entitling the creditor to retain possession until *all* his claims have been settled, can arise by contract or custom and is an important feature of business practice. Solicitors have a general lien on their clients' documents; bankers and stockbrokers a similar lien on customers' share certificates; warehousemen on customers' goods held in store; and, probably, printers on the books they have printed. A lien is a passive right providing the creditor with a defence if sued for the delivery of the goods. If he insists on retention he has to accept any concomitant inconveniences, such as the need to store, preserve and insure them. *The violin restorer who allows my Amati to be damaged by heat from his sitting room fire, is liable to me for the damage.* Moreover, it is only in special circumstances (e.g. a load of perishables) that the creditor is allowed to sell.

Destruction of Common Law Lien

299 A lien is destroyed if the debtor tenders the amount due, or if the creditor abandons it (e.g. by claiming the goods on other grounds) or sells them, or accepts an alternative security. It is also destroyed if possession is lost (e.g. by a builder incorporating light fittings into a concert hall) and this is true even if the delivery was made by mistake or to a third party, unless the debtor fraudulently induced the mistake.

Equitable Lien

300 The equitable lien is the converse concept. It is not necessarily dependent on physical possession, and gives a right, in the last resort, to sale. It is based upon the notion that if I have in my hands property for which I ought to pay you, I am a trustee for you and will not be allowed to keep it unless I pay. The creditor has his equitable lien even though he is not in possession. Such liens arise sometimes by agreement, but more often out of a business or personal relationship; for example, between partners or between trustees and their beneficiaries, between spouses who have made payments on each other's behalf or between buyers and sellers of land, for the seller has a lien on the land until all the money is actually paid, and the buyer has a lien on the land and documents in favour of his deposit.

301 Equitable liens are lost by abandonment, of which taking alternative security is the commonest case.

Pawn or Pledge

302 A pawn is a bailment* of identifiable personal property as a security for a debt or engagement. It is always a contract transferring possession to the lender (pawnee). The ownership remains with the borrower, who can, therefore, sell the pawn and so install the buyer in his own shoes. He is entitled, in the absence of contrary agreement, to redeem it at any time during his lifetime. Conversely, from the moment that the creditor acquires possession, he has a special interest which he may transfer, without destroying his rights and, if a time for repayment has been agreed,

he may demand repayment and then sell. Such a sale must be businesslike and he must account to the debtor for any surplus. It follows from the nature of the creditor's special interest, that he can sue anyone who wrongfully deprives him of possession.

Pawnbrokers

303 The foregoing general statement is modified in the case of dealings with pawnbrokers, that is professional lenders of money upon pawn. Most such agreements, unless they involve credits of more than £5000 are regulated by the Consumer Credit Act 1974. Under a regulated agreement the lender must, at the time when he receives the pawn, give a pawn receipt ("pawn ticket") in a prescribed form. This is an important document approximating to a document of title. The pawn is redeemable within six months or the agreed duration (longer or shorter) of the credit period. When time is up, the creditor may realise the pawn, but the debtor, unless the sum involved is less than £15, may redeem at any time before *actual* realisation. The debtor redeems by tendering all the money due and the pawn receipt. If he has lost the receipt, he must tender a prescribed statutory declatation.

Balances on Realizatin

304 If there is a surplus on realisation, the pawnbroker must account for it; if a deficit, the balance of the debt remains due to him, Unless the sale was below market value or entailed unreasonable expenses, in which respective case the balance will be calculated by reference to the market value or to reasonable expenses.

Bill of Sale[1]

305 In common law lien and pawn, the creditor has the thing upon which the security is based, in his possession. When a loan is secured by a *conditional or security bill of sale,* it is the borrower who remains in possession of the thing. This, without special arrangements, can create problems. For example, he may try to borrow again on the strength of his ostensible ownership of the thing or quietly sell it, and conversely an ill-educated borrower

---

[1] So called absolute bills of sale can be used to transfer the ownership in movables or to create security for payment otherwise than in money.

may have difficulty in understanding exactly what he has signed, or be tripped up by special clauses.

306 A bill of sale, then, must exceed £30 and must be exactly in the form set out in the Bills of Sale Act 1882, with a schedule of property which it affects. It must be signed by the borrower and witnessed by a solicitor, and it must be registered within seven days at the Supreme Court. Moreover, this registration must be renewed every five years. Copies are sent to a local register.

307 In form, the bill transfers the title to the property, but obliges the lender to transfer it back if the money mentioned in the bill is repaid at the time or in the manner described in the bill. It is thus, in effect, a mortgage adapted to the mobility of the subject matter. The creditor is entitled to enforce his ownership by seizure, however, if, but only if, the borrower fails to pay when he should, or fails to perform a covenant contained in the bill (e.g. to insure the sculpture), or if he becomes bankrupt or is distrained* for rent, rates or taxes, or fraudulently removes or permits removal of or suffers execution* upon the goods, or fails upon demand to produce his last receipts for rent, rates and taxes.

Debentures

308 Debentures have a common characteristic, namely, that, whatever their form, they are issued by a company as an acknowledgment that it owes money at a, generally, fixed rate of interest; the debenture usually contains a covenant to pay at a named place on a certain day (the redemption date) and it often contains a floating charge,[1] or a fixed security upon certain property, in which case it is commonly called a *mortgage debenture* Debenture stock (representing secured fractions of the debt) is issued for sale to the public and changes hands on the stock exchanges in much the same way as ordinary shares, but since individual debenture stock holders may not be sufficiently conversant with the company's affairs to know whether or when they should enforce their rights, most debentures are executed in favour of a trustee (such as a firm of accountants or a bank) as a watch-dog on their behalf.

---

[1] See paragraph 312-3 below.

Priority of Debentures

309 Debenture holders are entitled to their interest before any of the shareholders can be considered for dividends, and they are entitled on liquidation, to be paid their capital in priority over unsecured creditors and shareholders.

Convertible Debentures

310 Debentures sometimes provide for conversion at the holder's option, instead of redemption, that is to say, for the substitution of shares in the company for payment in cash. Such conversions are, usually, offered for earlier dates than the redemption date. Acceptance of such a conversion changes the status of the holder, who ceases to be a secured creditor and, by entering the society of the shareholders, becomes, to the extent of his new holding, a potential debtor. It is, therefore, important to have some knowledge of a company's solvency and prospects before accepting conversion. Convertible debentures represent a method of raising short or medium term loans for a confident business.

311 Trustees whose powers of investment are confined to those of the Trustee Acts, cannot accept a conversion offer unless their fund has been divided for wider and narrower range investment.[1]

Floating Charge

312 A floating charge is imposed on all, or a named part of, the assets, for the time being, of a business. It is not properly a charge at all but a right, upon the happening of a certain event, to impose one. It casts so to speak, a shadow under which the business' operations - buying, processing, selling, and so forth - continually pass. *The grants and box office takings continue through the system, paying for salaries and debts as if nothing had happened, but if the named event occurs, the charge fastens upon everything in its shadow, and becomes a fixed charge.*

313 Floating charges solidify in this way when a company or business is wound up, or a receiver is appointed or when the security

---

[1] See paragraphs 593 et seq.

appears to be in jeopardy. The creditor, thereupon, has priority over holders of later charges and unsecured creditors but, of course, his rights are postponed to those of debenture holders or other holders of floating charges ahead of him. For this reason, it is common for prospective lenders upon floating charges, to insist that no debentures or prior charges shall be created without their consent.

Overdrafts

314 While liens are a convenient part of the machinery for raising smaller bank overdrafts, a floating charge is often a convenient security for a larger one, for it enables money to be injected into a business without disturbing its functioning and with only a potentiality of change in the legal status of its assets.

Mortgages

Things Which can be Mortgaged or Charged

315 Though most mortgages (or their equivalent charges) are secured on land, other things can be, and often are, charged in this way. Local authorities habitually mortgage their rates, and private persons can charge assets such as their life insurance, their holdings of stocks and shares, or their copyrights. Such charges are generally simpler than mortgages of land, but in the following paragraphs the mortgage system is described primarily by reference to land.

General Nature of Mortgages and Charges

316 A mortgage is an interest in property created by a debtor (mortgagor) at the behest of a creditor (mortgagee) as a security for the performance of an obligation, usually the payment of a debt. The interest thus created is a long lease subject to a, so called, *provision for cesser on redemption* whereby the lease comes to an end if the obligation is performed sooner. If the debtor is himself a tenant, he may mortgage his terms of years by a sub-lease.

It is possible, and not uncommon, to create more than one mortgage in the same property: these later mortgages are created by granting leases or sub-leases, as the case may be, for a period one day longer than the preceding mortgage.

317 These securities, being leases, are good against all the world and, therefore, if the debtor sells his interest, he must, like any other landlord, do so subject to the tenancy created by the lease. The buyer, who thereby acquires the burden of the obligation, will, in theory, pay the value of the interest less the cost of the burden. In practice, the mortgage will contain a provision that it will be paid off out of the proceeds of a sale: hence, the buyer will pay the full amount, and acquire the interest free of the burden, while the debtor, by discharging the obligation will terminate the lease. Similarly, the mortgage will enable the creditor, in cases of extreme default, to sell the debtor's interest, recoup himself and account to the debtor for any surplus, with a similar end result.

Legal Mortgages and Charges

318 This type of *legal mortgage* must be created by deed, and so must a *charge by way of legal mortgage*, which is in a simpler statutory form. This charge gives exactly the same protection to a creditor as a legal mortgage and has some other technical advantages, notably, that freeholds and leaseholds can be charged in the same document. Nowadays, most mortgages are made in this form.

Sub-Mortgage

319 A legal mortgage can itself be mortgaged by means of a sub-mortgage, just as a tenant can confer a sub-tenancy.

Equitable Mortgages

320 In addition to the legal mortgages, there are three classes of equitable mortgage. A deed is not required to create these, but there must be either a written note or memorandum signed by the debtor, or some act of part performance which is unmistakeably referable to an intention to create the charge. The important difference between the legal and the equitable mortgage is that a legal mortgage is good against all the world, but the equitable one will not burden someone who acquired the burdened property for full value and who did not know and need not have known, of the charge.

321 Firstly, then, if the debtor mortgages only an equitable interest, the mortgage is equitable. This can happen where, for example, he is charging his interest as a beneficiary under a subsisting trust ("Borrowing on his prospects").

322 Secondly, a contract to create a legal mortgage, creates an equitable one as long as the legal mortgage has not been brought into existence (e.g. if the debtor disappears or dies) before executing the necessary document. A well known form of such a contract is a *mortgage by deposit of title deeds*, in which the debtor, in return for a loan, hands over the title deeds of the property charged, to the creditor. This is a sufficient act of part performance to supersede the need for a writing, but in modern practice, such a deposit is usually accompanied by a deed setting out the terms of the mortgage.

323 Thirdly, if, by a signed writing, I express the intention that a particular debt or obligation is to be discharged or met out of a particular and defined piece of property, the result is an equitable charge, for I have constituted myself a trustee of the property for the purpose.[1]

Debtor's (Mortgagor's) Rights

324 Victorian melodramas about wicket creditors (who drive widows and orphans into the snow when, after six months, the mortgage debt is unpaid) are based upon a misunderstanding of the literal words of a common law mortgage. A mortgage is a security only. Therefore, as long as the debtor performs his obligations (particularly the usual obligations to pay interest and to preserve and insure the property) the creditor is seldom allowed to interfere with it. He is, for example, discouraged from going into possession under his lease. Even if the debtor defaults on his obligations, the creditor must account for profits, and for surpluses on sale.

Equity of Redemption

325 Secondly, because the mortgage is a security for the redemption of a debt, a provision in it which impedes or substantially diminishes ("clogs") the debtor's right to redeem is void. This "equity of redemption" is the bedrock of the law of mortgages. It has the incidental effect of rendering mortgages unintelligible to the layman, for though most of them seem to provide for redemption of the debt at the end of six months, in fact equity does not permit a creditor to realise his security as long as the stipulated rate of interest and the other covenants are observed. On the other hand,

---

[1] See paragraphs 59-60.

it does require the debtor to give at least as much notice of redemption as the original redemption period.

326 The sanctity of the equity of redemption has the effect of making many types of provisions void. These include terms secured by fraud, or which are oppressive or which are repugnant to the general principle of redemption. Save for a debenture, a mortgage cannot be irredeemable. The right of redemption cannot be postponed to a very late date, or restricted to certain persons or particular occasions or to part only of the property. A provision which effectively converts a mortgage into something else, for example, by giving the creditor an option to purchase, is equally void, and so is a clause such as a tied house provision in the case of a pub, which continues after the mortgage is redeemed. This rule against associated continuing advantage has, however, one recognised (perhaps unreal) exception, namely, where the parties wish to settle a number of matters all at once and one of these happens to be a loan. In such a case, if the various other matters are really independent issues, they will be treated as such even if they and the mortgage are set out in the same document. *I want for example, the sole American agency for your orchestra for five years, at usual commission rates; you want £100,000 to reconstruct your London practice hall. The mortgage on the hall and the agency agreement are included in the same document. You pay off the mortgage after two years. The agency agreement remains binding.*

Redemption, Discharge, Transfer and Release

327 A mortgage is redeemed by tender of the amount due, including all arrears of interest, even those which are statute barred.* The creditor endorses a vacating receipt* on the mortgage. This gives the name of the payer, the amount and date of the payment and is signed by the creditor. If there is only one mortgage, it is, thereby, discharged, but if it is redeemed by a second or later mortgagee, it is transferred to him so that he then occupies the original creditor's position. In addition, a mortgage can be effectively vacated if the right of redemption is released by the debtor in return for a total release of the debt.

Leases by the Debtor (Mortgagor)

328 Despite the existence of the lease under a legal mortgage, the debtor can grant leases to other tenants which are effective as between him and them, but do not bind the creditor. In addition, so long as the mortgage does not expressly forbid them, there are certain types of leases which do bind the creditor as long as a counterpart, executed by the debtor and his tenant, is delivered to him.

The Creditor's (Mortgagee's) Immediate Rights

329 The first mortgagee is entitled to possession of the title deeds, and this, in effect, gives notice to all the world that the property is mortgaged, for the debtor will have to explain the absence of the documents to anyone who wants to deal with the land. When the mortgage is redeemed the deeds must be given up to the person who redeems it. He, of course, may be a later mortgagee.

330 The creditor is entitled, *if the mortgage is by deed*, to insure the property against fire and add the cost to the amount secured, but he cannot do this if the debtor insures it or if the deed otherwise provides.

The Creditor's Rights on Default

Recovering the Debt

331 When the date named for repayment has passed, the creditor, like any other creditor, *may sue for the debt*. This does not affect the mortgaged property, save to discharge the mortgage when the judgment is satisfied.

Possession

332 Strictly speaking, a creditor is *entitled to possession* under his lease but, in practice, he will want it only if the mortgage payments are so far in arrears that he intends to exercise his eventual powers of sale.[1] The reason is that, if he takes possession, he has to account strictly not only for the profits he receives but for those which he ought to receive if he acts prudently.

---

[1] See paragraph 334.

Receivership

333 Instead of taking possession, the creditor can, if the mortgage is made by deed, *appoint a receiver* who is deemed to be the debtor's agent but intercepts the profits for the creditor's benefit. At least two events must have occurred before a receiver can be appointed:

i) The date for repayment named in the deed must have passed, and
ii) One of three contingencies must have arisen, viz, either notice demanding repayment must have been given and such payment or some of it must have been in default for three months; or interest payments must be at least two months in arrears; or some provision in the deed must have been broken.

Sale

334 Instead of appointing a receiver on the happening of the two events, the creditor may *sell the property* free of his mortgage. He must try to get the best price and he cannot, directly or indirectly, acquire the property himself. With the proceeds he must discharge prior mortgages, if any (supposing he is a second or later mortgagee), recoup himself and pay the balance to the person next entitled - who may be a still later creditor - or the debtor.

335 The choice between sale and receivership is a business decision. If the market is low, receivership may be better than sale: if high, the other way round.

Foreclosure

336 A creditor can, after the date for repayment has passed, apply to the court for a *decree of foreclosure*, which abolishes the debtor's right to redeem and transfers the property to the creditors. In practice, sale is usually a more attractive remedy because of the expense of court proceedings and the safeguards with which the debtor's position is hedged. Foreclosure actions are, therefore, rare and usually arise only to disentangle situations complicated by the existence of several mortgages.

Consolidation of Mortgages

337 A creditor is entitled, if a mortgage deed mentions the matter, to *consolidate his mortgages*. This means that, if a debtor makes different mortgages of different properties to the same creditor, the creditor is entitled to refuse redemption of one without redemption of the other or others. This is now a very technical doctrine capable of enormous complication.

Priority of Mortgages of a Legal Estate

338 Though creditors can fairly rank for payment in the order in which their security was created, it is equally fair that they should take steps to make the existence of their security known to later prospective lenders. Hence, the first mortgagee must take possession of all the deeds, while any later one (whether legal or equitable) must register his mortgage in the local Register of Land Charges.* The priority of registrable mortgages then depends upon the date of registration, and such a mortgage is void as against a purchaser of the mortgaged land unless registered before the completion of the purchase.

Fraud or Carelessness by First Mortgagee

339 If the first mortgagee does not take the deeds, or all of them, he risks the possibility that some other mortgagee may come in and take them, in which case he may lose his priority, if he behaved fraudulently or carelessly.

Priority of Mortgages of Equitable Interest

340 Priority of mortgages of equitable interests depends on the order in which the owner of the *legal* interest (usually the trustee) receives written notice, but a creditor who knows or ought to know of an existing unnotified mortgage cannot give himself priority by getting his notice in first. This is a situation which might arise where several loans were being raised from different lenders almost simultaneously in order to raise a single global sum. The rule can be important to the sort of trust where the legal estate is vested in a holding trustee, and the managing body needs to raise funds.

Position of Charitable Trustees

341 Since charitable trustees cannot part with the trust property without the consent of the Charity Commissioners, it follows that, since a mortgage might deprive them of the property, they need the same consent for a mortgage.

Torts

In General

342 A tort (French=wrong) is a civil wrong for which the injured party ("plaintiff") may obtain unliquidated damages (that is, a monetary award separate from itemised expenses) from the person ("defendant") who inflicted the wrong. Some torts are also crimes; no act is a tort if simply it is a breach of contract or a breach of trust or an infringement of a statutory right, or if the only remedy is an action for a liquidated (i.e. itemised) amount, or for a non-pecuniary remedy such as an injunction. These non-pecuniary remedies are, if necessary, available to a plaintiff in tort, but only if, as a matter of law, he is *capable* of obtaining unliquidated damages too.

Contract and Tort Contrasted

343 Two central differences between tort and contract (the other major branch of the civil law) may, for convenience be noted here. The law of contract is a law on agreements: the law on tort a law on conflicts and, secondly, arising as a matter of practicalities out of this difference, in contract the parties are, within very wide limits, defining their relationship themselves, but in tort the areas of conflict are defined by the law. Since, however, the human condition becomes, with the advance of science and technology, ever more complicated, opportunities for conflict arise from time to time which nobody ever foresaw. Litigants who come before a court are entitled to have their dispute settled even if it is novel. Most torts have long been defined, but some have been discovered recently. As a separate tort, negligence by an act dates from 1932, by words from 1963, intimidation from 1964. The law may define torts, but the definition cannot necessarily be known in advance.

344 The following diagram represents an attempt to name and, as far as possible, classify the thirty three known torts and the four which seem to be emerging. The words "per se" (Latin=by itself) signify that the plaintiff is entitled to his remedy without proof of actual damage: "per quod" (Latin=by reason of which), that he must prove the actual damage which he has suffered.

TORTS

PER SE

TRESPASS GROUP
1 To land (Quare Clausum)
To the person
2 Battery
3 Assault
4 False Imprisonment

5 Malicious Prosecution
6 Abuse of Process

7 To chattels (but not in road accidents)

CONVERSION GROUP
DETINUE
1 Taking
2 Detention
3 Wrongful Delivery
4 Wrongful Disposition
5 Destruction
6 By Estoppel
(7 Refusal of Lawful demand)

1 **RYLANDS v FLETCHER** and analogues
2 Escape of Fire
3 Animals
4 Dangerous Premises (but licensing)

5 Breach of Statutory Duty)

INJURIOUS LIES
1 Libel (Civil)
2 Slander Actionable per se

PER QUOD

NEGLIGENCE
1 Donoghue v Stevenson
2 Hedley Byrne v Heller
3 Dangerous Chattels
(Res Ipsa Loquitur)

NUISANCE
(not public or statutory)

CONSPIRACY
INTIMIDATION
INDUCING BREACH OF CONTRACT
LOSS OF SERVANT

EMERGENT TORTS
? Invasion of Privacy
? Abuse of Statutory Power
? Infringement of Status
? Malicious Interference with business

3 Slander Simpliciter
4 Slander of Title
5 Passing off
6 Deceit and Imitating Trade Marks

Trespass

Principles

345 The underlying principle of trespass as a civil wrong is that the plaintiff is, or may be, the victim of an unlawful application of direct force. This force may, as in trespass to land, be, over a short period, imperceptible as when the roots of my trees invade your foundations, or perceptible as when I go into your cinema without a ticket, or put something, such as rubbish, on your property without your permission; or it may be unfelt, as when, in defiance of my contract, I sleep overnight in your theatre greenroom or as when I threaten you with violence (assault), or it may (as in battery) be felt when I hit you on the head with a hammer, or it may consist in an unlawful constriction of your liberty (false imprisonment) as when a burglar locks a cashier in a cupboard while rifling the till. Malicious prosecution and Abuse of Process, which may have the same ultimate effect as false imprisonment, are not applications of direct force, but it is convenient to mention them at this point. Finally, there is trespass to chattels* or goods, as when I smash your china. Damage to motor vehicles in road accidents, however, has escaped from the incidents of trespass, because proof of negligence is required.[1]

Remedies for Trespass

346 In all these cases, the victim is entitled to take measures, including reasonable force (e.g. throwing the intruder out, or cutting the roots) to defend his interest. Such force is "reasonable" if, having regard to all the circumstances, its purpose is carried out without inflicting needless or irrelevant damage or injury. A trespasser who violently resists expulsion has only himself to blame if his clothes, perhaps, are torn, but a broken leg may need explanation, and so may any injury inflicted outside the place from which he has been expelled. Moreover, except in the case of trespass by arboreal invasion, the victim is entitled, contrary to popular belief, to general damages (the technical name for a monetary award payable by the defendant for the injury to his rights) even though there was no actual damage whatever. He is, besides, entitled to compensation (special damages) for any actual damage and con-

---

[1] See paragraphs 357-360.

sequent expense (for example, doctor's bills, repairs to a fence, or a new suit). If the trespass is a continuing one, as when I dump my building materials on your land, the plaintiff is entitled to a new action each day it continues. If he has reason to think that it will be repeated, as sometimes happens when there is a personal element in a quarrel, he may obtain an injunction to stop the repetition. No question of fault or negligence is relevant, for a person is entitled to be protected civilly as well as criminally in the peaceful enjoyment of his rights.

Public Access and Trespass

347 In arts administration, the law on trespass to land most commonly applies where somebody came lawfully upon the property (*because the art gallery was open to the public, or because he had bought a ticket to a concert and then misbehaved*). The misbehaviour may itself be a separate trespass, *for example, an attack on an attendant*, or it may be an interference wiht the purposes for which other people are there, *for example, by persistently blowing a whistle during a performance*, but whatever it is, it will in the end, or instantly, amount to a departure from or an abuse of the purpose for which he was admitted to the premises. Strictly speaking his permission to be there will have implicitly ended with his misconduct, and he may be expelled, by force if necessary, as a trespasser without further ado. In gross and undoubted cases (*e.g. one who squirts a fire extinguisher at the band*) this should be done. In less flagrant or more doubtful cases he should be told to desist or leave, and then be removed if he does neither.[1] Moreover, he is liable for any damage which he may have done: therefore it is wise somehow to get his name and address - though the likelihood that he will be worth suing is commonly slight.

Criminal Acts and Forcible Expulsion

348 It should be observed that where misconduct is criminal (*for example, the commission of public acts of indecency*) the perpetrator can never be lawfully on the premises since he and the owner cannot make a legal contract to admit him for that purpose. It is not necessary to call in the police to effect a forcible expulsion, though it may be a convenient way of ensuring that the disturber

---

[1] For money back see paragraph 209.

goes quietly. On the other hand, it is best to invite the police in if a crime has been or seems likely to be committed. It may be cheap and convenient to employ elderly part-time doormen on occasions of habitual calm (e.g. a performance of *The Messiah*) but it is wise to engage persons of greater strength and agility if there is any likelihood of trouble. This is proper provided that they use only reasonable force.[1]

Conversion

Definitions

349   If, without your consent, I take away some physical object (e.g. conjuror's equipment) which is in your possession, or if having got it lawfully I refuse to give it up when asked, or give it up to someone else instead, or if I destroy it or if, having borrowed it, I deny that it is yours, I am guilty of conversion and you are entitled to damages and may, but will not necessarily, secure it's return. The essence of this tort is an act or series of acts of wilful and un-justified interference with any chattel[2] in a manner inconsistent with another's rights and so as to deprive him of its *use and possession*. It is no defence that I made a mistake about the possession or that I did not mean you to suffer loss, or that I was acting for someone else or (though it may affect the amount of the damages) that deprivation of possession was only temporary. Nor can I allege in defence that you are not the owner, for conversion is a wrong against a possessor, and as against a wrong doer possession is paramount. The only person entitled to take a thing from another is one who, at the moment of taking, has a better right to possession. *A burglar who steals my television set is converting it. If a second burglar then steals it from the first, he is committing a conversion against the first burglar as well as me.* People interfere with other people's goods at their peril.

Limits

350   This doctrine has its limits. Mere receipt of chattels is no conversion. *If George hands over your saxophone to me, I do not begin to convert the saxophone until I have somehow witheld*

[1]   See paragraph 346.

[2]   But for conversion actions in copyright, see para 252.

possession from you. Similarly, if George deposits it with me and I hand it back without ever knowing that it is yours; I commit no conversion because I have not affected your rights, only the position of the instrument. It follows that if George sells it to me we have both committed a conversion, for such a transaction is a denial of your rights. A more difficult case arises where you leave your motor car in my car park and my car park attendant lets George take it away. In such a case, I may [perhaps] be liable for my employee's negligence but George is guilty of the conversion not I or my attendant.

Specific Restitution

351 In an action for conversion the plaintiff is always entitled to damages but the court will order the return (specific restitution) of the thing itself instead of, or as part of the damages, only at discretion in special circumstances, for example, if the thing is a unique object such as a work of art, or an heirloom with a special value to the plaintiff rather than anyone else. Hence, if the defendant has improved it, he will be entitled to an allowance.

Rylands v. Fletcher

The Caged Tiger

352 If, on land which I occupy, there is something dangerous and not referable merely to the natural condition of the land (e.g. a cliff) two things are possible. Either you may, perhaps, go onto the land and suffer injury, or the dangerous thing may escape from the land and do damage. Who pays whom and under what conditions? The law has developed in different directions, according to whether the injury has occurred on my land or off it. The reason is plain: people outside my land are the unguarded and probably unaware public upon whose members I cannot unilaterally be allowed to impose a risk, but on my land I may exercise my rights of ownership without unauthorised disturbance from outsiders, who may be intruders (e.g. burglars) or meddlesome friends (e.g. a visitor's children), or contractors (e.g. a carpenter) called in to do a job, and whom I may

---

[1] See paragraphs 357-60.

or may not have warned. When my caged tiger leaps across my boundary fence, he leaps into a different legal world. The law on liability for damage done by dangerous escaping things is known as the Rule in *Rylands v Fletcher*.[1]

P. 244

Rylands v. Fletcher Applied

353 Where an occupier of land brings onto it anything likely to do damage if it escapes, he is bound at his peril to prevent the escape and is liable for all the direct consequences of failure to do so even though he may not have been guilty of any negligence. In *Rylands v. Fletcher* water escaped from a new mill pond, down a disused mineshaft and flooded a neighbour's mine. The principle has been applied to the accumulation of noxious sewage in a sewer, the garageing of a motor car with the brake off, to someone who allowed caravan dwellers on his land to commit nuisances to neighbouring property, and to herbicide sprayed from an aircraft. The person liable is the occupier who is in control.

Natural or Unnatural Use of Land?

354 Unfortunately this simple principle has been complicated through the importation of a distinction between natural and unnatural uses of land. If in the process of a natural use of my land, I have there something dangerous which escapes and hurts you, it seems that I am not liable unless you prove my negligence. The distinction between natural and unnatural use can, therefore, be highly important: if there is a central core of cases where it is obvious enough, the edges are more than usually woolly. It seems that supplying domestic water and gas are natural but building a garage is not.

Defences

355 Assuming, however, unnatural use, the defences available are very limited. They are firstly, the plaintiff's consent. *The commonest example is water from an upper level of a building entering a flat lower down. Here the various occupiers are held to have consented to the state of the roofs and piping,* and must, therefore, prove negligence (as when I let my bath overflow). The second, more obvious defence is the plaintiff's own default. *If I turn off*

---

[1] 1868 LR. 3HL. 330. The other matters are collectively treated under the heading "Condition of Premises" see paragraphs 214-248.

the common water main for repairs in my flat and fail to tell you, I have only myself to blame if when I turn it on again the flood upstairs brings down my ceiling. Thirdly, and analogously with the first two, the act of a stranger, though often difficult to prove, is a good defence. *A trespasser from an open air Pop Festival camps on my land in my absence. Sparks from his camp fire cause a fire on my property which spreads to your's.* I am not liable to you, Fourthly, there is the diminishingly successful defence of

356 Act of God. It consists in attributing an accident to an exceptional natural cause without human intervention. What is exceptional depends on circumstances. Rainfall must be of astounding violence to qualify in the western parts of the British Isles. A heavy snowstorm in England has been considered sceptically. Lightning is probably an Act of God in most places.

Lastly there is the defence of statutory authority, which can occasionally be raised by a public body such as a local authority or a nationalised industry. *If gas escapes from a defective gas main and blows up my house, the Gas Board can plead that it has laid the main under statutory authority and that it is bound to maintain the supply. I will then have the more difficult task of proving negligence.*

Negligence

Two Sorts of Negligence

357 In English law the word "negligence" appears in two different contexts, either as an ingredient in another tort or as a separate tort in its own right. One difference lies in the liability for damages. If negligence, in the sense of carelessness, is part of another tort then the liability for damages is determined by the nature of that other tort, but if negligence is being pursued as a separate cause of action, the plaintiff must prove actual damage in order to succeed. This difference seems more theoretical than real because motor accidents and statutory duty defences under *Rylands v Fletcher*[1] probably exhaust the possible examples, and in these the proceedings would not be launched if there had been no actual damage in the first place. A second difference of some

---

[1] See paragraphs 355-6.

importance is that where negligence is part of another tort the plaintiff has to jump two hurdles: he must prove the ingredients of the main tort *and* the negligence. In "independent" negligence he only has to prove the negligence: this, as will be seen is not always as simple as it looks, and there is a necessary difference of definition.

The Independent Tort of Negligence

358 In the independent tort of negligence, the plaintiff must show i) that the defendant owed to him a duty of care; ii) that he was in breach of that duty; iii) and that by reason of that breach the plaintiff suffered loss. The main source for the concept is *Donoghue v Stevenson* ([1932] AC 562) in which a lady swallowed some ginger beer containing a decomposed snail. A friend had stood her the drink, which came in an opaque glass bottle, in a café; the café proprietor had no idea that the drink was contaminated and no question of contract could arise because the lady had not herself paid for the drink. She, however, successfully sued the manufacturer. The principle has since been applied not only to manufacturers, but to assemblers, builders, and distributors, to articles other than food and drink, including underwear, lifts and hair dye, and even to advice carelessly given. The classes of persons to whom the duty is owed has equally widened. The original principle was that the goods should be sold in such a form as to reach the ultimate consumer with the same original defect and without reasonable possibility of intermediate examination. It has been extended to any person through whose hands it passes, and perhaps even to casual passers-by. Finally, it is essential to prove injury to body, goods or finances.

Res Ipsa Loquitur — the thing speaks for itself

359 The *Donoghue v. Stevenson* type of negligence is concerned mainly if not wholly with injuries caused by things defective in themselves, but another type is more often related to negligent acts. If a barrel roles out of my drink store and injures you, a passer by, the defect is not in the barrel but in somebody's handling of it, and you are the very opposite of a consumer. You have suffered an injury, but your difficulty is to prove how it happened, for the facts, in so far as they are known at all, are known only to one or two persons working with my authority in the building. In such cases, many injured people would go empty away for lack of evidence, if the law did not come to their rescue with a special rule of evidence applicable in such cases. This is known as *res ipsa loquitur* (Latin="It speaks for itself") defined in 1865 as follows: "There must be reasonable evidence of negligence, but where the thing is shown to be under the management of the defendant or his servants and the accident is such as in the ordinary course of things does not happen if those who have the management use proper care, it affords reasonable evidence in the absence of explanation by the defendant, that the accident arose from want of care". The principle has been applied to bags of flour falling from a warehouse window, stones found in a bun, and a sudden bad skid by a car. The plaintiff proves the injury and leaves the defendant to explain it. This rectifies the evidential balance, for the plaintiff need not call the defendant's employees who will probably be unwilling or recalcitrant witnesses, and if the defendant does so, the plaintiff may cross-examine them.[1]

The Standard of Care

360 The standard of care required needs some consideration. It represents the sort of circumspection which an ordinary reasonable person might show in the circumstances. He is not expected to show superhuman foresight but, on the other hand, he can reasonably be supposed to have regard to the gravity of a possible injury (*e.g. to the good eye of a one-eyed employee*), its likelihood (*e.g. small children playing with fire*), and the importance of the object to be attained as compared with the burden of his precautions. Railway accidents would probably not happen if trains never went faster than 10mph, but nobody would use the railways.

Nuisances

Sturgess + Bridgeman (change of use + nuisance)

General

361 The lawyer's idea of nuisance hardly resembles the layman's use of the word. In the law it is a highly technical term, but

---

[1] See paragraph 33.

unfortunately it means, according to context, one of three quite widely differentiated ideas. These are *private nuisance, public nuisance* and *statutory nuisance.* It is wise to treat these separately, but it is helpful to know that the word is derived from a French word meaning harm. Many things (passing helicopters or amorous roof-top cats, for example) may be nuisances in the lay sense that I find them ugly and irritating, but unless they do or may do harm they are not nuisances in law.

Private Nuisance

362   I commit a private nuisance if I do or permit something on *my land* which causes damage adversely affecting the use and enjoyment of *your land* nearby. It is an injury by one user to the use of property by an other, and as such in its nature it lasts or is likely to last a substantial time. *If I wake you up by blowing a bugle at 2am, I may irritate you personally, but I am not affecting you in your capacity as an occupier of property. If, however, I establish a bugle playing school and give nocturnal lessons, I may be doing so.* The second may be a private nuisance, the first is not. *If on the other hand, vibrations from my factory cause your cistern to fall on your wife, she may fail in an action for nuisance if you own the house and she does not.*

363   Private nuisances take two forms. Firstly, there are interferences with easements[1] for the benefit of your land, running across mine, for example, *obstruction to private rights of way, or puncturing your pipes across my garden.* Secondly, there is emission from my land of something which affects the enjoyment of yours, for example, *animals, electricity, fumes, gas, germs, heat, noise, smell, smoke, vibration, water or weeds.* A single emission may constitute a nuisance if the damage is lasting (*for example, if my water overflows into your attic and the resulting damp brings on dry rot*), but more often there will be a continuing or recurrent emission. This must, however, be serious.
A vague buzzing was not considered a nuisance to a church con-gregation, but it may be wise to take steps to minimise door slamming and acceleration noises where many motor cars regularly leave a car park at night.

---

[1] See paragraphs 194 et seq.

364 Much can depend upon the character of the neighbourhood. *A person who chooses to live in a tannery district, cannot complain of smells.* On the other hand, it is not a defence to allege apart from the general character of the neighbourhood, that the plaintiff came to the nuisance, for this would take much land out of the market, nor that the activity confers a public benefit, nor that no other place is suitable for it, nor even that every care and skill was used to avoid committing the nuisance. If a nuisance cannot be prevented, it must be legalised by Act of Parliament or agreed with the neighbours. This can be important to a place of entertainment where there is a good deal of noise.

Public Nuisance

365 I commit a public nuisance if I interfere with the rights of the Queen's lieges generally; the commonest example is an obstruction in the public highway, where all the lieges have a right to pass and repass. The types of such obstruction are numerous: *digging a trench, dumping a vehicle, felling a tree into the highway, inserting a stile into a public footpath where none existed before.* In civil law their peculiarity in that proceedings may be taken only by, or with the consent of the Attorney-General; a private person cannot sue unless he has suffered damage peculiar to himself over and above that done to the public at large, and even then he must relate (report) his complaint to the Attorney-General in whose name the action is begun. Such actions, called relator actions, proceed at the relator's expense. They may arise, for example, *where the habitual sale of hot dogs from a van attracts crowds, litter and smells to the front of my box office door, and interrupts my concerts.*

366 Relator actions are not common, partly because the Attorney General is a long way off, but more practically because many such nuisances are offences against the Road Traffic Acts or byelaws, and are handled by the police, or because for some obstructions, such as builders' scaffolding, there is a system of licensing operated by the district council.

Statutory Nuisances

367 The Public Health Acts from 1936 onwards contain provisions for preventing the possible effects on public health of a number of

defined acts or neglects. These are called statutory nuisances. The district council or London Borough may, serve an abatement notice on an occupier of property where the statutory nuisance exists, requiring him to put the matter right within a defined time. If he fails to do so, the council may apply to the magistrates for an order authorising it to enter the premises and to do what the occupier has failed to do. A private person aggrieved by a statutory nuisance may likewise apply to the magistrates who may order the district council to act. It may charge the occupier and if he refuses or neglects to pay, the money can be recovered by legal proceedings.

368 This is essentially administrative process and is concerned with things prejudicial to health such as unhealthy, decayed, dilapidated or fouled premises; animals kept in such conditions; accumulations and deposits; trade or manufacturing dust or effluvia (which includes steam), smoke other than smoke from a private house, and dark smoke from any source, water storage containers liable to contamination, and tents, vans, sheds and other similar structures which are overcrowded or deficient in sanitary arrangements. Nowadays, the commonest applications of this legislation concern defective WC's and badly ventilated places such as attics and basements.

Injurious Lies

General

369 In addition to the infliction of damage by verbal negligence (such as badly conceived advice from someone who is expected to know better) the civil law provides remedies for six types of injurious lies. Three of these torts, namely (civil) *libel* and the *two forms of slander* are injuries to personal reputation collectively known as *defamation* and are notable because parties in defamation cases cannot obtain legal aid. The others, *slander of title, passing off, and deceit and imitating trade marks,* have no collective name, for their histories and origins differ; their common practical feature is that they are concerned with certain shadey business practices. In this murky field, there are, in addition, a considerable number of interventions from the criminal law. There is a separate and

different crime of criminal libel, there are many frauds in which words form an element, and there is the Trade Descriptions Act 1968. In all these areas an offender may find himself being fined or imprisoned for some contravention of the criminal law, but if his offence happens to coincide with one of six torts arising out of injurious lies, his liability to the person he has injured remains.

Defamation

370 "A man disparages the good name of another when he publishes to some third person words or matter which are false and which injure his reputation . . . such disparagement, if embodied in some permanent form . . . it is called *libel,* if expressed in some fugitive form . . . it is called *slander.*" [1] It is presumed that libel causes injury and a similar presumption arises in slanders imputing crime, infectious disease (e.g. syphillis), unchastity in a woman (despite the pill), or which disparage a person in his office, profession, calling, trade or business. In other cases of slander the person alleging injury must prove actual damage. The abolition of stage play censorship has exposed the stage to possibly more dangerous, and certainly, more capricious forms of attack by way of the laws of defamation and criminal libel.

Five Ingredients of Defamation

371 Questions of injury apart, defamation always has five components. There must first be a *publication,* that is to say a making known.[2] In this context the word 'publication' has no connection with the multiplication of material by mechanical or other means. Scurrilous words in a private letter, or whispered at a cocktail party can constitute a publication, and though defamations are normally conveyed in words, they can be conveyed in some other way such as cartoons or an exhibition of them, films, pictures or even gestures, provided, secondly, that the utterer makes the publication *to a third party.* To write or speak wholly false and insulting allegations to somebody alone about himself, may be disagreeable for him or insulting but it is not defamatory because there is no

---

[1] Gatley on Libel and Slander Fifth Edition (1960) p3. In view of the Rehabilitation of Offenders Act 1974 this famous quotation probably needs some revision.

[2] Cf the biblical "tell it not in Gath, publish it not in the streets of Ashkelon". 2 Sam 1v.20.

third party in whose eyes his reputation may be lowered. Moreover, if he is foolish enough to tell someone else, he cannot complain, for then it is not the utterer who has made the publication. Conversely, a person who hears of a defamatory statement and passes it on, is himself publishing it. This is why printers as well as publishers are sometimes sued for libel.

372 Thirdly, at any rate in civil libel, the matter published *must be false*. It is not defamatory to say something, however nasty, about somebody if it is true. The difficulty, of course, is to prove the truth.

373 Fourthly, the matter must be thought to refer *to the plaintiff*. This apparently obvious rule has some less obvious ramifications. If I name a fictional character and write libellously about him, I am guilty of libel if it turns out that there really is a person so named and that people thought that he was meant. If I write similarly about a real person and another answers the description, he may hold me liable: this is why newspapers tend to report such uninteresting detail as age and address. If I write something defamatory of a class of persons, a member of that class may be able to show that he had personally been defamed: in one case a newspaper alleged that working people were badly treated in Irish factories, and a plaintiff convinced a jury that this was understood to refer to his factory at Portlaw (Co. Waterford). The bigger the class, however, the more difficulty a plaintiff will have in proving the personal reference. On the other hand a defendant may expose himself to proceedings for criminal libel if his published matter tends to set one body of people in violence against another

374 Fifthly, it is the *reputation* which the matter must injure, that is to say, it must bring the plaintiff into hatred, ridicule, contempt or expose him in some real sense to revulsion or cause him to be shunned. It is not necessarily defamatory to express oneself intemperately about someone, and an insult may be offensive to a man's dignity without injuring his reputation. Moreover, political and social ideas change, so that what is and what is not defamatory changes with the times and the places. The following examples are given, solely by way of illustration, of this variability. Some would

presumably not be held defamatory at other periods: What is defamatory in Somerset may be acceptable in London.

> *Hatred.* To call a man "a German" (during World War II); "a Jewish international financier" (1937); "a Czech" (1964).
> *Ridicule.* To represent Mr Dunlop, who invented the pneumatic tyre and was a plain and ordinary citizen of Dublin, in advertisements as a foppish gentleman (1921).
> *Contempt.* To publish a rubbishy, ill written article under the name of a reputable author who did not write it, and thereby lower his literary reputation (1913). To attribute insanity to someone (1863), or insolvency to a trader (1700), or lesbianism to a woman (1942), or, apparently, incompetence in magical skills in a witch (1981).
> *Revulsion.* An imputation of venereal disease (1948) or probably any skin disease, or an imputation of crime punishable with imprisonment.

375 On the other hand it is not necessarily defamatory to expose a person to these disadvantages, if the opinion of those with whom he associates is, in an objective sense, to be discounted. To say of a criminal that he has set the law in motion may lower him in the eyes of other criminals, but is not defamatory (1937).

Innuendo

376 Many of the examples given so far, reveal a further important feature of the law of defamation, namely *innuendo.* A statement may on the surface seem innocent, but may, at some deeper or more specialised level be directed at the plaintiff and damaging to his reputation. *Some may regard the statement, that so-and-so is a great lover in and out of working hours, as complimentary, but if he happens to be a medical practitioner he may successfully establish an innuendo of unprofessional conduct. To say that someone is always late may be greeted with a smile by everyone except an actor.* Many words, too, have cant meanings. The word "pansy" had to be explained to the court in 1943. No doubt "gay" would have to be similarly explained in 1984.

Innocent Defamation

377 Just as a defamatory statement made about a fictional character may rebound onto its author, so he may be at risk with a statement

in whose innocence he believes, if it turns out to be defamatory of a real person because of facts unknown to him but known to those who hear it. The law's dilemma is much the same in both cases. Somebody is bound to suffer. Should it be the victim or the defamer? *I tell a reporter that I am engaged to Mary. His paper publishes it. My wife, Joan, whom I occasionally visit, promptly sues the paper. The innuendo is that I have all along been living in sin with her. She only has to find a couple of witnesses to say that they thought the worse of her, and her case against the newspaper is made.* "Liability for libel does not depend on the intention of the defamer, but on the fact of defamation". As will be seen[1] an offer of amends under the Defamation Act 1952 may help an unintentional defamer in such circumstances, but innocence as such is no defence: the principle is that a man publishes a defamatory statement at his peril, for it is notoriously difficult to catch up with a lie once it has escaped from the mind of its perpetrator.

Seven Defences

378 It follows that once the five elements of defamation have been proved, the defendant can escape only by bringing himself within at least one of seven well recognised defences. These are, i) absolute and ii) qualified privilege, iii) consent, iv) justification or truth, v) fair comment, vi) apology and vii) offer of amends.

Absolute Privilege

379 The nature of this defence is that the injury to the plaintiff is of no account in comparison with the paramount need to protect freedom of expression in five particular circumstances. It applies and applies only to statements made in parliament and parliamentary papers; in courts during judicial proceedings and in fair, accurate and contemporaneous newspaper reports of them; by one officer of state to another in the course of his official duty; in reports of the Prices and Incomes Board; and in communications between husband and wife.

Qualified or Conditional Privilege

380 There are, in addition, four types of case where privilege can be claimed for a statement, provided that it is made without malice

---

[1] See paragraph 387.

(which does not necessarily connote spite) that is to say honestly, to the right people and without an ulterior or improper motive. The first and commonest is a statement made in performance of an actual legal or moral duty to somebody who has a duty or interest in receiving it. Actuality and mutuality are essential. Thus, an employer may answer questions about a former employee from someone proposing to give the employee a job. You may accuse someone of a crime in answer to questions by the police. Councillors are privileged in respect of communications made to one another or council officials in the fulfilment of their functions. Company officials have a similar privilege, and so would a trade protection association or a bank which gave information about a person's financial status to someone entitled to have it. A parent who warns a son or daughter against the character of someone whom he or she proposes to marry, is in the same position.

381 The second category of conditionally privileged statements are those made in pursuance of a moral or legal duty to protect a lawful interest. This protects complaints to M.P.'s about the conduct of public authorities. It has been held to cover a letter, published in the press, attacking the decision of four artistes simultaneously to terminate their contracts (1969), to complaints by a landlord to his tenant about the conduct of the tenant's lodgers, and to communications between shareholders in a company in furtherance of their common interests.

382 Thirdly, there are the many reports, mostly in newspapers. These need not be *verbatim* but must be fair and substantially accurate, and, if they are, then they fall into two classes: namely, those privileged i) *without any explanation or contradiction* and ii) *subject to explanation or contradiction*. The first are cases resembling cases of absolute privilege such as proceedings in Commonwealth parliaments and courts, international organisations and courts, and registers and notices kept or issued by courts and government departments. The second comprises reports of decisions by associations (such as artistic, learned, professional or sporting bodies) about any individual member; discussions of meetings called to consider questions of public concern; proceedings of public bodies such as local and licencing authorities, and public companies, and summaries of notices

issued by public authorities. In these instances, a defaming newspaper or broadcasting station cannot plead qualified privilege if it has been asked by the plaintiff to publish a reasonable letter or statement of explanation or contradiction and has refused or neglected to do so or has done so but inadequately. Such publication must be in the newspaper concerned, or, in other cases, in the manner of the original defamatory statement.

383 Fourthly, confidential communications between a solicitor and his client are privileged.

Consent.

384 It is a complete defence that the plaintiff consented by, for example, inviting the defendant to repeat what he said before witnesses.

Justification (or Truth).

385 "The law will not permit a man to recover damages in respect of an injury to a character which he either does not or ought not, to possess." It is, thus, a defence to prove that the statement is substantially true. In this context proof of conviction is conclusive evidence that the plaintiff committed the offence, but a danger lurks in connection with social penalties such as expulsion from a club or being disbarred; such occurrences happen for reasons other than ill conduct. A man may no longer be able to afford the club subscription, or may be disbarred at his own request in order to become a solicitor. Where the statement is derived from a rumour, the truth of the rumour, not merely its existence must be proved.

Fair Comment.

386 If a matter is of public interest, or is (like a book or a play) submitted to public scrutiny, ostensibly fair comment upon it is not actionable even if it is intemperately expressed. But such comment must be honest; it must not amount to a statement or imputation of fact; it must not be actuated by malice; and it must not mis-state the matter commented upon. Fair comment is the literary and artistic critic's standard defence.

---

[1] The list is much larger and Section 7 of the Defamation Act 1952 should be studied for particular cases.

Apology and Amends.

387 An apology is, by itself, no defence, but, in the case of a libel in a newspaper or other periodical which was published without malice or gross negligence, the paper can publish an apology at the earliest possible moment and pay money into court. If the damages awarded are less than the money paid in, the plaintiff pays his own costs. Alternatively, a defendant (not necessarily a newspaper) can claim that the words were published innocently, and make an offer of amends which includes an offer to publish a sufficient retractation and apology and to notify as far as practicable those into whose hands the defamatory document or record may have come. If the offer is accepted, no proceedings for defamation can be taken against the offeror and the court settles any questions of costs. If it is refused, the defendant can plead the offer in the subsequent action, but will have to prove that he did not know that the words referred to the plaintiff or that they were defamatory of him.

Slander of Title and Slander of Goods

388 These two torts differ from defamatory slander in that they can be expressed in any way, written or otherwise, and consist of false statements made maliciously (not merely carelessly) to third parties about a plaintiff which result in those parties doing something to the plaintiff's injury and which they would not have done if they had not been deceived. Such a statement may not be defamatory at all. For example (Slander of Title) I stop the sale of your house by claiming that a new road will soon be built across the site, or damage your business by publishing in a newspaper that you have ceased to trade, or (Slander of Goods) I cause your theatre-bus contract to be terminated by telling people that your buses are unsafe, or broadcast allegations that your warehouse is damp, so that you lose storage contracts thereby. It is not, however, actionable merely to say (or advertise) that one's goods are better than someone else's. The tort consists in the false attribution of a specific defect, and damage.

Deceit

389 Deceit is the tort of making a wilfully false representation of fact to a person intending that in reliance upon it he will act and that, in consequence of such act, he suffers harm. The representation can

be in words or by conduct, and must *amount* to a positive assertion: active concealment of a fact, for instance by telling part of the truth or "painting over" counts as a positive assertion, and so does failure to correct a misrepresentation after its character has become known to its maker. There are, in addition, a number of statutory obligations of disclosure, relating mainly to prospectuses and investments. Mere passive silence, without more, is not, however, actionable; a "fact" in this context does not include a promise; and an action for deceit cannot be brought for a representation as to credit, unless the representation is in writing and signed by its maker. It should be noted that the false statement, to be actionable, must be made with the intent that the person to whom it is made shall act upon it, and that the latter acts in the manner intended. For example, if, as a result of a fraudulent prospectus, I pay money to the issuing company for its shares and suffer loss, I can sue the company, but if, having read the same prospectus, I buy on the market shares already issued, I cannot for I have not done what the company intended.

Passing Off

390 It is actionable to use, without his consent, someone else's reputation to make a business advantage. The basis of this tort is the deception of the public leading to appropriation of another man's established goodwill, and it can take many forms, for example selling a book by falsely putting a well known author's name on the title page, trading under a name which so closely resembles another that the public is misled, or similarly misusing or imitating a publicly understood trade name for particular goods, or deceptively imitating their appearance. A plaintiff who is likely to suffer injury can obtain an injunction to prevent the practice; if he has already suffered injury he may obtain an injunction and, at his option, damages or an account of the profits which the defendant has made. Where, however, the complaint arises from a defendant's own name being similar to the plaintiffs, the latter must embark on the difficult, but not always impossible task of proving that the defendant was acting dishonestly. In principle anyone is entitled to use his own name, but company names are controlled (mainly for similarity) by the Registrar of Companies who may refuse to register an unsuitable name.

Imitating Trade Marks

391 As soon as a trade mark is registered it becomes actionable to use or deceptively imitate it in relation to the classes of goods for which it is registered. This gives an earlier, cheaper but narrower protection than a passing off action, for the latter cannot succeed where the plaintiff has not had time to build up good will.

Contract

392 In paragraphs 129 to 149 there is an account of the difference between contractual operations and transfers of ownership or title to possession. From the point of view of the law of contract, the various forms may be summarised thus:

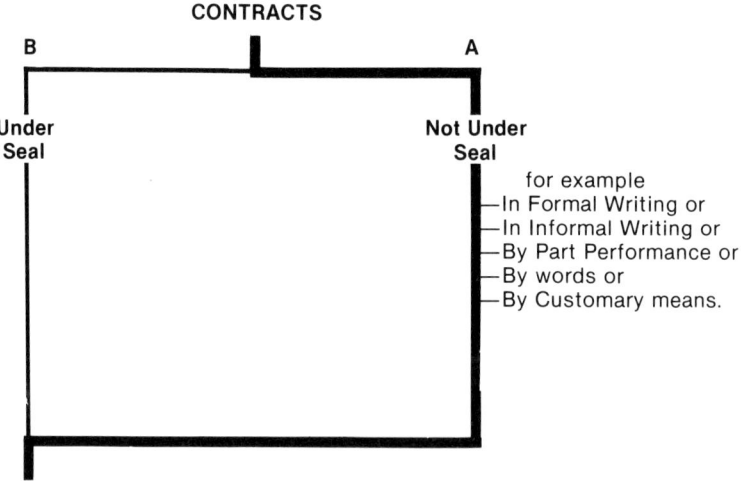

Sequence A, in the diagram, shows the run-of-the-mill agreements (however named) by means of which we carry on our daily business. These have been exhaustively analysed over the centuries. The sequence, however, shows only the things which may have to be produced or proved to show that a contract exists. Most of this chapter is concerned with the nature and intrinsic validity of contracts themselves, for what is proved to exist might turn out not to be a contract at all.

The Seven Elements of a Contract

393 Every English contract not under seal contains the following elements:

    i) Qualified parties
    ii) An offer
    iii) An acceptance
    iv) Consideration
    v) Intention to enter into a legal relationship
    vi) Legality or rather lack of illegality
    vii) Morality or rather lack of immorality

Preliminary Warning on Qualified Parties

394 Rational agreement cannot be expected from a lunatic or a drug addict on a trip, nor mature judgement from a child, nor understanding of an offer in one language by someone who only speaks another, nor proper authority from a repudiated agent, nor capacity from a corporation created for one purpose but negotiating for something quite different, nor real consent from someone under threat. For reasons of convenience, however, it is proposed to consider the characteristics of contracts as made between capable and qualified parties at arms length, and then return to the relatively few exceptional ones later.

The Offer

395 One party has to make an offer by which, if accepted, he intends to be bound. The offer need not be made to a particular or identified person. The board in a cinema foyer setting out the prices of the various tickets and the availability of tickets in each class, is an offer to anyone who sees it. The board in the foyer forbidding smoking is a condition of the contract if the offer is accepted. It is, however, to be distinguished from an invitation to treat. Price labels on goods in shop windows are not offers (though often treated as if they are), but invitations to treat. They do not even guarantee that the goods are available for sale. The shop keeper may raise his price or refuse to sell altogether. The customer may offer less. Whether a form of words is an offer or an invitation to treat depends on the facts and circumstances of the case, which include the customs of the trade. Thus it is well known that a person cannot enter a cinema without a ticket, and that the box

office will only sell available tickets at the prices displayed on its board. The board thus sets out a course of conduct upon which a prospective customer can rely.

Counter-offer and Acceptance

396 To make a valid agreement, that which is offered must be accepted exactly, including (if such be the case) the mode of acceptance prescribed in the offer ("Acceptances to reach the Lucrative Bank Ltd by 11am on 15th August 1982" or "Ring 123-45-6789"). Before accepting an offer, it is obviously wise to make sure of its real meaning. Many apparently standard terms (e.g. "season") have provoked conflicts of interpretation which have been solved, if at all, at great expense. Some words have a customary meaning within a given profession only, or one which differs from the normal.

397 An attempt to accept part but not all of an offer, or to make conditions, no matter how small the difference, is in law a refusal followed by an offer (usually called a *counter-offer*). At this stage, then, there is no agreement at all, and the original offeror is free either to make an offer to someone else, or to accept the counter-offer.

Customary or Unspecified Methods of Acceptance

398 If no method of acceptance is prescribed in the offer, then the method (if there is one) usual or customary in the trade must be used. If there is no such customary method, any method may be used. Problems, however, arise where there are delays or difficulties of communication. When parties are negotiating orally, face to face or by telephone, the acceptance must be such that the offeror clearly understands that the offer is accepted. *If, for example, a radio telephone conversation is interrupted by static, the acceptor must continue to repeat his acceptance until it is understood.* Analogous considerations apply in bilingual or multilingual negotiations through interpreters.

Postal Negotiations

399 In the case of postal negotiations, the rules are different. A letter of acceptance which has been properly addressed and stamped is binding when it is posted, even if it does not arrive: but this general principle is subject to some qualifications. It applies only if no other method of acceptance has been prescribed, and not if the circumstances were such that the parties could not reasonably have contemplated the rule at all, as, for example, where a woman accepts a proposal of marriage but her letter does not arrive. Logically, a valid postal acceptance will bind both parties, and the acceptor cannot, therefore, recall it before it arrives, for example, by telephone; this is the view of many Commonwealth courts, but oddly enough it does not seem to have been considered by an English court. It is, therefore, still possible to argue in England that it binds the offeror only, because he, being responsible for the mode of acceptance, must take the risks inherent in the ones he permits.

400 Total silence can never be an acceptance and an offeror cannot impose it, for example by some such sentence as, "If I do not hear from you by Tuesday I shall assume that you accept".

Withdrawal of the Offer

401 There are four cases in which an offer may be, or may be considered to have been, withdrawn. These are revocation before acceptance, lapse through time expiry, the failure of a condition, and death.

Revocation.

402 It is a fairly obvious proposition that an offer can be revoked as long as it has not been accepted, but the way in which the rule works is not always simple. Clearly, the intending acceptor must know of the revocation: but it has been held that this knowledge need not be the result of any communication from the offeror, and that so long as the information seems reliable it may come from any source. *The theatre separately offers me and my friend George discount tickets for the pantomime; when George goes round to pick his up, he learns that they are sold out and tells me. The theatre (assuming it can prove that I knew) incurs no liability if I quickly slip in an acceptance.* Secondly, the rule on postal withdrawals is different from the rule on acceptances. A postal withdrawal is effective only when it *arrives. I write to Miss Gong Bang in Formosa, offering her a concert engagement. I post the letter on 1st October. On 8th I post another letter revoking it. On*

11th she accepts by telegramme, confirmed by letter. On 20th my revocation reaches her. Only then would it become effective, but, as the acceptance was posted on the 11th, it was never effective at all.

403 Thirdly, there is some lawyers' controversy cver the case where a contract (misleadingly known as a unilateral contract) is in the form of a promise for an act. *I offer by advertisement a reward for the recovery of my lost picture. The offer is accepted when the picture is put in my hands. If I see my picture being carried along the street towards my house, can I revoke the offer before the man reaches my doorstep? Or, if I buy equipment on your behalf on hire purchase, but undertake to make it over to you if you pay all the instalments, may I revoke just before the instalment is paid?* The better, but not completely established English view, is that by putting an intending acceptor to trouble and probably expense, I have undertaken not to revoke until a reasonable time (which must depend on the facts) has passed. This opinion is supported by the practice in the use of the increasingly numerous, mainly international, bankers' commercial credits.*

Lapse.

404 If an offer is expressed to expire at a certain moment, an acceptance after that moment is obviously ineffectual. Where there is no such expression, the acceptance must be made within a reasonable time, and reasonableness will depend on the facts or upon the customs of the trade, and upon the spirit of the times.[1]

Failure of Condition

405 Offers are frequently made subject to some condition, *for example, that the currency exchange rate has not moved against sterling by more than, say 3% before acceptance.* Sometimes, too, cases arise, where hire purchase or third parties are involved. If I sign a hire purchase agreement, I am assuming that, when the finance company signs it, the goods will still be in the condition which led me to apply to the finance company in the first place; but supposing they are damaged by fire or thieves in the interval and the finance company innocently signs, there is still no contract

---

[1] In the horse and buggy era, a reasonable period for presenting cheques, theoretically unlimited, was thought to be three days. In the computer era, banks allow three months. Neither period has more than customary sanction.

between the finance company and me, because the supervening event has destroyed the condition on which my offer was made.

Death

406 An offer lapses immediately at the offeror's death if it contains an element personal to him, for example, to act as an agent, play in a concert or paint a picture, regardless of whether the acceptor knows of the death or not. It is, in principle, otherwise if the offer is, so to speak, a matter indifferent to him and capable of satisfaction out of his estate. In such a case, a contract will result from acceptance at anytime up to the moment when the intending acceptor is informed of the death. Conversely, an offer made to an individual who dies before acceptance is probably incapable of acceptance afterwards, because it was made to a living persona, and as that persona is no longer living it has ceased to be an offer.

Latent or Unperceived Contracts

407 It can happen that, in the course of negotiating a contract, a preliminary (or so called collateral) contract is settled, which paves the way for the main agreement. The commonest cases are found in the hire purchase of motor cars. *A dealer gives an assurance that a car is in good condition. As a result, the purchaser enters into a hire purchase agreement with a finance company.* The form of such agreements is that the dealer sells the car to the company which sells it to the buyer on hire purchase terms: they often contain a clause excluding warranties, descriptions or representations about the state of the vehicle. This may prevent the finance company from being sued, but not the dealer, for there are two contracts not one.

408 The other case of the unperceived contract, arises most commonly in membership of clubs, or participation in events or competitions (for example, a musical solo competition). By accepting membership or entering the event, a person agrees with the club or the sponsors to obey the rules. In form, he is making a contract with them. In fact, the rules also constitute a many-sided contract between every member and every other. Thus, if in entering my yacht for a race, I undertake to pay all damages and I sink another competitor, I am under a contract to *him* and must, under that contract, pay for all the damage even though, otherwise, under the Merchant Shipping Acts, my liability might have been limited to a fixed figure per ton.

409 Consideration

Consideration, in the law of contract, is a requirement peculiar to the Common Law of England and of countries whose laws are descended from it, such as the USA and the Old Commonwealth. In order to distinguish, as it were at a glance, between agreements which are meant to be legally enforced (e.g. the sale of a house) and those which are not (e.g. an invitation to a party) the law enforces those expressed in a deed[1] and refuses to enforce those not so expressed, *unless the parties to the contract must (put loosely) do something for each other.* This is sometimes called *quid pro quo.* It often appears in the wording of formal contracts as *"in consideration of the sum of £500, paid by the purchaser, the vendor undertakes to . . . ".* This salutory rule makes it mostly unnecessary[2] to argue whether the parties did or did not mean to make their (unsealed) agreement legally enforceable, because if no consideration is present, it cannot be enforced anyway.

Reality of Consideration

410

Like all legal rules, this one has difficult or woolly marginal applications (and has been heavily attacked by academics) and since it was first applied in the 15th Century it has naturally been elaborated. It is not sensible to make too much of the snags, but it is necessary to describe the main limitations of the doctrine. Consideration then, consists in the conferment as part of, and under, the contract of a benefit upon the other party by doing something or by refraining from doing something, and each must so confer a benefit upon the other. It will be seen, that a party is not giving consideration if the benefit was already conferred before the contract was made, (e.g. a contract for a radio talk which has already been given), or if he has to confer the same benefit anyway - for example, under a different contract or because he is already legally obliged to do it. Such occurrences are not altogether uncommon. *If my agent engages your ballet company in America, and your agent not knowing this contracts the same company to me, the later of the two contracts cannot stand;* the police cannot make me pay for preventing a particular riot outside my concert

---

[1] See paragraphs 141-4.

[2] But see paragraphs 414-416 below.

hall, because they are under a general duty to prevent riots, but it would be otherwise if I had a contract with them which specified precautions which went beyond this duty.

Adequacy of Consideration

411 While, thus, the law requires a something for something, it does not pronounce on the adequacy of one something in comparison with another. *If I choose to pay £1,000,000 for a china orange, I cannot get the contract set aside merely because there appears to be a considerable disparity of value. The disparity, may (or may not) be evidence of fraud, duress, undue influence or supervening temporary insanity, but those matters are separate issues which have to be proved by evidence appropriate to themselves.* The reason for this, at first surprising, doctrine lies at the heart of the nature of contract itself. In the field of contract, the parties make their own arrangements as they wish and for their own reasons. "The Devil himself knoweth not what is in the mind of man." The courts have generally repudiated any idea that they know a man's business better than he does himself. They will not rewrite a contract simply because a party has second thoughts. They will hardly ever rewrite a contract at all.

Outside or Third Parties

412 Further, an important consequence of the doctrine is that in principle a third party, sought to be benefitted by an unsealed contract between two others, cannot enforce his intended benefit against the other two because *he* has not given any consideration. This rule is sometimes encapsulated in the tag "consideration must move from the promisee". The common example arises where a private businessman makes a normal contract in the course of the business but stipulates that the money be paid to his wife, or to a child or even to one of his creditors. I licence a quarryman to quarry stone in my land for 10 years in return for a minimum weekly royalty which is to be paid direct to you. I die within the 10 years. Can you force the quarryman to go on paying you? The answer is "No", unless you can prove that I made the contract as your agent or (perhaps) that you were my spouse and signed it together with me. The only watertight way of benefitting a third person who gives no consideration is to make the contract as a deed.

Novation* and Promissory Estoppel*

413 A contract can be replaced by another contract but the new one requires consideration just as much as the old. Hence (for example) a payment of a smaller sum can never, by itself discharge, save under seal, an obligation to pay a greater, though the same smaller sum accompanied by a bottle of claret (or, in the old cases, a beaver hat) will do so. This prevents burdensome one-sided changes in contracts, but the rule's full rigour could have unjust results, for example, where, as in the famous *High Trees* case, a landlord lowered his rents throughout World War II and then sued the tenant for the remitted balances back-dated to the beginning, after it was over. The tenant had given no consideration, but the court imported into the case the old rule of evidence, restated as a rule of equity called estoppel*. The landlord was not allowed to go back on his promise. The result is a two-tier effect. There must, initially be consideration, but if an alteration is required then, if the change is to be more burdensome, there must be further consideration, but if less, there need be no consideration if the disburdened party has altered his position in consequence of the promise.

Intention to create legal relationships

414 Absence of consideration eliminates the need to investigate whether a legal relationship is intended, but in a few instances its presence is not conclusive. *If you and I agree to dine out, you paying for the food, I for the wine, consideration is obviously present, yet neither would contemplate serving writs on the other.* Purely social arrangements are not contractual.

415 Secondly, there is a presumption, that dealings between spouses or between parents and children are not meant to create contractual relations. The presumption can be rebutted by the facts of the case.

416 Thirdly, in business dealings, the presumption is the other way, but it can be rebutted if the parties have so agreed in the contract. Such an agreement, sometimes called an *Honour Clause,* prevents the parties taking each other to court, provided that it is unambiguous. Otherwise, a party might be taken unawares by difficulties of language. In a retirement pensions case, the prospective pensioner took the less advantageous of two alternatives, because the employer promised, in addition, an *ex gratia* payment. In defaulting on this promise, the employer argued unsuccessfully that the words *ex gratia* meant that the payment was *non-contractual*. The court held that it might have other meanings too.

Illegal, Immoral, Void and Voidable Contracts

417 Apart from those contracts which are unenforceable by one of the parties because of the absence of the correct form,[1] there are some sorts of contracts and some matters which may be found in them of which the law disapproves. One way of classifying them is to consider what happens if you apply to the court for enforcement.

Voidability

418 At the least objectionable level is the *voidable* contract. This is one which was accepted by a party who was induced to do so by a misrepresentation, or by a bodily threat (duress) or by undue influence such as may be exercised by a nurse upon a very sick man. The weaker, or deceived party, may repudiate the contract without any ill consequences to himself, but it remains in force until the repudiation happens. Hence, things done before that event have a lawful life, especially where third parties are concerned. *I buy George's motor car as a historic model. I sell it to you before I discover that it is not. You acquire a valid title, because I had one. If I now repudiate the contract with George, this will not affect you. I shall be entitled to damages from him for the loss, if any, which I have suffered.*

419 It is in the nature of this type of situation that the person entitled to repudiate, is equally entitled to affirm. He must do one or the other within a reasonable time after he knows of his right, and whichever he does, he cannot change his mind. Moreover, the choice can as well be inferred from conduct as expressed in words. I subscribe for shares on the faith of a misrepresentation in a company prospectus. When I discover the lie, I may return the shares and get my money back; but if I accept and retain a dividend, or try to sell the shares on the stock market, I have affirmed the contract because my conduct is inconsistent with a decision to return the shares.

---

[1] See paragraph 137-138.

Void But Not Necessarily Illegal Contracts

420 Contracts which may be void but not necessarily illegal include: *Contracts prejudicial to the status of marriage,* whether by restraining an unmarried person's freedom to marry, (e.g. in a circus performer's contract) or for procuring, for reward, a marriage between particular people, or which encourage marital infidelity, or which provide for a future (as opposed to an immediate) separation, are void.

Contracts in Restraint of Trade

421 Stipulations whereby somebody undertakes not to exercise a trade, profession or vocation, except for agreements for sole agency, and tied-house agreements in the catering industry, are presumed void unless the party to whom the undertaking is given can show that it is reasonable as between himself and the other party, and also not detrimental to the public. The possible variations in this field are limitless, but most of them may be collected into four groups, viz:

> (i) Restraints upon employees
> (ii) Restraints upon vendors of businesses
> (iii) Restraints upon businesses imposed by business associations ("horizontal restraints").
> (iv) Restraints upon distributors imposed by manufacturers, or upon retailers by wholesalers ("vertical restraints").

Restraints upon Employees

422 An employee may be restrained from misusing his employer's trade secrets and from exploiting his customer contacts, but only to the extent that the restraint is necessary to protect the employer. In particular, the courts look closely at the geographical area of the restraint (*is it necessary to a business in Newcastle that an ex-employee should not set up a similar business in London?*) and its duration - a life ban may be held void, but not necessarily; it all depends on the facts. The law is also suspicious of indirect restraints. A company whose pension scheme is conditional upon pensioners not engaging in any activity in competition with the company, may have difficulty in justifying the condition.

423 Contracts for the appearance of a well known star, commonly, include a clause forbidding her to appear at any other place in the catchment area within a month either side of the contracted date.

Sales of Businesses

424 The law is slightly less suspicious where the restraint is connected with the sale of a business. When I sell my theatre as a going concern, I am selling also its reputation and goodwill. It is reasonable that I should not immediately use my funds (which probably include the purchase money) to build a new theatre next door, or perhaps within the catchment area, however defined, but if the area contains a developing new town it may be right to limit the ban to a short period of years.

Horizontal and Vertical Restraints

425 A person in the same trade as others who, for their own profit, agree upon mutual restraints, gets little sympathy from the courts if he tries to get out of his obligations, unless they are so burdensome that they eliminate competition altogether. The same may be said of vertical restraints, save that, as the parties are not always at arms length, the courts are apt to approximate the position of the restrained party more nearly to that of an employee. In both types of case, however, the arrangement may attract the attention of the Restrictive Practices Court. Agreements for the production, supply and processing of *goods* have to be registered with the Director of Fair Trading if they restrict prices, conditions of sale, quantities to be produced or persons or areas to be supplied, and he has to bring any such agreement before the Restrictive Practices Court, which, amongst other things, considers whether it is in the public interest. It may declare it void. One such agreement, which the court upheld, was the Net Book Agreement whereby a given edition of a book is sold at every bookshop at the price fixed by the publisher, who gives all bookshops the same discount. It was recognised that mutual undercutting by bookshops would rapidly destroy the systematic dissemination of books.

426 Betting

A wagering contract is a contract which two people, ''professing to hold opposite views touching the issue of a future uncertain event, mutually agree that, dependent upon the determination of that event, one shall pay or hand over to the other a sum of money or other stake; neither of the contracting parties having any other interest in that contract than the sum or stake he will so win or lose . . .''. Such an agreement is void and no proceedings can be brought to recover anything due under one, unless it is really a prize in a competition. The importance of this in the general law arises from its relationship with insurance, for an insurance policy is void as a wager if the parties have no interest in the subject matter.[1]

Infants*

427 A contract with an infant for necessaries, and a contract of employment beneficial to an infant is valid; what is necessary or beneficial is a question of fact;an electric guitar will probably be necessary to a pop singer; a contract of employment on the normal conditions and at the normal rates prevailing in the relevant industry will generally be beneficial. On the other hand, a loan of money to an infant, a mortgage or other security for a loan and an account stated given by an infant is absolutely void, and so is a guarantee given by someone else (for example of an overdraft), and such transactions cannot be ratified after majority. Between these two extremes, all other contracts can be repudiated by the infant at at any moment up to the end of a reasonable period after he comes of age, but remains valid till then. This is a matter of great importance because of the existence of youthful musicians and pop groups, some or all of whose membes may be infants, as well as other youthful practitioners of arts such as ballet. The fact that the contracts are invariably negotiated through adult agents is ir- relevant, for the agent has no greater authority than his principal[2]

Illegality

428 Secondly, some types of contract are for various reasons void, but a number of these are also illegal. Stated in very general terms, the difference is that the courts will not help either party to an illegal contract, (e.g. to commit an offence) and will treat the whole agreement as a contractual nullity, whereas it may assist parties to some merely void contracts to put things right. As usual this gen- eralisation is subject to variations in particular cases.

---

[1] See paragraph 465.

[2] But see paragraphs 472 et seq.

429 Illegal contracts include *Contracts to commit an offence.* The obvious cases need no comment, but sometimes there may be a less obvious vitiating element. An international contract, *for example, to transport a theatre company from England to U.S.A. may involve a breach of exchange regulations.*[1] On the other hand, the English court will not treat a contract as illegal if it breaches a foreign law not reflected in the law of England, unless it is intended to be performed in the foreign country. *I may sell a case of whisky to a Saudi Arabian here. If he chooses to take it home, he risks corporal punishment, which is his affair, but if I make a contract with him to import whisky into his country, an English court will treat it as illegal if the Saudi law is brought to its notice by proper evidence.*

430 A murderer can never benefit from his own crime. In other cases of unlawful killing, the convicted killer cannot, without an order of the court, or, in the case of social security benefits an order of the appropriate Commissioner, acquire a benefit in consequence of the killing. If I, being the beneficiary under your life insurance, am convicted of the manslaughter of you in a stage accident, I shall not, without such an order, be paid by the insurance company, nor, for that matter, can I similarly take a legacy under your will.

431 Secondly, the courts will not assist the parties to *contracts involving the commission of any tort,* for example, to publish a libel, *or a fraud,* for example, to rig the stock market by share purchases at a fictitious premium.

432 Thirdly, *contracts with an alien enemy,* for example, *with an Argentinian Company operating in France during the Falklands War,* are illegal.

433 Fourthly, *contracts to prejudice the administration of justice.* This is really a kind of fraud. The less obvious examples include agreements not to plead the Gaming Acts as a defence in an action on a cheque given for lost bets (i.e. to pretend that there was a genuine contract), or not to appear in the public examination of a bankrupt.

---

[1] Mostly suspended in 1979.

Defrauding the Revenue

434 Agreements designed to avoid taxes are common and many are lawful. In most cases where they are illegal, there is an element of concealment. If a number of people agree to endow an apparently charitable trust and then pay the trust funds towards their children's education, there may, depending on the precise facts, be an illegal agreement. Similarly, if a contract of employment entitles an employee to charge the tax payable upon his salary as expenses, there is a fraud on the Revenue, and if the employer defaults, the employee cannot recover even arrears of salary.

Sexually Immoral Contracts

435 A contract contemplating *future* fornication or adultery is illegal, even if the contemplated sexual intercourse is not to take place between the parties, and regardless of its actual wording. Direct references to the subject are naturally rare. A lease to a prostitute for the purpose of her profession is illegal. *A contract of employment between a theatre and a chorus girl which is really a method of supporting her as the manager's mistress* may come into the same category.

In neither case is the agreement necessarily illegal because of the character of the woman. A prostitute is entitled to have a home, and there is nothing illegal in being a man's mistress. It all depends on the particular facts.

436 An agreement to pay for *past* sexual intercourse fails for lack of consideration,[1] but if made under seal it will be enforceable.

Assignments of Contracts

The Problem

437 *A contract exists between you and me, whereby I have to deliver goods to, or do something for, you and you have to pay. For reasons which may be good as well as bad, I want to assign my place in the transaction to George. No difficulty arises if I seek and*

---

[1] See paragraph 410.

get your consent, for this ends the contract and substitutes a new one between you and George, but supposing that you refuse consent, or supposing that, at the critical moment, I cannot find you, or that I am injured and unable to carry on, or any other supposition, how far can I go in assigning my obligations and rights to George?

Obligations

438 It is well settled law that I cannot divest myself of the responsibility by shifting the burden to George. In the very common case of building subcontracts, for example, the fact that I have contracted the electrical wiring to him does not excuse me, if the wiring is improperly done. I remain liable to you, and so George to me.

Rights

439 The rules of assignment of rights are more complicated. I can assign my right to be paid to George by a statutory assignment. This must be in writing, it must be absolute (i.e. not dependent on any condition or happening) and you must have notice of it. George can then force you to pay him. An assignment in which one of the components required by statute is missing, is called an *equitable* assignment. If it is not in writing, George may ask me to join him in suing you but if I refuse he sues you and me instead. If notice has not been given, another creditor who *has* given notice will be entitled to be paid before George. If the assignment though, in proper form, is not absolute, he cannot enforce it.

Discharge of Contracts

Discharge of Contract by Performance

440 In most contracts the parties do exactly what they have agreed. They part, each with his purpose achieved, and the contract which regulated their relationship vanishes. *I pay your price for the cabbage: you hand over the cabbage. Between us there is nothing more to be done. Though the consequences, of course, remain, they do not normally involve us together. You bank the money without my help: I eat the cabbage without yours.* What, however,

happens if the contract is not exactly performed? What, indeed, is exact performance?

Exactitude of Performance

441 The fundamental rule, to which, however, there are important exceptions, is that performance must be precise to create a right to payment. If I deliver to you more goods than you ordered, I cannot force you to choose the right amount from the total delivered. You may, if you wish, treat the contract as discharged by breach and reject the lot; it was even held that a consignee could reject the correct quantity of tinned fruit in cases of 24 because the contract stipulated that they should be in cases of 30. It originally followed from this rule of precision that partial performance gave no right to payment, and this was manifestly unjust where the contract was for work or services. A builder was entitled to nothing until the house was built: the mate of a ship out of Jamaica, nothing until the ship had reached Liverpool. In the former the work had to be abandoned at a late stage. In the latter the mate died a few days before arrival. Nothing was payable in either case.

Partial Performance at Breach

442 The first exception to this rule arises where a party has caused the breach himself. Here the other may sue either for breach of contract or for the value of work already done, whichever will suit him best. In cases involving a large service element, the time factor will be important. *I agree to paint your portrait for £1000. If you countermand the order next day it is better for me to sue for breach of contract, for my damages will amount to my profit on the contract. If you countermand the day before the portrait is to be completed, I sue you for my work and trouble, which might well be more.*

Divisibility or Indivisibility?

443 The second exception arises where one party is entitled to demand performance independently of whether he performs his part of the bargain. *A tenant, for example, cannot withold rent simply because the landlord has failed to carry out repairs which he has undertaken to perform in the lease.* In such cases it is a question of fact whether the parties meant the mutual promises to be *in-*

divisible or *divisible* from each other; the law tends to presume indivisibility, but in some cases it will hold the opposite presumption: *for example, if I build bricks into your house but do not complete the job or if I, a singer, contract to sing in six of your concerts but am prevented by influenza (or bloody mindedness) from appearing at the sixth, or if a hundred cases of whisky are to be delivered by me to your bar at a rate of ten cases a week, there is a right to payment for work and things already done or delivered.* This type of exception is, however, related to the so-called rule of an *implied contract for partial performance.* If there is an opportunity for you to reject the part performance, then an acceptance by you can be inferred, but if there is no such opportunity it becomes necessary to explore other evidence. *The builder who abandons work on a building on my land and leaves me with an incomplete building will not, for that reason alone, be able to recover for his work and materials, unless the work has been substantially performed.*

Substantial Performance

444 The third exception, then, is known as *substantial performance. Where, for example, the contractor has completed building operations but not the decoration he cannot be refused all payment, but if he sues for payment on the contract he can be met with a counter claim for the failure to decorate.*

Tender and Legal Tender

445 Performance, however, may take the form of a tender. *If I agree to deliver ten tons of fuel oil to your concert hall "within the last 14 days of March" and you to pay on delivery, I have performed my part by appearing at the right premises with the oil at 8.30 p.m. on 31st March, and if you then reject the oil because your boilerman has gone home, I can treat the contract as breached and sue for damages.* In the case of a tender of money the position is slightly different. If the contract stipulates for payment in a particular way, that way must be observed. If there is no stipulation, the exact sum must be produced in so-called *legal tender,* i.e. Bank of England notes up to any amount; cupro-nickel or silver coins above 10p up to £10; below 10p up to £5 and bronze up to 20p only. There is no

right to ask for change. If the tender of money is not accepted, the debt of course continues in existence, but if you now sue me for the debt, I pay the money into court and you bear all the costs of legal proceedings thereafter.

Frustration of Contracts

446 It sometimes happens that after a contract has been made some supervening event frustrates the purpose which the parties had in mind. The number of possibilities is large but most of them can be gathered together under the following four headings.

Disappearance of the Subject Matter

447 Firstly, if a physical thing, the subject of the contract and essential to its performance, ceases to be available by the act of **none** of the parties, the contract is discharged. *I agree to make my music hall available to you for the performance of concerts on specified days. The hall is accidently burned down.* The contract is at an end. Of course if you could prove that I had set it on fire I would be in breach of the contract.

448 It seems, however, that this doctrine of frustration may not apply to leases or to contracts for the sale of land. In one such case the land, the subject of the contract, was compulsorily purchased by a local authority before the conveyance was executed. The purchasers wanted their deposit back, the vendors demanded the right to convey and be paid in full. The vendors succeeded, with the practical consequence that the purchasers became entitled to the compensation money.

Destruction of the Essential Object of the Contract

449 In the field of the arts, there are performances involving a high degree of expenditure, organisation, training, sensibility, and unity of conception, atmosphere and execution. Stage plays, operas, and symphony concerts are the obvious, but not necessarily the only, examples. The members of the audience buy their admissions in the expectation of a unified, intellectual or aesthetic experience. Now suppose that something happens which is outside the management's control and which "spoils the whole evening"

by destroying the cumulative nature of the experience. *The conductor, perhaps, has a heart attack during the last movement of the symphony; somebody in the front row of the dress circle leans too far and crashes to his death in the stalls; a drunk vomits over the people below; or, as in a well known example, a man is unable to control his laughter, and ruins a whole act. As a result the audience wants its money back.*

In such cases, there seems to be no direct authority, yet on general principles, the contract would seem to have been frustrated.

Non-occurrence of Essential Event

450 Thirdly, if the contract is founded wholly upon the occurrence of an expected event which, through no act of the parties, does not happen, the contract is discharged. The classic examples occurred in connection with the letting of rooms along the processional route for the coronation of King Edward VII. Because of the King's appendicitis the processions were cancelled.

Government Interference

451 Fourthly, there are the many examples of interference by government action. A declaration of war may make it illegal to carry out a contract, originally legal, due for performance in any enemy country, or a change in the law may have a similar effect at home.

Legal Consequences of Frustration

452 Apart from contracts for the sale of specific goods which, without the fault of a party, have perished before the risk has passed to the buyer, the effect of frustration, apart from discharging the contract, is that prepaid money may be recovered and, conversely, that if one party has before the frustrating event, conferred a benefit on the other, he may recover compensation for it. Under contracts for large single sums, this is a practical rule, but in the case of numerous repayments to angry and unidentifiable ticket holders, it is hardly workable. One may suggest two solutions. The one is to print on the ticket a condition that the management reserves the right to deduct a certain percentage from refunds arising out of events beyond its control during a performance. The other is to insure.

Breaches of Contract

453 Finally, it often happens that a contractual relationship is vitiated by the breach of one of the parties to it. In all such cases the innocent party can sue for damages, but in two of them he may, if he wishes, to go further. These cases are *repudiation* and *fundamental breach*.

Repudiation

454 Repudiation occurs where, before a contract is due to be performed, one of the parties indicates that he will not perform his side of the bargain, *for example, I agree in April to employ you as a theatre manager from 1st June, but change my mind and tell you on 11th May that you will not be required*, or where a party puts himself in a position where he cannot perform it: *I have agreed to sell my Botticelli to you, and then sell it to someone else before the time for delivery.*

Fundamental or Minor Breach?

455 Fundamental breach is harder to describe. It is a breach of a promise in a contract which is of such importance to the innocent party that he would not have entered into the contract unless he had been assured that that promise would be performed. The status of the promise has to be gathered from either the express words of the contract or its general nature taken as a whole, and it must be apparent to the person who made it. "If a man offers to buy peas of another and he sends him beans, he does not perform the contract." In an apprenticeship case, the master, described in the contract as an auctioneer, appraiser and corn factor, undertook to teach the apprentice these three trades. Half way through the period the master ceased to be a corn factor.

456 In both types of case (save in a lease) the innocent party has an option somewhat similar to that which obtains in a voidable contract.[1] He may affirm the contract and, therefore, remains bound by it himself, or he may treat it as discharged and sue for

---

[1] See paragraphs 418-419.

the breach. In the former case, his affirmation will be good even if he does not make it in words, as long as it is clear from his acts. In the second case, he must make his decision known to the other party, and once he has done so he cannot retract.

Quasi Contracts or Restitution

457 In addition to the cases of a part performance permitting the terms of a contract to be proved[1] there are many private transactions in which a common sense of justice infers some kind of legal relationship, but which lack one or more of the distinguishing marks of a true contract. There may be no consideration, or no precise agreement, or indeed no agreement at all, and yet there may arise a legitimate grievance deserving a remedy.

Quantum Meruit [2]

458 Quantum meruit is the generic term for the situation in which work has been done or goods supplied but no payment has been defined in advance. In such cases the court will if necessary fix the proper amount. There are four main instances where this can happen:-

i) An agreement to do work or supply goods at a reasonable (but unnamed) price.

ii) The substitution of a new agreement for an old one. "If I order from a wine merchant 12 bottles of whisky at so much a bottle and he sends me ten bottles of whisky and two of brandy *and I accept them*, I must pay a reasonable price for the brandy."

iii) Work already done under a contract which has been discharged by the defendant's breach. *I agree to write a book for a fee for your series. When I have written half the book you abandon the series.* I can sue you either for breach of contract or reasonable renumeration for work done. *remuner-*

iv) Work done under a supposed contract which turns out to be void. *I am appointed managing director of a company. It turns out some months later that the directors who appointed me were*

---

[1] See paragraph 139.

[2] *Lat* = Whatever he deserved.

unqualified and could not bind the company. I cannot sue under the supposed contract for it does not exist, but I can recover payment for work alreadty done.

Money Paid under a Mistake of Fact

459 Money paid under a mistake of fact (but not of law) is recoverable provided that the fact, if true, would have made the payer liable to pay. This distantly resembles the Quantum Meruit case iv) above, but here the contract may be valid but there is a mistake of another sort. *An insurance company pays up on a claim that goods have been lost: in fact thay have been sold.* The distinction between a mistake of fact and one of law is, however, less simple than it looks and full of traps. In particular a plaintiff may be caught by a supervening regulation, or by the result of a test case.

Money paid in pursuance of an ineffective contract

460 This distantly resembles Quantum Meruit Case iii). I have paid the money but the consideration then fails (for example, *if I pay a deposit for land which you cannot, as it turns out, sell).* If the failure is total, I may either sue for damages for breach or for the return of the money. If the failure is partial only, I must sue on the contract for damages.

Money had and received to the plaintiff's use

461 In this limited case, at least three parties are concerned. *George pays money to me and tells me to pass part of it to you; or some of George's money has come into my hands from a fourth party, and George tells me to pay it to you. You can, in either case, force me to pay you, if, but only if, I have notified you of George's instructions.*

Money paid to the defendant's use

462 This is the converse of the preceding case but is legally more complicated. Save in maritime salvage, a plaintiff who, benevolently or officiously, without the request of the defendant has paid money or taken trouble on the defendant's behalf, is entitled to nothing but thanks, but if he was forced to pay by a legal constraint, he will be entitled to have his money, but only if the

defendant must have been legally bound to pay it. *The most usual case is that of a co-guarantor of a debt. If he pays the whole of the debt he is entitled to sue the defaulting principal for the whole, or his co-guarantors for contributions.*

Necessaries supplied to persons under an incapacity

463 Where necessaries are sold to *and delivered* to an infant, or to someone who by reason of mental incapacity or drunkenness is incompetent to make a contract, he can be forced to pay a reasonable (not necessarily the actual) price for them.

Insurance

464 Insurance policies are contracts governed, in addition to the ordinary law of contract, by special rules of their own.

The Insurable Interest

465 If I insure something in which I have no interest at all (save the premium and the prospect of payment) the policy is void because it is really a bet.[1] My interest, however, does not have to be directly proprietorial. *A travelling theatrical company may insure its scenery and effects even though they belong to the management, because without them it may not be able to perform;* large managements avoid the need to insure actors' health by retaining understudies, but some smaller ones insure against perils to health, though, by definition, they have no property in the actors as such.

Frankness and the Proposal Form

466 One who takes out a policy of insurance is dealing with matters peculiarly within his own knowledge. It is therefore reasonable that he should disclose to a prospective insurer every *material circumstance*, that is to say "every circumstance which would influence the judgement of a prudent insurer in fixing the premium or determining whether he will take the risk". Hence insurers make a practice of requiring a prospective customer to complete a questionnaire called a *proposal form*, and this habitually requires (in one way or another) the customer to agree that his answers to

---

[1] See paragraphs 426.

the questions shall constitute the basis of the contract. This stipulation is a trap for the unwary, for it has the effect of making the accuracy (as opposed to the honesty) of the answers a condition of the validity of the policy, and of requiring very exact and complete answers to questions which are sometimes deceptively drafted. A policy of house fire insurance was held void because the assured had said that no proposal by him had been declined by any other company. Another company had in fact refused to insure his car. In another fire insurance case the insured had honestly replied, "No" to the question "Has there ever been a fire in the building"? The house was in a terrace, and another house owned by someone else in the same terrace had had a fire some years before. As long ago as 1908 the Court of Appeal waxed indignant at some of the practices which it was forcd to uphold.

Average and the Prohibition on Profiteering

467 An insurance policy other than a policy for life insurance is meant as an indemnity against loss, not as a means for realizing an unwarranted profit, for the prospect of unwarranted profit is a direct encouragement to crimes such as arson, and anyhow, as to the excess over the true loss the transaction would be a bet. *Hence if I insure my china orange for a million pounds, its loss does not entitle me to a million pounds, but only to the £3 which it will cost to replace.* Conversely, if I have numerous miscellaneous items in my house, collectively insured at only half their value, I am entitled to only half the value of any one of them which happens to be stolen. A similar principle is applied where there is a collective insurance of objects in different ownership (for example in a warehouse, museum or ship) and it becomes necessary to sacrifice some in order to save the rest. The owners of the saved properties may have to contribute to the loss of the owner of the sacrificed property if there is no insurance cover to deal with the problem.

Life and Endowment Policies

468 These policies are agreements to pay a fixed sum upon the death of a person or upon his attaining a certain age. They are not indemnity agreements, but the definition of an insurable interest in a life is noticeably tighter than in other branches of insurance law, being confined in practice to the insured's own life or the life of his or her spouse, debtor or trustee.

Types of Insurance and Insurers

469 Insurance terminology is often misleading. Policies are commonly classified under four major headings, viz, Marine, Fire, Life and Accident. These groups each contain varieties which are analogous, not subordinate to the main headings, and there is also a vast mass of rare, special or unclassified risks.

Marine insurance is concerned with ships and aircraft, goods and people carried in them, and freight, against perils of the sea and air and other risks such as detention through restraints of princes and peoples, wars and civil commotions. This market is directly affected by the rules on limitation*, whereby in a marine or air accident an owner's liability is limited to a rather low figure unless the claimant can prove personal responsibility by the owner.

Fire insurance is concerned with buildings or other property and the risks which occur to or in them; the class includes losses not only by fire but by natural calamity (e.g. earth tremors, or floods) or theft. The amounts insured invariably have an upper and often a lower limit, and certain types of risk (e.g. civil commotion) and also fair wear and tear are often excluded. In no branch of business is it more important to "read the small print". In particular two phrases in habitual use are usually riddled with exceptions* and exclusions*. These are the "Comprehensive Policy", which is never wholly comprehensive unless certain, quite onerous, conditions are met, and the policy supposedly covering "All Risks".

Accident insurance is concerned with accidents to persons including the insured, his employees and to third parties in motoring accidents or who may come upon his premises.

Miscellaneous but Important Possibilities

470 In addition there are many unclassified risks which it is the business of a good administrator at least to foresee. These can only be illustrated. *Bad weather may interfere with a pageant, or open air performances. A leading soprano may catch a cold and lose her voice. The launching meeting for a grand appeal may have to be cancelled because of a sudden general election, or a strike.*

Insurers

471 The world of insurers can be considered in two groups: the so-called Tariff Companies and the Underwriters. The insurance (or assurance) companies in effect offer commodities in the shape of standardised printed policies which deal with the most commonly recurrent problems. These can be varied for amount insured, but in other ways only to a limited extent. Underwriters, on the other hand, all practice at Lloyds, the City of London insurance market; they deal in the same sorts of insurance as the companies and, in addition, among them there can usually be found one or more willing to accept a risk which an insurance company does not find worthwhile. Lloyds underwriters must, however, be approached through an insurance broker, who also, of course, deals with companies. Brokers are experts and are paid by a small commission; their existence makes it feasible to shop around in the market for insurance tailored to one's needs and one's pocket. Anyone with substantial interests may be wise to consider using a broker.

Agency

Basic Description

472 Where a person, called the principal, appoints another, called the agent, to act as his representative, the relationship between them is called "agency". There is a special contract between the principal and the agent for the purpose of bringing the principal close to a third party to whom, very often, the agent is already known. The contract confers upon the agent an authority (varying with the purpose which the principal has in mind) and any further contract made by the agent in the exercise of that authority has the same consequences for the principal as if the latter had made it himself. So far as the *third party* (i.e. the person with whom the further contract is made) is concerned, the principal acquires all the rights and assumes all the liabilities, and the agent drops out and ceases to be a party to the further contract.

Agent Distinguished from Independent Contractor

473 This basic rule implies a distinction between an agent and an independent contractor. An agent acts for one side in setting up a contract with the other. An independent contractor makes contracts for his own benefit with both. *I wish to buy a 1,000 tons of bananas. My West Indian agent makes a contract on my behalf with an exporter. I am directly liable to the exporter.* Alternatively, *I go to an English importer. He buys them from the same exporter and resells them to me. I end up in either case with a 1,000 tons of bananas at, perhaps, the same cost, but in the second case I am not liable to the West Indian exporter but to the English importer (who of course, is liable to the West Indian).*

Creation of Agencies

474 Agencies can be created directly and expressly, or by any one of four inferential methods.

Express agency

475 Authority to execute a deed must be given by deed, but otherwise there are no formalities for creating an express agency: a telephone conversation may be enough. For reasons which will appear, it is wise to set down and agree the terms in writing, particularly if the agent is operating far away or in a specialised field where his work is hard to understand.

Inferential Agencies

Cohabitation

476 Firstly, a woman cohabiting with a man as his wife or mistress is *presumed* to be able to contract on his behalf for household necessaries suitable to his mode of living. This type of presumptive agency only runs to household matters and does not, of itself for example, enable her to negotiate a job for him, and it can be ended if, for example, the man gives notice to the local shops that they must not give her credit. It is uncertain if a man has a similar presumed agency for a woman, but there seems to be no objection of principle.

Agencies of Necessity

477 Secondly, there is a limited class (which the courts are reluctant to widen) of agencies of necessity. These arise in accidents and emergencies usually to ships or other carriers loaded with perishables. Here the master or carrier may contract without any authority on behalf of the owners, if the contract is clearly for their benefit, for example, to "save something from the wreck".

Agencies by Ratification

478 Thirdly, there are agencies by ratification. A supposed agent, who is most often in such cases a local manager, contracts without any authority from the principal, commonly the person or company which employs him. Assuming that the contract is not void, for if it were there would be nothing to ratify, the principal may ratify the agency provided that two conditions are met. The first is that the principal must be competent to make the contract at the time when the agent makes it. A contract made on behalf of an infant for something which is not a necessity may perhaps come into this category. An attempt to contract on behalf of a company which is being formed but not yet in formal existence certainly does, and so does a contract with a foreign principal where commercial relations have been interrupted by hostilities. The second condition is that the purported agent should unequivocally have identified the principal on whose behalf he professes to act. If he has, for example, really made the contract for his own behoof no one else can unilaterally come in and take it over.

Agencies by Estoppel

479 Fourthly, there are the agencies by estoppel*. These are really agencies by default. In theory an agent cannot act save by the will of the principal, but if a purported principal knowingly allows somebody to negotiate and contract on his behalf without interposing, and the third party acts upon the supposition that the agent is really an agent, then the principal is not allowed to deny the agency. Such cases usually arise where a long standing habit has been broken on one side, but the other has been insufficiently informed; for example, where someone has retired from a partnership, he may be bound by contracts made by it with people who had no reason to know of his retirement, or where a longstanding agency has been terminated, but the people with whom the agent has hitherto habitually dealt, have not been told.

The Third Party's Rights or Duties

480 Assuming that an agent is contracting within the scope of his authority, a third party's position will vary according to (i) whether he knows that he is dealing with an agent, and the identity of the principal, or (ii) whether he knows that he is dealing with an agent but does not know the identity of the principal, or (iii) whether he believes that the agent with whom he is dealing is the principal.

481 In cases (i) and (ii), the presumption is that the contract and legal relationship is with the principal, and the agent drops out, but this presumption can be displaced if the third party and the agent expressly agree that the agent as well as the principal shall be liable, or if the contract can be understood in no other way or if there is a trade usage governing the point. The issue is important where an agent is contracting on behalf of a minor (e.g. a pop group), and it may be desired to make him, as well as the minor, liable. Where the principal's identity is undisclosed it is obviously easier to argue that the agent is liable, but the question still remains one of fact.

In both cases, there are some special rules in particular instances. Thus, if an agent makes a contract under seal on behalf of another, he is liable and entitled under the deed, but his principal is not, unless the principal gave him a power of attorney to execute the deed. Secondly, the presumption of the principal's entitlement and liability can sometimes be displaced in the case of negotiable instruments such as cheques.

482 In case (iii) a third party who had no reason to doubt that the agent was the principal, can make the agent personally liable, and where he discovers the facts he can choose which he will sue, leaving the agent, if necessary, to recover from the principal.

The Undisclosed Principal's Right of Intervention

483 Where an authorised agent has contracted in his own name without disclosing the agency, the principal may spring from behind the curtain and enforce his rights against the third party, provided that the agency existed at the time when the contract was made, and that the contract neither expressly nor implicitly excludes him, for in such cases there is no contract to which he is a party.

Payments to Agents

484 It sometimes happens that in the course of business, payments are made to agents who, through fraud, carelessness, or bankruptcy fail to pass the money on. This can arise either where a principal has paid money to an agent to make a purchase or settle a debt ("purchasing agent") or where a customer has paid an agent for goods or services secured through him from his principal ("selling agent").

485 The fundamental presumption is that as the contract is between cutomer and principal, the debtor still owes the money if he has paid the wrong person, just as he would if he had paid any other wrong person. He must pay, and try to recover from the agent. This presumption can, however, be displaced if, in the case of a purchasing agent, the seller made it clear that he looked only to the agent for payment. In the case of a selling agent the rule is more stringent, for the general presumption is that he is not entitled to receive payment on behalf of his principal and that therefore the customer remains liable unless he can demonstrate that the agent had actual express authority to receive payment.

Unauthorised Acts by Agents

486 An agent does something for which he has no authority. He has taken a chance, or made a mistake or abused his position. What are the consequences for the other parties and for himself?

The other parties

487 If a principal is bound by a contract made with authority, it is easy to see that he is not so bound where he has given, or could give, none. For example, *if a managing committee has no power to buy goods on credit, an order for goods "on account" given by its secretary will not bind the committee.* The rule can be important if the agent goes bankrupt after disposing of property without authority, for the money so obtained does not form part of the agent's assets in the bankruptcy, and can be fully recovered by the principal — if it can be found.

Authority by Estoppel

488 There is, however, a difficulty arising from the differing vision of the principal and the ("contractor") third party. The *actual* authority which I give (in whatever way) to my agent, may seem to be rather different to the contractor. I can in some instances be made liable for acts which I have apparently but not actually authorised; for the most part, the contractor can only know what I or the agent tell (or otherwise represent to) him, and on that he is entitled to rely. If, for example, agents always behave in accordance with the custom of a particular trade, it will avail me nothing to plead only that my agent had no authority to behave in that way: I must show, further, that I told the contractor. This is authority by estoppel[1], comparable with agency by estoppel and can result in my being unable to deny an authority of which, as a matter of fact, I was entirely ignorant.

The agent's rights

489 If I pretend to act on behalf of a named principal who does not ratify, I cannot base any rights upon that lie, and I am estopped* from denying it if I try to make a claim in my own name. Thus, *if I bid, falsely, at an auction on behalf of a well known picture dealer and pay the deposit*, I shall not be allowed to say that I was the principal when I personally try to get the deposit back. If, on the other hand, I pretend to be an agent but do not name the principal, I am entitled to maintain proceedings in my own name. The reason for the difference is that a prospective contractor will, or may, have relied upon the principal's credit or reputation if he thinks that he knows who he is, but if he does not know (or probably care) he must be relying on me.

The agent's obligations

490 The agent's obligations depended, in a sense, upon his state of mind. If he tells a deliberate lie (e.g. *that a habitually indecent comedian is "not blue"*) and causes damage, he may be sued in tort for deceit.[2] If, however, he honestly but wrongly believed that he had authority, he is not liable for deceit, and he cannot be made liable on the contract either, because he, under the basic rule of agency[3] has dropped out.

491 This rather extreme doctrine applies, nowadays only where the authority began as a genuine authority but was terminated by some later event unknown to the agent and the contractor, such as the death of the principal in India. It is otherwise where such a supervening event is not in issue; a person professing to contract as agent for another is held to have made a promise that the authority exists, and the third party with whom he is dealing gives sufficient consideration for the promise, by entering into the transaction, to convert it into preliminary (or so called collateral) contract. It is upon this preliminary contract that the agent can be made liable.

---

[1] See paragraph 479. [2] See paragraph 389. [3] See paragraph 472.

Termination of Agencies

492 An agency is automatically ended at the moment when the principal or the agent *dies,* and the deceased's estate is not liable for any contracts made, however, innocently, after that moment. A similar rule applies when either is a company which has been liquidated, but as a liquidator may continue the trading activities of the company for the benefit of creditors, the *commencement* of liquidation proceedings does not necessarily terminate any given agency. An agent, in such a case, may wish to terminate the agency himself and prove in the liquidation.

493 *In bankruptcy* proceedings (for example, of an extravagant film star) the rule is more complicated. The making of a company receiving order* terminates any agency retrospectively to the time of any act of bankruptcy* committed within three months before the order, but the *advantage* of any contract is saved to the agent or third party if they were acting for value, and did not and could not have been expected to know of an act of bankruptcy.

494 *Supervening insanity* ends a contract of agency as between the principal and the agent, but the insane principal remains liable to third parties who did not know of his condition. ''Insanity is not a privilege''.

Termination of Agencies by the Parties

495 Like any other contract an agency can be ended by an agreement between the principal and the agent, but where one wishes to terminate and the other does not there may be special results. Though the variety of possible agencies is unlimited, most gather for this purpose, round two extremities. In the one, the agent is active and bound to further (generally on a commission basis) the principal's interests, and is commonly precluded from undertaking work inconsistent with the agency. *If there is hardly enough work for one bumblophone player in the world, the artist's agent who undertakes to manage a second such player is obviously breaking the terms of his agency with the first - unless, of course, the first foolishly agreed in advance to let him.* This agency is obviously

---

[1] See paragraph 52.

comparable with an employer-employee relationship, save that the integration into the employer's concerns is lacking. In such a case, unless the contract itself provides for notice, either party may end it by giving reasonable notice, whose length a court will, if necessary assess on the basis of all the facts.

496 At the other extremity, the principal and the agent are hardly bound to each other at all. The arrangement is simply that the principal *will* pay a fee or commission if the agent does something. This is commonly the case in property dealings: the estate agent is not bound even to try to sell my house, but if he does he gets his commission. Here, in the absence of any specific arrangement, the agent may back out whenever he likes, the principal at any time before the happening of the event which imposes an obligation upon him.

Agency Coupled with an Interest

497 In all instances, however, a principal cannot revoke an agency if for the advantage or protection of the agent it is coupled, at the time of its creation, with an interest. *You lend me £10,000 and I give you authority, as security for the loan, to collect rents from my tenants; I cannot revoke the authority until I have repaid the loan. On the other hand, If I give you such an authority and then later and independantly you lend me £10,000, I can revoke the authority when I like unless the loan agreement itself says otherwise.*

Employment

498 It has been whimsically said that the place which you want to find on the map is always at a point where several map sheets meet. Employment is one such area in the map sheets of law and politics. All employments are founded in specialised contracts, but the occasions when work is interrupted may be ruled by the law of torts. These are well recognised parts of the Common Law into which, however, statutes, varying with the temporary complexion of the government and of EEC legislation, make increasingly complicated incursions. The laws on workers and employers com-

binations, on national insurance and social security, on freedom of movement and on taxation, all have their practical and legal bearing and immensely complicate the difficulties of exposition.[1]

Contracts of Employment or Service

499 A contract of employment (or in the older terminology, a contract between master and servant) is as much a contract as any other, and, save for the exceptions necessitated by the nature of the relationship or statutory interventions, the ordinary rules of contract as to offer, acceptance, consideration and so forth apply to it.[2]

500 The distinguishing feature of such a contract used to be simple: an employer was entitled not only to control what work the employee was to do, but the manner in which the work was done. Then it was said that there were four marks of a contract of service: 1) the employer's power to select his employee; 2) the payment of wages or other remuneration; 3) the employer's right to control the method of doing the work; and 4) the employer's right to suspend or dismiss.

Modern Distinction from Other Contracts

501 These tests, though useful, are none of them now of universal application. Where high grade staff with professional qualifications are employed, such as eminent journalists or theatre directors, the employer can have little control of what work the employee is to do or how he is to do it. In other cases the employer may have control over the manner in which a worker is to work for him and the work may be of a kind usually done by employees, but the worker may nevertheless be an independent contractor, and in such cases may be known as a "labour only" sub-contractor. The modern test distinguishes between the employee who is employed as part of the business and whose work is an integral part of the business, and the worker whose work is not integrated into the business but is only accessory to it or is done by him on his own account.

---

[1] I know of no single work in which this subject is fully covered. Even if a genius appeared who could do it, he would be frustrated by politically inspired fluctuations in the rules, which often occur between putting pen to paper and publication.

[2] See paragraphs 392 et seq.

502 Whether or not the relationship of employer and employee exists is a question of fact, although the interpretation of the contract is a matter of law. It is possible for a person to be the employee of another even if a third party can appoint or dismiss him, or has powers of direction and control in regard to his work, or pays him his wages. A person may be an employee' even if he is remunerated otherwise than by wages, or is only employed at will. A person may be an employee part-time or to different employers, and a contract for exclusive personal service does not necessarily establish the relation of employer and employee. A person may be an employee and not an agent although he is remunerated by commission only.

503 On the other hand, a contract to render services to a third person is not a contract of employment and a sub-contractor is not the employee of the contractor employing him. A person may occupy the position of contractor in respect of one matter and of employee in respect of another to the same person. An employee of a sub-contractor is in principle not the employee of the main contractor; an employee of one employer may become the employee of another for a particular occasion where services are lent.

Sex Equality

504 Every contract of employment is deemed to contain an equality clause providing for equal pay and conditions as between employees of different sex in like work, unless (as in acting, or in particular circumstances of decency or privacy) the essential nature of the job makes the sex a genuine occupational qualification.

Closed Shop Provisions in Contracts

505 A term or condition of any contract for the supply of goods or services is void if it requires a party to the contract to recognise a trade union or negotiate with a trade union official. *Thus, if I, an employer, do not wish to recognise the Holeborers' Union, I can, when buying square pegs, ignore a provision in the contract with the supplier making such recognition a requirement of supply.*

Closed Shop Ballots

506 Closed shop agreements made since 14 August 1980 have to be approved in a ballot by a majority of either 80% of those entitled to vote or 85% of those who voted. There is also provision which will ultimately result in all closed shop agreements requiring such approval every five years, but these will probably not be put into effect before November 1984.

Strikes and Lockouts

507 Anyone is entitled to put an end to a contract by giving the notice required by it or implied by law, and if this happens in the case of a contract of employment, its revival has to be renegotiated in the same way as any other contract. It was thought illogical for the law to uphold *simultaneously* a fundamental breach of a contract by way of a strike or lockout (especially of a secondary character) and the continuance of the contract, unless such a possibility were written into the contract itself. To this extent the expression "right to strike" was self contradictory, and this logical incompatibility has lain at the bottom of the confusion in industrial relations, which has been a feature of the last century.

Interference and Unfair Industrial Practices

508 Before the rise of trade unions, interferences by outsiders in contractual relations were discouraged or prevented by the law of torts. The courts developed three, or perhaps four, doctrines or separate torts, namely:

Inducement of Breach of Contract
Conspiracy
Intimidation
(Perhaps) Interference in Business Relations

Apart from doubts about the last, these torts still exist. In so far as they affect employment their influence is restrictively regulated by Industrial Relations and Employment legislation, but the almost god-like immunity of trade unions from legal process has, since 1980 been reduced by enactments enabling employers to sue them for limited damages where such an employer is a victim of secondary industrial action. The limitation on the amount of damages depends on the size of the union, and certain, especially benevolent, union funds are protected from seizure.

Unfair Industrial Practices

509 The legislation also created a new group of remediable wrongs. As will be seen the actions included in this group resemble torts in many ways, but they are not torts because the task of adjudicating upon them is not entrusted to the courts, but to a separate and specialised structure of institutions which can award compensation but not unliquidated damages. The simplest definition of an unfair industrial practice is a practice about which the victim may complain to an industrial tribunal.

510 To understand the Unfair Industrial Practice and these institutions, some account of the three or four torts forming part of their context is necessary[1] and also the general common law rules which have been developed over the years.

511 Since the reduction of the immunity of trade unions from action in the courts, the economic torts have assumed a greater importance than they previously possessed

Economic Torts[2]

Inducement to Break an Enforceable Contract

512 This is an ancient action whose modern form (1853) arose when a theatre manager obtained damages from a man who had induced a well known opera singer to break her contract to sing at the theatre. Apart from straight persuasion, this tort can be committed by physical means such as kidnapping the opera singer, or wrecking the stage before a performance, or by dealings inconsistent with the contract such as buying something which the seller is under convenant not to resell, or by interfering with a source of supply. The tort is not committed if the defendant did not know of the contract, or if he merely advises someone to break it. He must have created a reason for breaking it. It is no defence that this was done in good faith or without malice towards the plaintiff, but moral duty can be a defence, for example (1924) where a protection committee induced a theatre manager to break a contract with

---

[1] See paragraphs 512-4.

[2] No satisfactory collective name for these torts exists. I have adopted this one, but the reader is warned against importing into this subject a legal cohesion which is at present doubtful.

someone who paid his chorus girls so little that they had to resort to prostitution.

Conspiracy

513 Conspiracy, as a tort, is a combination between two or more people or entities to injure somebody's interests or to further their own by unlawful means. It is not committed if the means are lawful and the real purpose to promote the legitimate interests of its members or even a lawful good cause, even though it incidentally injures those of the plaintiff. A boycott of a dance hall which operated a colour bar has not been held not to be a conspiracy.

Intimidation

514 Intimidation consists in administering unlawful threats, by which harm is inflicted through interference with the liberty of others to do as they please. This can take two forms: a direct threat to the plaintiff himself to act against his own interest or a threat to others to act against the plaintiff's interest. *If I threaten to slash your face, or your mother's, if you continue to act at George's theatre, you can, in either case, sue me for Intimidation, and if you have in fact broken the contract, George can sue me for inducing the breach.*[1]

Interventions by Statute and Common Law

515 Statutes have made far reaching inroads into the relationship between employer and employee. The tendency of recent legislation has been to give the employee something akin to a right of property in his job. In particular there are provisions on the terms and form of contracts, the place and mode of payment of the wages, the deductions which may be made from them, the minimum wages which may be paid, and on payments to be made on redundancy. Legislation also restricts the employment of children and young persons and women, forbids discrimination according to race or sex, controls hours and conditions of work in particular employments, and imposes on certain employers a duty to employ a quota of disabled persons.

---

[1] See paragraph 512.

The Natural Vagueness

516 In real life, moreover, many parts of such contracts tend to be left vague. I engage carpenters and painters to make scenery for my theatre. I am *at this moment* contemplating a production of *"Hamlet"*, but neither they nor I know what I may wish to produce next year. It might be *"The Importance of Being Earnest on Ice"*. Employers and job seekers are seldom learned in the law, and come to quick agreements orally expressed. Thousands of such agreements are made daily. It would be surprising if things did not happen which nobody foresaw or bothered to express, and since it is the function of the law to quieten disputes, it has been forced to develop rules to fill gaps if the contracting parties have not filled them themselves. In addition there are rules of law which must be obeyed whatever the contract says.

517 Form and the Written Statement

The contract, that is the agreement by which the employer and the employee are bound to each other, may be in writing or merely in spoken words, or it may be a mixture of the two, but not later than thirteen weeks after the beginning of the employment, the employer must give a written statement identifying the parties, specifying the date when the employment began and the date when it expires if it is for a fixed term, and giving the particulars of the following terms of employment as at a specified date not more than one week before the statement is given:

the scale or rate of remuneration, or the method of calculating it;
the intervals at which remuneration is paid;
any terms and conditions relating to:-

> hours of work, including any terms and conditions relating to normal working hours;
> entitlement to holidays, including public holidays, and holiday pay;
> incapacity for work due to sickness or injury including any provisions for sick pay;
> pensions and pension schemes;
> the length of notice which the employee is obliged to give and entitled to receive to determine his contract of employment; and the title of the job which the employee is employed to do.

518 If there are no particulars to be entered in the statement under any of the above heads the fact must be stated. It must also state (mainly for pensions reasons) whether any employment with a previous employer counts as part of the employee's continuous period of employment with the present employer and, if so, the date on which the continuous period of employment began.

519 The statement must also specify any disciplinary rules applicable to the employee; and by description or otherwise, a person (apparently not a trade union official) to whom he can apply if he is dissatisfied with any disciplinary decision relating to him, and a person to whom he can apply to seek redress of any grievance relating to his employment, and how he can apply; and, where there are further steps consequent upon any such application, explain them.

520 The particulars to be given and the matters to be included in the note need not be set out in detail if it refers the employee to some document which he has reasonable opportunities of reading in the course of his employment, or which is made reasonably accessible to him in some other way.

Distinction between the Contract and the Statement

521 It should be understood that the statement records the contents of the contract. It is not the contract itself. Hence changes in the contract may be negotiated, and, when they are settled changes must be made in the statement accordingly. This must be done within a month of the change.

522 An employer is not bound to provide these statements if the employee is his parent, spouse or child.

523 If an employer fails to provide a statement where or when he should, or the employee disputes its correctness, the latter may apply to an Industrial Tribunal which can settle the statement itself as if the employer had done so. It cannot include matters not required by the legislation.

Collective Agreements

524 Unlike the common American practice, collective agreements between bodies representing workers and employers do not, as such, bind individuals on either side unless the trade union or employers' association was acting as each individual member's authorised agent. In practice such a collective agreement is made binding through the medium of a Contract of Employment, which actually, or by clear reference, incorporates its terms. A restriction on the employee's right to strike, if contained in such a collective agreement, does not bind him unless the agreement:

> is in writing;
> expressly states that the restriction may be incorporated in the contract of employment;
> is reasonably accessible at the place of work;
> and
> has been made with trade unions, all of which are independent.*

525 There is also a curious (but apparently little used) provision that on a reference by the Secretary of State to the Industrial Arbitration Board, the Board can require an employer to observe recognised terms and conditions of employment and, in effect, insert them into the relevant contracts of service. To this extent a collective agreement can be forced on an employer, but not an employee, who was not a party to it.

Implied Duties of an Employee

526 An employee must obey his employer's lawful instructions and serve him faithfully. He is not bound to do more than his contract requires, but he must not wilfully obstruct the employer as he goes about his business. If, in violation of his duty to serve faithfully, he takes advantage of the opportunities of his position to enrich himself, he is accountable to his employer for the proceeds; he is also similarly accountable for goods found by him in the course of his employment, and he must take proper care of any property of the employer entrusted to his charge. He may take physical measures in his employer's defence.

Employee's Relations with Trade Competitors

527 An employee must not in his spare time work for a trade competitor of his employer, even though no disclosure of confidential information takes place, nor must he accept from his employer's client an offer of work which he had been doing until then as his employer's employee.

Unjustified Absences

528 He must not absent himself from work. If he does so without good cause he is liable in damages to the employer, and if the absence is inconsistent with the proper discharge of his obligations it may justify dismissal.

Skilled Employees

529 If an employee is engaged to do work in which he is particularly skilled, he must do it with reasonable care and is liable in damages to the employer if he fails to do so or causes the employer to become liable to third parties. This rule applies only where he is lawfully working on the subject matter in which he is skilled.

Good Faith

530 An employee is under an obligation of good faith both during his employ and after he leaves it. Thus, he must not disclose his employer's secrets, other than information that the employer intends or is committing a crime, fraud, or other misdeed unjustifiable in the public interest. If he invents or discovers something in the course of his employment he becomes a trustee of it and must disclose it to his employer; and he must not canvass his employer's customers with the intention of diverting their custom to himself.

Employer's Obligations [1]

531 Generally the obligation to pay wages will be regulated by the contract itself or by statute, but sometimes no price will have been agreed in advance. So long as it is clear that the work was to be remunerated, the employee is entitled to a *quantum meruit*.[2]

---

[1] For Health and Safety at Work see paragraphs 224-230.

[2] See paragraph 458.

532 While an agreement to pay more for doing what is already required by the contract is bad for lack of consideration, it becomes enforceable if the employee is no longer bound by the original contract, because, for example, the work has become more dangerous or arduous or because its nature has changed.

Payment at End of Contract Periods

533 An employer must pay the remuneration due for each period contracted, but is bound to do so only at the end of the period. This period is, unless otherwise stated in the contract, the period by reference to which pay is calculated. Hence an employee on an annual salary is entitled to be paid only once a year unless there is provision for payment by instalments, and an employee who leaves without notice during a period is not entitled to payment for any part of it. For this reason workers paid by the day, even if in practice they receive the money weekly, are at an advantage, since they are entitled to be paid wages accrued to the end of the last full working day.

Illness

534 If an employee is absent through illness, the amount to which he is entitled depends on the contract. Hence the employer is not automatically entitled to deduct state sickness or injury benefits from his pay, unless the contract so permits, nor similarly, can he make deductions for breaches of contract, or suspend an employee unless permitted to do so by the contract. Only a very prolonged absence will justify terminating the employment.

Out-of-Pockets

535 An employee is entitled to be reimbursed for outlay in the course of the employment on the employer's behalf and to be indemnified for any loss or damage caused by obedience to the employer's lawful instructions, but not if the liabilities or expenses were not implied in the general nature of the employment. *I must pay for my motor mechanic's broken spanner, but not for his case of champagne.*

Accident Insurance

536 An employer other than a local authority or nationalised industry must insure his employees with an authorised insurer* against injury or disease arising out of the employment in Great Britain. The policy must be a so-called approved policy (which must not contain certain exclusions or exceptions tending to put the cover in doubt by requiring the employer to do certain things) and for at least £2,000,000 per occurrence.

Injuries at Work

537 An employer is bound to see that his employees do not suffer injury through his personal negligence or failure to superintend or control the undertaking. He is liable for injury inflicted in the course of work by one employee on another and cannot contract out of this liability. On the other hand his liability may be reduced if the plaintiff employee's negligence contributed to the injury.

Termination of Employment other than by Dismissal

538 Apart from the ordinary events which discharge and contract, an employee may refuse to continue where he unreasonably apprehends injury or death, or where he is severely ill-treated.

Termination on Dissolution of Partnership

539 If the employer is a partnership, the dissolution of the partnership by a death terminates the contract, but dissolution by a voluntary arrangement operates as a wrongful dismissal and so does the transfer of a business from one company to another.

Termination on Bankruptcy or Liquidation

540 Bankruptcies and compulsory liquidations of companies do not necessarily terminate an employment, but a voluntary liquidation does. In all such cases the employee becomes entitled to prove for his unpaid wages.

Ordinary Dismissal

541 Apart from the cases where there is a *dismissal procedures agreement* in force, or where either party may end the contract because of the conduct of the other, an *employer* must give the following lengths of notice to an employee who has served continuously with him for the following lengths of time:

---

[1] See paragraphs 440-446.

Period of Service	Length of Notice
Under 1 month	None
1 month to 2 years	One week
2 to 12 years	One week for each year of continuous employment
12 years or more	Three months

An *employee* for over 1 month must give at least one week.

Contracts may provide for longer but not shorter periods, but an employee may waive his right on any particular occasion or accept payment in lieu. Work outside Great Britain* counts only if the employee ordinarily works in Great Britain, and the work abroad is done for the same employer. A strike or lock-out does not break the continuity, but the week in which it occurs is not counted. On the other hand a week does count if the employee could not work because of sickness, injury, pregnancy or confinement, or because of a temporary cessation, or if, by custom or arrangement, his absence counts as work. A week for these purposes is a seven day period (ending on a Saturday) involving at least 16 hours work.

"Unfair Dismissal"

542 "Unfair dismissal", a technical term defined by statute, is the principal category of unfair industrial practice. It includes certain acts which, in an ordinary sense, are not dismissals, and the definition of "unfair" is specialised. Its most important consequence is that, apart from certain excepted groups, employees who are subjected to treatment, as so defined, are entitled to seek redress from an Industrial Tribunal but not the Courts. The excepted groups include those employed under the terms of their contract for less than 21 hours a week, those ordinarily employed outside Great Britain*, the employer's spouse, parent, grandparent, step-parent, child, grandchild, stepchild, or full or half brother or sister, those who have reached normal retiring age and usually those who have been employed for less than 26 weeks.

543 An employee is treated as dismissed if, but only if:
   i) the employer terminates his contract of employment, whether or not by notice;

ii) the employee is employed under a contract for a fixed term, and the term expires without being renewed under the same contract, unless the employee agreed in writing before the expiry of the term to exclude any claim for unfair dismissal in such a case; or

iii) the employee terminates the contract with or without notice in circumstances such that he is entitled to do so without notice by reason of the employer's conduct.[1]

544 Where an employer has given an employee notice to terminate his contract and where during the obligatory period of that notice the employee gives written notice to terminate the contract sooner than the date on which the employer's notice is due to expire, the employee is still taken to be dismissed by the employer, and the reasons for the dismissal are still the reasons given in the employer's notice.

Dismissal Procedures Agreements

545 Dismissal procedures agreements are negotiated between independent* trades unions and employer's associations. They must conform with certain statutory requirements, and can be designated by an order of the Secretary of State for Employment. They then bind both sides and replace the ordinary rules on unfair dismissal.[2] A typical agreement requires an employer to have given an employee first a verbal warning and then a written warning, each for different "offences" before taking any disciplinary action such as suspension or dismissal. Large employers simplify such obligations by using printed warning forms.

In certain circumstances such orders can be revoked.

The Fairness of a Dismissal

546 In principle a dismissal for conduct will be held unfair if the employee is given no opportunity to explain himself. Hence the employer must state his reasons and conduct some sort of investigation. In all cases the burden is on him to prove that a dismissal is fair, but the legislation deals specifically with the main cases.

---

[1] See paragraphs 537 and 538.

[2] See above.

547 It is *statutorily fair* to dismiss an employee for failing to join a closed shop unless he objects to joining it on grounds of conscience, conflict with professional ethics or deeply seated conviction, or unless he obtains a declaration from a Tribunal that he has been expelled from or refused admission to a trade union, or unless the closed shop agreement was made after he took up the employment or, in the case of an agreement which came into force after 14 August 1980, it was not approved in a ballot held during the five years before the dismissal by a majority of 80% of those who voted, or 85% of those entitled to vote.

548 It is *statutorily unfair* to dismiss an employee for joining or proposing to join a trade union, or for taking part in its activities in his own time, or in agreed working time, or for refusing to join or for leaving or refusing to remain with, a union which is not independant*. To plug loopholes in these rules certain types of discrimination are also statutorily unfair. Thus if an employee is dismissed for redundancy, and the circumstances constituting the redundancy applied equally to his mates in the same undertaking and they remained in employment while the dismissed employee was selected for redundancy, for any of the reasons set out above, or in contravention of a customary arrangement or agreed procedure, and there were no special reasons justifying a departure from that arrangement or procedure his dismissal would be statutorily unfair.

549 Where an employee is dismissed in connection with a strike, a tribunal must not decide if the dismissal or subsequent failure to re-engage is fair or unfair unless he is apparently a victim of discrimination.[1]

Statutorily Acceptable Reasons
550 The employer must show not only that he has, having regard to equity and the substantial merits, acted reasonably, but that his reasons fall within one of the statutorily acceptable classes. These are (a) redundancy, (b) (gross) misconduct, (c) incapability relevant to the nature of the employment, (d) lack of qualifications (if any) necessary to act in it, and (e) any other *substantial* reason

---

[1] See paragraphs 548 and also 574.

(e.g. a travel agency employee who married an employee in a rival agency). Though union pressure must be ignored in deciding if a reason is good, a redundancy caused by union action can be a good reason, and a tribunal can order a trade union rather than the employer to pay or contribute to the compensation awards, provided that the complainant or employer applies before judgment to have the trade union joined in the proceedings.

Conciliation and Complaint

551 An employee may seek the good offices of ACAS* or he may make a complaint of unfair dismissal to an Industrial Tribunal, which can refer the matter to ACAS, or deal with the complaint itself. Such a complaint must be made within three months of the dismissal taking effect unless the Tribunal gives leave to complain out of time.

552 The Tribunal may order reinstatement if the complainant wants it and has not caused his own dismissal, and if it is practicable for the employer to comply; failing this it must consider ordering re-engagement upon such terms as it thinks just. If an order is not fully complied with, the Tribunal must award compensation payable by the employer to the employee. This may consist of three parts, a basic award related to the age of the employee, a compensatory award and a special award. The *basic award* is calculated for each full year worked continuously with the employer as follows:

Between the ages of	Wages per year worked
18 and 22	½ a week
22 and 41	1 week
over 41	1½ weeks

Where, however, the dismissal is for trade union reasons[1] it must not be less than £2000, but this amount can be reduced if his conduct justifies reduction.

In addition, where the dismissal is for trade union reasons, [1]he is entitled to a special award which (subject to an upper limit of

[1] See paragraphs 547-548.

£20,000) equals the greater of one weeks pay multiplied by 104, or £10,000, or if he requests and is refused reinstatement, one weeks pay multiplied by 156 or £15,000, but if his basic award has been reduced, his special award must be reduced in the same proportion. The compensatory award is limited to £6,250 or such less amount as is thought proper taking into account five points, viz:

(i) immediate, and (ii) future, loss of wages,
(iii) manner of dismissal
(iv) loss of protection and
(v) loss of pension rights.

There are also provisions on sex and racial discrimination.

Redundancy

Redundancies Procedure

553 An employer who proposes to dismiss an employee as redundant must notify the Secretary of State for Employment and must consult the representatives of the relevant recognised trade union, that is to say the union which the employer has recognised or which ACAS* has recommended for recognition. He must make such notification and begin such consultation at the earliest opportunity before the dismissal and in any case:

Numbers at any one establishment to be made redundant	Period within which dismissals are to take place	Consultation to begin before dismissals are to take effect
100 or more	90 days or less	90 days at least
10 or more	30 days or less	30 days at least

The employer must give the union representative in writing i) the reasons, ii) the numbers and descriptions of employees, iii) the total number of such employees employed at the establishment, iv) his method of selecting those to be dismissed, v) the method of carrying out the dismissals, having regard to any agreed procedures, and vi) the period over which they are to take effect. He must consider and reply to representations made by trade union representatives and, if he rejects any of them he must state his reasons. If he fails to comply with these requirements the union can complain to the Tribunal.

Protective Award

554 If the Tribunal thinks that the complaint is well founded, it can make a Protective Award that is to say it can require him to pay any employee for a period, which can vary between 28 and 90 days. This is not a punitive jurisdiction, but is intended to safeguard the end period of an employees contractual rights; there are provisions for ensuring that the employer does not have to pay both under the contract and under the award, and for enabling an employee to complain to the Tribunal if the employer is not complying with the award.

Redundancy Procedure Agreements

555 There are certain collective agreements for dealing with redundancy procedures. Where such an agreement has been brought into force by a departmental order it replaces the provisions described above.

The Redundancy Fund and Redundancy Payments

556 An employer must make a redundancy payment to any redundant employee who is over 18 and under 65 except his or her spouse or someone ordinarily working outside Great Britain*. The basic amount is calculated by a formula which appears below, but the actual amount payable can be reduced to take account of pension rights, provided that the employer gives written notice to the employee claiming to reduce the payment on that ground. Such a notice will be declared ineffectual by a tribunal if the pension does not become payable wthin 90 days of the end of the employment; but otherwise a pension (or its lump sum equivalent) of at least one third of the last annual total of wages or salary will exclude a redundancy payment, altogether, and there will be adjustments allowing for pensions of less than that amount and for commencement dates within the 90 days.[1]

---

[1] There is so far unused ministerial power to provide for reductions taking account of compensation for unfair dismissal.

Employer's Rebate

557 When the right amount has been calculated *and paid,* the employer may become entitled to a Rebate from the Redundancy Fund controlled by the Secretary of State. To ensure his right to the Rebate he must give at least 14 days written notice (or 21 days if ten or more employees are involved) before the employment is to end, to the Department's local office and must make the claim for the actual amount within 6 months afterwards. This claim must, of course, give the date when the employment ended, and set out the method by which the redundancy payment was calculated, and it must be accompanied by the employee's signed receipt for the money.

558 The Rebate in 1983 was 41% of the amount paid, but the Department has power to reduce or withhold it if the employee received shorter notice than he should have received, or if the employer has without excuse failed to give the local office the 14 or 21 days notice before the employment ended. The Rebate is only payable against Redundancy Payments made to employees in respect of employment between 18 and 65. Thus, if the employer is bound by some agreement to make payments for work outside this period, he can receive nothing from the fund in respect of them.

559 The formula for calculating the Redundancy payment is based upon the minimum weekly wage payable to the employee at the end of the employment, but not exceeding (in 1983) £130 per week. It is the aggregate, reckoning backwards from the end of the employment, of the amounts shown below; not, however, exceeding 20 years-worth.

Years of continuous employment	*Amount per year*
Age 18 to 22	½ a weeks wage
Age 22 to 41	1 weeks wage
Age 41 to 65	1½ weeks wages

Other Dismissals

Summary and Unlawful Dismissal

560 Most cases of dismissal will, if put to the test, be handled by an

Industrial Tribunal on a complaint of unfairness, but there remain a residue which still may arise under the Common Law, and are handled by the Courts. Generally speaking, these two jurisdictions and procedures are mutually exclusive.

561 An employee may be dismissed without notice for:

a) **Wilful disobedience** to lawful instructions going to the root of the contract of employment

b) **Misconduct** of a grave kind involving, for example, dishonesty towards the employer or the commission of the sort of offence (not necessarily in working hours) which makes it unsafe to retain him.

c) Habitual or gross, but not an isolated instance of minor, **neglect** of the duties of his job.

d) **Incompetence** in a skilled employee. This arises because the employee has warranted his skill to get the job, and the employer is not bound to retain him if he has not got that for which he is being paid.

e) **Very long or incapacitating illness.**

f) **Conduct incompatible** with his duty of good faith, such as taking a secret commission or secretly entering into transactions in which his interests conflict with those of his employer.

562 An employer, dismisses an employee wrongfully if he terminates the employment before the expiration of the term agreed, for some reason other than a) to f) above, or if, though he could have dismissed the employee for such a reason, he condoned it. An employee who alleges wrongful dismissal may treat the contract as broken and sue for the breach, or treat it as rescinded and sue for work done but so far unpaid (whichever is to his greater advantage) but he cannot do both.

More on Strikes and Lockouts

563 From the foregoing account of the law, it will be obvious that the previous law on strikes and lockouts has not remained unaffected. The law now provides that for purposes of notices of dismissal and redundancy payments the employment is not considered to have been interrupted if the employee goes back to work with the same employer. On the other hand, he is not entitled to have a week

during which he was actually on strike counted for these purposes. In real life the effect of most such interruptions is to suspend rather than end the contract, for when work is resumed it will usually be on the terms of the original contract modified, in favour of the strikers or the employer as the case may be, to deal with the points at issue in the stoppage. This, on the other hand, is not necessarily the case where there is no direct issue between the employer and the strikers, who are taking "secondary industrial action" in support of colleagues of a different establishment or industry. In such cases the aggrieved employer has his Common Law rights (but limited as to amount) to sue for breach of contract or in tort.

Discrimination

564 Apart from sex discrimination[1] there are rules on discrimination against married people; and against "victimisation" (that is by treating less favourably a person who invokes the law on sex discrimination and equal pay).

Time Off

565 An employer must allow time off during working hours to an employee

(i)   for trade union duties if he is an official of a union which the employer has recognised, and must pay him;

(ii)   for public duties such as acting as a JP, member of a tribunal, councillor, member of a health or water authority or the

(iii) governing body of a primary or secondary school; and

(iv) to look for work if given notice of dismissal because of redundancy,
and the employee can complain to the Industrial Tribunal if he does not.

Medical Issues

Suspension or Dismissal on Medical Grounds

566 If an employee is suspended on medical grounds or on the basis of the Health and Safety at Work Code of Practice, he is entitled to be

---

[1] See paragraph 504.

paid up to 26 weeks but not if he had been in the employment for less than 4 weeks, nor for any period when he was incapable of work by reason of disease, nor if he has refused suitable alternative work or arrangements for securing his availability for work. If he is dismissed instead of suspended, he is qualified to complain of Unfair Dismissal if he has been in the employment for 4 weeks (instead of the usual 26).

Pregnancy

567 Special arrangements apply in cases of pregnancy. The general principle is that a pregnant employee is entitled to maternity pay from her employer, and to return to work. It follows that the occasions when she can be fairly dismissed for pregnancy are limited to cases where the pregnancy prevents her from adequately doing her work or from doing her work without contravening a legal restriction on the employer, and even then she must be offered a new contract for work suitable to her condition and not less favourable as to the circumstances of her employment than that which previously obtained. Moreover, the new contract must come into effect without a break (other than a weekend).

568 Her rights, however, depend upon whether she had been employed continuously for two years with the employer up to the 11th week before confinement, and she must give her employer at least three weeks notice before her absence begins, that the absence is due to pregnancy or confinement and, if such be the case, that she intends to return. The notice must be supported by a medical certificate.

Maternity Pay

569 Maternity pay is 90% of six weeks pay less the maternity allowance payable (even if not paid) under the Social Security legislation. It is payable in six weekly instalments beginning when the notice and medical certificate have been produced.

Maternity Pay Rebates

570 The legislation provides arrangements whereby the employee will receive the foregoing statutory right or any more favourable rights under a contract but not both, and in such a way as not to disadvantage the employer, who can claim a Rebate from the

Maternity Pay Fund in much the same way as he can make claims on the Redundancy Fund. This Rebate is the amount which he has paid plus the relevant Secondary Class I National Health Insurance Contribution.

Right of Return

571 The employee can exercise her right to return to the same employer or his successor at any time before the end of the 29th week (inclusive) from the week of her confinement, as long as she gives at least a week's notice of the date on which she means to return. In effect she is entitled to her old job on the same or better terms, but if this is impossible she must be offered suitable alternative employment in circumstances not less favourable than before. Both sides can postpone the date of return by up to 4 weeks but she must have her reason medically certified.

572 If she cannot return on the notified day because of an interruption of work at the place of employment, she can return when work is resumed. If she does not notify a date of return and there is an interruption of work, she can notify a day within 14 days of its termination, even though it falls outside the 29th week.

573 Her rights are, as usual, supported by a right to complain to the Industrial Tribunal, but the Tribunal must not find that she has been dismissed if the employer has less than six employees and finds that it is not reasonably practicable to reinstate her or offer her another suitable job, or if any employer finds it equally impracticable for any reason other than redundancy, and has offered her suitable alternative employment which she has either accepted or unreasonably refused.

574 Maternity does not affect rights to redundancy payments where the redundancy happens to arise before the notified day of return, but an employer who refuses to allow the employee to return on grounds of redundancy cannot be treated as having dismissed her unfairly.

Temporary Replacements

575 Where an employer engages a replacement for a pregnant employee who is temporarily absent, he may fairly dismiss him to make way for the returning employee, provided that the replacement has on engagement been informed in writing that this will happen.

Insolvency of Employer

Employee's Priority

576 If an employer becomes insolvent* the employees are specially protected in the case of two groups of sums which they may be owed. The **priority group**, consisting of sums which the insolvent's trustee or liquidator must pay in priority to other creditors, comprises five amounts which the employer was legally bound to make even though they were of no direct commercial advantage to himself, viz:

(i) guarantee payments*;
(ii) pay due while under suspension on medical grounds;
or (iii) when carrying out trade union duties;
or (iv) when taking time off to look for work or arrange for retraining;
or (v) under a protective award.

577 The **redundancy** group, comprising five types of debt, for which the employee can request repayment out of the Redundancy Fund. These comprise:

(vi) arrears of pay not exceeding £130 per week up to 8 weeks;
(vii) amounts due in lieu of notice or for failure to give notice;
(viii) holiday pay up to six weeks, due within the previous 12 months;
(ix) any basic award for unfair dismissal;
(x) and any reasonable reimbursement of the whole or part of an apprentice's or articled clerk's premium.

578 It should be noted that there may be delay of up to six months in paying these sums, unless the amounts claimed are corroborated by the trustee or liquidator.

579 In addition, the Fund can become liable to pay unpaid employer's contributions to an occupational pension scheme, but here it is the duty of the trustees or managers of the scheme, or others competent to act on its behalf, to make the request, and payment may be delayed for the like purpose as payments for the Redundancy group. Employees and occupational schemes can complain to the Industrial Tribunal if money due is not paid.

Contracting Out

Restrictions

580 A provision in a contract which apparently excludes or limits the operation of the Employment Protection Act 1975 or precludes anyone from complaining to or bringing any proceedings before a tribunal or from making any proper reference, claim, complaint or application to ACAS* is void except:

(i) a provision in a collective agreement excluding rights to guarantee payments or in respect of redundancy if an exemption order* is in force in respect of it;

(ii) any union membership agreement so far as it affects the rights of an employee to participate in certain union activities; To opposite)

(iii) any agreement to refrain from instituting or continuing proceedings before a tribunal where a conciliation officer has taken action; and

(iv) certain agreements between employers and unions or employees to the extent that the agreement varies or supersedes an award made by the Central Arbitration Committee.

Jurisdiction of Industrial Tribunals

581 Industrial Tribunals can deal with the following:

(i) A complaint by an employee that the employer has failed:

a) to provide him with a written statement of reasons for his dismissal;

b) to pay him under a protective award;

c) to give him, or pay him for, time off for trade union duties; or to look for work or arrange for training;

d) to give him time off for trade union activities or public dities;

e) to pay him during suspension on medical grounds;

f) to pay her maternity pay;

g) to pay him a guarantee payment*;

(ii) A complaint by an employee that:

    h) action has been taken against him on account of trade union membership or activities;

    (i) the Secretary of State has failed to make him payments from the Redundancy Fund in respect of sums due from it on the employer's insolvency.

(iii) A complaint by an employer that the Secretary of State has failed to pay him a maternity pay rebate;

(iv) A complaint by a trade union that an employer has dismissed or proposes to dismiss workers as redundant without having consulted it;

(v) A complaint on behalf of an occupational pension scheme that the Secretary of State has failed to make payments to the scheme's funds on an employer's insolvency;

(vi) An application by an employee for interim relief pending determination of a complaint for unfair dismissal, or for the revocation or variation of such interim relief;

(vii) An application by an employer for the revocation or variation of an order giving such interim relief;

(viii) A reference by an employer or employee to determine what particulars ought to have been included in an itemised pay statement;

(ix) An appeal by an employer on the ground that the Secretary of State:

    a) has reduced a redundancy rebate on the employer's failure to notify him of his redundancy proposals;

    b) has refused to pay him a maternity pay rebate; and

(x) A claim for damages in certain cases permitted by ministerial order. No such orders have so far been made.

Offences

582 A number of criminal offences exist within the field of employment law. The principal ones are:

failure by an employer to notify redundancy proposals to the Secretary of State, and

failure by a liquidator or trustee to provide accurate information in insolvency cases.

Trustee Investments

Origin of Powers and Restrictions

583 Trustees are allowed to invest their trust funds only in a manner permitted by law. The most restrictive code of such permissions is found in the Trustee Investments Act 1961, but, mainly in the case of private trusts created, for example, by will, the investment powers of the trustees may be enlarged (but cannot be reduced) beyond the scope of the Act, provided that the additional powers are conferred in the very instrument creating the trust. Such additional powers can, indeed, be so wide as to enable trustees to invest funds exactly as if the money were their own.

584 In the case of funds belonging to a local authority, this will never, and in the case of charitable and other public funds seldom be, the case. The Trustee Investments Act 1961 is thus the main personal protection for the trustee. If ordinarily he makes rash investments, he may be required personally to replace the resulting losses, because he is bound, as a trustee, to act prudently, but if losses result from investment carried out in accordance with the Act of 1961 he will be exonerated.

Statutory Securities

585 The Act defines statutory securities, and a trustee who invests in securities outside the definition does so at his peril. With a few exceptions the definition excludes stocks not repayable in sterling, stocks not quoted on a stock exchange, and securities not fully paid up. The statutory securities are classified into Narrower Range Investments and Wider Range Investments. Trustees may, without special action, invest in the narrower range, which is itself divided into those on which written advice is not required, and those on which it is. Broadly speaking narrower range investments are those in which the capital is considered safe by reason of an official guarantee or the security of a mortgage or debenture.

586 The difficulty is that in a period of inflation the fixed interest investments represented by the list of narrower range securities, decline steadily both in market value and in real value, and many funds invested in such securities before 1914 (when the modern inflation set in) had by 1960 lost up to 95% of their real value. To combat this, the 1961 Act defined this new class of Wider Range Investments. These are other securities (ie. equities) issued by a United Kingdom company, units in unit trusts designated under the Prevention of Frauds Act 1958, and building society shares, and it permitted trustees to invest in such securities, but only if they first took an irrevocable step.

The Division of the Fund

587 The irrevocable step is that they must formally divide the fund into two exact halves, one for Narrower Range, the other for Wider Range Investment. Such a division can be made once only and, once made, an asset from one part can be transferred to the other only against an equal compensating transfer in the opposite direction, and any new money coming to the fund must be apportioned so as to increase the value of each part by an equal amount. If property comes to the narrow range part, which ought to be in the other, it must either be converted into a narrower range investment or transferred to the wider range part with a compensating transfer. This sometimes happens, for example, where conversion rights in convertible debentures are exercised. On the other hand, if property (save interest or dividends) accrues to the trustees as owners of an investment in either part (for example, a bonus issue) it belongs to that part, unless it was secured by a payment (e.g. on a Letter of Rights) in which case it must be treated as an investment.

588 It is not, of course, envisaged that the two parts shall remain equal; indeed the countrary is to be expected, but the Act enjoins trustees to diversify investments.

Advice

589 Trustees cannot claim to have sought proper advice unless it was given or confirmed in writing. Proper advice is advice by a person whom the trustees reasonably believe to be qualified by his ability or practical experience in financial matters. It will not be invalidated simply because the adviser gives the advice in the course of his employment. In practice it may be thought wise to secure the advice of a stock broker, stock jobber or investment consultant.

Narrower-Range Investments Not Requiring Advice

590 Defence Bonds, National Savings Certificates, an Ulster Savings Certificates, Ulster Development Bonds, National Development Bonds and British Savings Bonds.

591 Deposits in the National Savings Bank, ordinary deposits in a trustee savings bank and deposits in a bank or department thereof certified under section 414 (3) and (5) of the Income and Corporation Taxes Act 1970.

Narrower-Range Investments Requiring Advice

592 Securities issued by H.M.Government in the United Kingdom (UK), the Government of Northern Ireland or the Government of the Isle of Man, (other than those mentioned in paragraphs 600 and 601) being fixed-interest securities registered in the UK or the Isle of Man, Treasury Bills or Tax Reserve Certificates.

593 Any securities whose interest payments are guaranteed by H.M. Governments in the UK or Northern Ireland.

594 Fixed-interest securities issued in the UK by any public authority, or nationalised industry or undertaking in the UK.

595 Fixed-interest securities issued in the UK by the government of any overseas territory within the Commonwealth or by any public or local authority within such a territory, being securities registered in the UK.

596 Securities issued in the UK by the bodies mentioned in paragraph 605 being securities registered in the UK and in respect of which the rate of interest is varied by reference to one or more of the following:

    (a) the Bank of England's minimum lending rate;
    (b) the average rate of discount of allotment on 91-day Treasury Bills;
    (c) a yield on 91-day Treasury Bills;
    (d) a London sterling inter-bank offered rate;
    (e) a London sterling certificate of deposit rate.

597 Fixed-interest securities issued in the UK by the International Bank for Reconstruction and Development, being securities registered in the United Kingdom, and fixed interest securities issued by the Inter-American Development Bank or by the European Coal and Steel Community.

598 Securities issues in the UK by
  (i) the International Bank for Reconstruction and Development or by the European Investment Bank or by the European Coal and Steel Community, being securities registered in the UK or
  (ii) the Inter-American Development Bank, being securities in respect of which the rate of interest is variable by reference to one or more of factors (a) to (e) mentioned in paragraph 596 above.

599 Debentures issued in the UK by a company with a paid-up capital of more than £1,000,000 incorporated in the UK, being debentures registered in the UK, unless the company has failed to pay dividends in the previous 5 years.

600 Stock of the Bank of Ireland, and Bank of Ireland 7 per cent Loan Stock 1986/1991.

601 Debentures issued by the Agricultural Mortgage Corporation Limited, or the Scottish Agricultural Securities Corporation Limited.

602 Loans to any local authority charged on all or any of its revenues or on a fund into which all or any of those revenues are payable; in any fixed-interest securities issued in the UK by any such authority for the purpose of borrowing money so charged; and in deposits with any such authority by way of temporary loan made against a receipt for the loan by the treasurer or other officer of the authority so that, if requested to charge the loan as aforesaid, it will either comply with the request or repay the loan.

603 The definition of local authority for this purpose includes not only any local authority in the United Kingdom but

    (a) any authority all the members of which are appointed or elected by one or more such local authorities;

    (b) any authority the majority of the members which are appointed or elected by one or more such local authorities being an authority which has power to issue a precept to a local authority in England and Wales, or a requisition in Scotland, or to the expenses of which such a local authority is or can be required to contribute;

    (c) the Receiver for the Metropolitan Police or a combined police authority; the Belfast City and District Water Commissioners;

    (d) the Great Ouse Water Authority and other river authorities; any district council in Northern Ireland.

604 Any such securities issued in the U.K. by any authority mentioned in paragraph 603, secured upon revenues of the authority or on a fund in respect of which the rate of interest is variable by reference to one or more of factors (a) to (e) mentioned in paragraph 596 above.

605 Debentures or guaranteed or preference stock of any incorporated statutory water undertakers which, during each of the ten years immediately preceding the calendar year of the investment, paid a dividend of not less than 3½ % on its ordinary shares.

606 Deposits by way of special investment in a trustee savings bank or in a department (not being a department certified under section 414 (3) or (5) of the Income and Corporation Taxes Act 1970) of a bank any department of which is so certified.

607 Deposits in a building society designated under section one of the House Purchase and Housing Act 1959.

608 Mortgages of freehold property in England and Wales or Northern Ireland and of leasehold property in those countries under leases with, at the time of investment, not less than sixty years to run, and in loans on heritable security in Scotland.

609 Perpetual rent-charges on land in England and Wales or Northern Ireland and fee-farm rents (not being rent-charges) issuing out of such land, and in feu-duties or ground annuals in Scotland.

610 Perpetual rent-charges on land in England and Wales or Northern Ireland and fee-farm rents (not being rent-charges) issuing out of such land, and in feu-duties or ground annuals in Scotland.

611 Certificates of Tax Deposit.

Wider-Range Investments

612 Any equities issued in the UK by a company with a paid up capital of more than £1,000,000 incorporated in the UK, unless it has failed to pay a dividend for five years.

613 Shares in any building society designated under section one of the House Purchase and Housing Act 1959.

614 In any units, or other shares of the investments subject to the trusts, of a unit scheme, if there is in force at the time of investment an order under section 17 of the Prevention of Fraud (Investments) Act 1958, or as the case may be under section 16 of the Prevention of Fraud (Investments) Act (Northern Ireland) 1940.

GLOSSARY

mainly of expressions marked*

Abatement
1) Self remedy for a nuisance by one injured by it.
2) The termination of certain court proceedings by a supervening cause which removes one of the parties.
3) The amount by which particular debts or legacies have proportionably to be reduced if there is not enough money to pay them all out in full.

ACAS
Stands for the Advisory, Conciliation and Arbitration Service of the Deprtment of Employment.

Account Stated
An admission by a person that he owes a sum of money to the person named in the account.

Administrator
A person (usually a close relative) appointed by the court to wind up a deceased's affairs, when no valid will exists or when one exists but it names no executor.

Arbitration
The settlement of a dispute by extra-judicial means. It is a form of contract (to abide by the arbitrator's decision) and enforceable as such.

Assault
In civil law this means the threat of violence to the body, not the violence itself. (See Battery) In criminal law, however, it does mean the violence itself.

Assignment
The transfer of the remaining period of a lease, by one tenant to another. This usually needs the landlord's consent.

Bailment
The committal of moveable property to another by putting it into his possession. I bail my hat to the hotel when I hand it over to the cloakroom attendant.

Banker's Commercial Credits
This is mainly an international practice designed to circumvent a triple combination of difficulties, viz:
i) an intending seller of goods or services such as a play may not be able to finance production and transport, ii) the intending buyer or other entrepreneur may not be able to pay until he has resold the goods, or otherwise secured custom, and, iii) owing to distance or linguistic obstacles, the credit-worthiness of each is unknown

to the other. Hence three interlinked transactions, viz:
a) a clause in the sale agreement that the buyer must request his bank to open a
credit in the seller's favour, irrevocable by the buyer for a fixed period;
b) a consequent agreement to that effect, between the buyer and his bank, under
which he undertakes reimbursement, pays a commission and gives a lien on the
shipping documents or bills of lading;
c) the buyer's bank informs the seller that it has opened the credit in his favour
and undertakes to pay when the shipping documents are presented. The bank,
being locally informed, would not do this if it doubted the buyer's credit.

Bankruptcy
The condition of a debtor who cannot pay his debts in full **and** who has been
adjudicated bankrupt by the High or a County Court. The **effect** of adjudication
is to vest all his assets (with minor exceptions) in a receiver and eventually a
trustee for the benefit of his creditors. He is also disqualified from being a
company director or a member of a public authority, and must not enter into
commercial dealings without disclosing that he is a bankrupt.

Bankruptcy, Act of
Something done, suffered or omitted by a person, which entitles any one of his
creditors to petition the court for a receiving order against his assets. The
commonest acts of bankruptcy are failure to pay a debt exceeding £50 within two
months of a demand, failure to satisfy a court judgment, and fraudulent acts such
as assigning property to evade seizure, and going abroad to evade creditors.

£750

Battery
The tort of applying violence to the body. "The least touching in anger."
(See Assault)

Bond
A deed whereby a person, called the obligor, binds himself to pay a specified sum
to another, called the obligee, on a specified day. A single bond is a bond merely
to pay money. A double or conditional bond is a bond to do something by a
certain day or pay money; hence performance of the promised act discharges the
obligation to pay.

Cause of Action
A legal rule which an aggrieved party can enforce if he has sufficient evidence to
bring himself within it.

Chattel
Property which at Common Law could be protected only by a personal action for
damages, not for the possession of the property itself; in effect anything except an
interest (including a mortgagee's interest) in land. The word is related to *cattle*.

Choses (*Fr = things*) in Action
All personal rights of property which can be enforced or claimed by action in the

courts and not by taking physical possession, eg, debts, insurance policies, patents and copyrights.

Choses in Possession
Rights of Property capable of being physically possessed.

Codicil
An addition to a will. It has to be executed in the same way as a will.

Contract under Seal
A contract in the form of a deed.

Conveyance
A deed which transfers a legal interest in land.

Corporeal Hereditament
A form of tangible property included in the definition of land. It consists of substantial and permanent objects including the land itself, buildings and other things such as fences and walls built into it, and trees (but not shrubs).

Council
See Local Authority.

Covenant
A deed or a provision in a deed whereby the covenantor undertakes something, for example, to maintain a fence, produce certain documents on demand, or make a periodical payment to someone.
In the last example, the obligation being absolute, the executant's income is deemed to be diminished by the amount covenanted and, provided that the covenant is made for a certain minimum period of years, the tax liability of himself and his covenantee will be altered.

"Darling of Equity"
One who has bought trust property for its full value and without actual or imputable knowledge of the trust. He cannot be forced to give up the property or to act as a trustee himself.

Deed
See Bond, Conveyance, Covenant, Deed Poll, Fine, Indemnity, Indenture.

Deed Poll
A deed with a straight edge (see Indenture). Nowadays, most commonly used to declare a change of surname.

Distress (vb distrain)
The seizure, under authority of a court order, of goods to satisfy a debt.

Easement
A private right, such as a right of way, existing for the benefit of one piece of land across another.

Equitable Interest
1) Any right, eg, under a trust, enforceable by equity.
2) Especially any interest in land other than a Fee Simple and a term of years absolute.

Equity
The concurrent system of principles derived from the notion of fair dealing, which supplements the common law, and which prevails over it in case of a conflict. It acts against the person, it does not heedlessly depart from the common law; it requires parties to be prepared to see justice done and not to have acted improperly. It operates primarily through trusts.

Estoppel
A rule which may be stated thus: If a person makes an assertion upon the faith of which another alters his position, the assertor is forbidden in a dispute with the other person to deny the assertion. It has been described as a shield, not a sword, ie, a resort for a defendant not a plaintiff.

Executor
A person named in a will to carry it out. (See Probate)

Exception
In an insurance policy against a generic type of risk, is a sub-class of that risk which the policy does **not** guard against eg, a policy against natural calamities may except damage by flood.

Exclusion
In an insurance policy is a limitation on the amount generally payable under the policy, eg, "£1000 exclusive of the first £10".

Exclusive Licence
A copyright owner's licence in writing, signed by him or on his behalf, which confers on the licensee the right, to the exclusion of all other persons, including the licensor, to exercise a right which would otherwise be exercisable solely by the copyright owner.

Fine (Obselete)
A three sided indenture (q.v.).

Great Britain
England, Wales and Scotland only. It does not include Northern Ireland, Isle of Man or the Channel Islands.

Guarantee Payment
A payment which an employer is bound to make to an employee for a particular day, not withstanding that he has no work to offer him on that day.

Incorporeal Hereditament
An invisible form of property included in the definition of land. Of the ten types of incorporeal hereditament only easements, profits, rents and rights of common are now important.

Indemnity
A deed undertaking to compensate (by money or in some other way) a person on the occurrence of a defined event.

Indenture (Obsolescent)
A deed written out twice on one sheet of parchment, each executed by two parties, and cut apart to that each party can keep a copy, but so as to leave indented edges which can be fitted together to prove authenticity.

Infant
A person under 18.

Injunction
An order by the court to a party to do, or to desist from doing, something. Disobedience may lead to imprisonment (of a somewhat comfortable kind) until the order is complied with.

Insolvency
The generic term for an inability to pay debts leading, in the case of an individual, to bankruptcy* and, in the case of a company, to compulsory liquidation.

Intestacy
The condition of dying without leaving a valid will.

Land Charges
Include restrictive convenants, estate contracts, equitable mortgages and charges, equitable easements and other permanent burdens on land.

Land Charges Register
A register kept in London and in various provincial towns where such land charges as are otherwise difficult to establish, may be registered under the name of the owner of the land they affect.

Legacy
A gift in a will to a specific person or for a specific purpose. It is paid out after the debts (including taxes) have been paid. If there is not enough to satisfy all the legacies, they are reduced proportionably to each other. (See Abatement)

Letters of Administration
An administrator's equivalent of probate. The administrator can **not** act to protect the property until after it is granted.

Licence — Removal of
The moving of an existing Justices' Licence from the premises to which it applies to other premises.

Licence — Transfer of
The substitution of a new licensee for an existing licence, without a change of premises.

Lien
The right acquired in advance, to take possession of a chattel as security for a debt.

Limitation
1) The limitation of shareholders' liability for company debts to the amount represented by their shares.

2) The limitation of the liability of owners of ships and aircraft for injury to goods and persons unless the injury is due to their personal actions. The liability is restricted in the absence of a special contract, to the following sums calculated on the empty weight of the ship or aircraft:

	Ships per ton	Aircraft
Persons	£124.55	£10,845 per person
Goods etc.	£40.18	£10.85 per kilo of goods

3) The period after which legal proceedings may not be brought to assert a civil right which, consequently, lapses. The main cases are:

Recovery of land	12 years
Action on a Deed	12 years
Action on a simple contract	6 years
Action in Tort except the next following	6 years
Action in respect of personal injuries by negligence, nuisance or breach of duty	3 years

Time begins to run from the violation of the right, or from the time it was discovered if fraudulently concealed, and there are provisions for extension where a plaintiff was prevented from proceeding because his own rights vested after the injury, and where his rights were more recently acknowledged.

4) The limitation under the Employment Act 1982 on the amount of damages which a successful plaintiff may secure in any one action in tort against a trade

union. The amount depends upon the size of the union's membership, as follows:-

Membership	Amount
up to 4,999	£10,000
5000 to 24,999	£50,000
25,000 to 99,999	£125,000
100,000 or more	£250,000

Local Authority
In **England:** The Greater London Council, London Borough Councils, The Corporation of the City of London, The Councils of Counties, Districts, and Parishes.
In **Wales:** The Councils of Counties, Districts and Communities.
In **Scotland:** The Councils of Regions, Districts and Islands.

Notice
1) Knowledge which a person actually has or ought, with reasonable dilligence, to have.
2) The period between the notified intention to assert a right, and its assertion.

Novation
The replacement of an existing contract by a new one.

Off-Licence
A Justices' Licence to sell liquor for consumption **off** the premises.

On-Licence
A Justices' Licence to sell liquor for consumption **on** the premises.

Precept
An order to a rating authority from another authority, to collect enough money from the ratepayers to cover the precepting authority's expenditure. The amount of the precepts received and the amounts needed by the rating authority itself are levied as a single consolidated rate.

Prescription
A title to property based on nothing but enjoyment by a person and his predecessors for a very long time.

Probate
The authority granted by the court to an executor to carry out the will. It is not granted until all the taxes have been paid, but he may act to protect the property before it is granted.

Rating Authority
In London the London Borough Councils, elsewhere the District Council. (See Precept)

Receiver
A person appointed by the court to intercept the profits and income and, if necessary, manage the property and assets of a person (eg, a bankrupt, a defaulting mortgagor or a company in liquidation) for the benefit of creditors.

Re-entry
A landlord's right, which must be specifically reserved in the lease, to repossess the land, the subject of the lease, if the tenant has broken a covenant in it.

Residuary Legatee
The person to whom a testator leaves the residue of his property.
(See Residue)

Residue
That which remains in a deceased's estate after the debts and specific legacies have been satisfied.

Specialty
An old word for a deed.

Specific Restitution
The return of an object to its owner instead of compensation for its loss.

Statutory Authority or Body
Any organisation created or authorised by an act of parliament, including local authorities, the Inner London Education Authority, Electricity, Gas and Water Boards, and British Rail. They may do only that which their statutes permit or which may fairly be inferred from such permission.

Statute Barred
See Limitation (3)

Surrender
The voluntary return to a landlord of the remaining period of a lease by the tenant.

Testator
One who has made a will.

Vacating Receipt
The receipt endorsed on a mortage showing that it has been redeemed.

Vesting Assent
A deed made by an executor or administrator transferring the property of a deceased to a person entitled to it.

ADDRESSES

A

ABSA (Association for Business Sponsorship of the Arts)
12 Abbey Churchyard, Bath.

ACME
15 Robinson Road, Bethnal Green, London E2.

Actors' Benevolent Fund
6 Adam Street, London WC2.

Actors' Charitable Trust
Bedford Chambers, Covent Garden, London WC2.

Advisory, Conciliation & Arbitration Service (ACAS)
11-12 St. James' Square, London SW1.

Arlis (Art Libraries Society)
77 Kinnerton Street, London SW1.

Arts Council of Eire
70 Merrion Square, Dublin 2.

Arts Council of Great Britain
105 Piccadilly, London W1.

Arts Council of Northern Ireland
181a Stranmillis Road, Belfast.

Association of British Theatre Technicians (ABTT)
4 Great Pulteney Street, London W1.

B

Ballet Rambert
Mercury Theatre, Ladbroke Road, London W11.

Barbican Arts Centre
Barbican, London EC2.

Bath Academy of Art
Corsham, Wilts.

BBC
Broadcasting House, Portland Place, London W1.

Birmingham School of Music
Paradise Circus, Birmingham 3.

Board of Customs & Excise
Kings Beam House, Mark Lane, London EC3.

Board of Inland Revenue
Somerset House, London WC2.

British Actors Equity Association
8 Harley Street, London W1.

British Council
10 Spring Gardens, London SW1.

British Institute of Recorded Sound
29 Exhibition Road, London SW7

British Library
2 Sheraton Street, London W1

British Museum
Great Russell Street, London WC1.

British Music Information Centre
10 Stratford Place, London W1.

British School at Rome
1 Lowther Gardens, Exhibition Road, London SW7.

British Theatre Association
9/10 Fitzroy Square, London W1.

British Theatre Institute
30 Clareville Street, London SW7.

C

Calouste Gulbenkian Foundation
98 Portland Place, London W1.

Camberwell School of Arts and Crafts
Peckham Road, London SE5.

Carnegie UK Trust
Comely Park House, Dunfermline, Fife, Scotland.

Central Register of Charities
St. Alban's House, Haymarket, London SW1.

Central School of Art & Design
Southampton Row, London WC1.

Central School of Speech & Drama
Embassy Theatre, Eton Avenue, London NW3.

Centre for Arts & Related Studies
City University, Northampton Square, London EC1.

Ceramics Institute
Federation House, Station Road, Stoke on Trent.

Charity Commission
14 Ryder Street, London SW1.

Charity Commission, Northern Office
Graeme House, Derby Square, Liverpool.

Chelsea School of Art
Manresa Road, London SW3.

Chichester Festival Theatre
Oaklands Park, Chichester, Sussex.

Church Commissioners
1 Millbank, Westminster, London SW1.

Composers' Guild of Great Britain
10 Stratford Place, London W1.

Companies Registry, England
Companies House, Crown Way, Maindy, Cardiff.

Companies Registry, Scotland
102 George Street, Edinburgh.

CORAA (Council of Regional Arts Associations)
31 Shelton Street, London WC2.

Courtauld Institute
Woburn Square, London WC1.

Crafts Council
11 Waterloo Place, London SW1.

D
Dartington Hall
Nr. Totnes, South Devon.

Department of Education & Science
Elizabeth House, York Road, London SE1.

Design Council
28 Haymarket, London SW1.

Duncan of Jordonstone College of Art
Perth Road, Dundee.

E
Eastern Arts Association
8/9 Bridge Street, Cambridge.

East Midlands Arts
Mountfields House, Forest Road, Loughborough.

Edinburgh College of Art
Lauriston Place, Edinburgh.

Electoral Reform Society
6 Chancel Street, London SE1.

Exeter College of Art & Design
Earl Richard's Road, North Exeter, Devon.

F
Falmouth School of Art
Woodlane, Falmouth, Cornwall.

G
Glasgow College of Art
167 Renfrew Street, Glasgow.

Glyndebourne
Lewes, East Sussex.

Greater London Arts Association
25/31 Tavistock Place, London WC1.

Guildhall School of Music & Drama
Barbican, London EC2.

H
Historic Buildings Councils, England
25 Savile Row, London W1.

Historic Buildings Councils, Scotland
25 Drumsheugh Gardens, Edinburgh 3.

Historic Buildings Councils, Wales
Welsh Office, Cathays Park, Cardiff.

Horniman Museum & Library
London Road, Forest Hill, London SE23.

I
ILAM (Institute of Leisure & Amenity Management)
ILAM House, Lower Basildon, Reading.

Incorporated Society of Musicians
10 Stratford Place, London W1.

Independent Broadcasting Authority
70 Brompton Road, London SW3.

Institute of Incorporated Photographers
Amwell End, Ware, Herts.

International Theatre Institute
31 Shelton Street, London WC1.

K

Kent Opera
Pembles Cross, Egerton, Ashford, Kent.

L

Laban Centre for Movement and Dance
Goldsmith's College, New Cross,
London SE14.

Leverhulme Trust
15-19 New Fetter Lane, London EC4.

Lincolnshire & Humberside Arts
St. Hugh's, 23 Newport, Lincoln.

London Chamber of Commerce &
Industry
69 Cannon Street, London EC4.

London Contemporary Dance Theatre
17 Dukes Road, London WC1.

London Festival Ballet
39 Jay Mews, London SW7.

Loughborough College of Art &
Design
Radmoor, Loughborough, Leicester.

M

Maidstone College of Art
Oakwood Park, Maidstone, Kent.

Malone Society
2 Church Street, Beckley, Oxford.

Manpower Services Commission
1 Cambridge Gate, London NW1.

Merseyside Arts Trust
6 Bluecoat Chambers, School Lane,
Liverpool.

Museums and Galleries Commission
2 Carlton Gardens, London SW1.

Musicians Union
60/62 Clapham Road, London SW9.

N

National Art Collections Fund
8 Duncannon Street, London WC2.

National Council for Drama Training
5 Tavistock Place, London WC1.

National Federation of Music Societies
Francis House, Francis Street,
London SW1.

National Federation of Women's
Institutes
39 Eccleston Street, London SW1.

National Gallery
Trafalgar Square, London WC2.

National Galleries of Scotland
The Mound, Edinburgh.

National Library for Scotland
George IV Bridge, Edinburgh.

National Library for Wales
Llyfrgell Genedlaethol Cymru,
Aberystwyth.

National Museum of Wales
Cathay's Park, Cardiff.

National Portrait Gallery
St. Martin's Place, Charing Cross Road,
London WC2.

National Society for Art Education
7a High Street, Corsham, Wiltshire.

National Society of Painters, Sculptors
& Printmakers
17 Carlton House Terrace,
London SW1.

National Theatre
South Bank, London SE1.

New English Art Club
17 Carlton House Terrace,
London SW1.

North Wales Arts Association
10 Wellfield House, Bangor, Gwynedd.

Northern Arts
10 Osborne Terrace, Newcastle upon
Tyne.

North West Arts
12 Harter Street, Manchester.

Norwich School of Art
St. George Street, Norwich, Norfolk.

O

Opera North
Grant Theatre, 46 New Briggate, Leeds,
West Yorkshire.

P

Patent Office
25 Southampton Buildings,
London WC2.

Percival David Foundation for Chinese Art
53 Gordon Square, London WC1.

Performing Right Society Ltd.
29-33 Berners Street, London W1.

R

Royal Academy of Dancing
48 Vicarage Crescent, London SW11.

Royal Academy of Dramatic Art
62-4 Gower Street, London WC1.

Royal Academy of Music
Marylebone Road, London NW1.

Royal Academy Schools
Burlington Gardens, London W1.

Royal Ballet
Royal Opera House, Covent Garden,
London WC2.

Royal Ballet School
155 Talgarth Road, London W14.

Royal Choral Society
Royal Albert Hall, London SW7.

Royal College of Art
Kensington Gore, London SW7.

Royal College of Music
Prince Consort Road, London SW7.

Royal College of Organists
Kensington Gore, London SW7.

Royal Commission for the Exhibition of 1851
1 Lowther Gardens, Exhibition Road,
London SW7.

Royal Drawing School
17 Carlton House Terrace,
London SW1.

Royal Fine Arts Commission
2 Carlton Gardens, London SW1.

Royal Fine Arts Commission for Scotland
22 Melville Street, Edinburgh 3.

Royal Institute of Painters In Water Colours
17 Carlton House Terrace,
London SW1.

Royal Literary Fund
11 Ludgate Hill, London EC4.

Royal Military School of Music
Kneller Hall, Twickenham.

Royal Northern College of Music
~~Addington Place, Croydon, Surrey.~~
184 Oxford Rd, Manchester M13 9R

Royal School of Church Music
Addington Place, Croydon, Surrey.

Royal School of Needlework
25 Princes Gate, London SW7.

Royal Scottish Academy of Music & Drama
St. George's Place, Glasgow 2.

Royal Scottish Country Dance Society
12 Coates Crescent, Edinburgh.

Royal Society of Arts
6-8 John Adam Street, London WC2.

Royal Society of British Sculptors
108 Old Brompton Road, London SW7.

Royal Society of Musicians
10 Stratford Place, London W1.

Royal Society of Painters In Water Colours
Bankside Gallery, 48 Hopton Street,
London SE1.

Royal Society of Portrait Painters
17 Carlton House Terrace, SW1.

S

SACLAT (Standing Advisory Committee on Local Authorities and the Theatre)
25 Buckingham Gate, London SW1.

Sadler's Wells Royal Ballet
Sadler's Wells Theatre, Rosebery
Avenue, London EC1.

St. Martin's School of Art
Charing Cross Road, London WC2.

Scottish Arts Council
19 Charlotte Square, Edinburgh.

Scottish Ballet
261 West Princes Street, Glasgow 4.

Scottish Education Department
New St. Andrew's House, St. James'
Centre, Edinburgh.

Scottish National Gallery of Modern Art
Inverleith House, Royal Botanic
Garden, Edinburgh.

Scottish National Portrait Gallery
1 Queen Street, Edinburgh.

Scottish Opera
Theatre Royal, Hope Street, Glasgow 2.

Sir John Soane's Museum
13 Lincoln's Inn Fields, London WC2.

Slade School
University College London, WC1.

Society of Authors
84 Drayton Gardens, London SW10.

Society of Theatre Consultants
9 Fitzroy Square, London W1.

Society of West End Theatre (SWET)
Bedford Chambers, Covent Garden,
London WC2.

Society for Theatre Research
77 Kinnerton Street, London SW1.

Society of Women Artists
17 Carlton House Terrace,
London SW1.

South East Arts Association
9-10 Crescent Road, Tunbridge Wells,
Kent.

South East Wales Arts Association
Victoria Street, Cwmbran, Gwent.

Southern Arts Association
19 Southgate Street, Winchester, Hants.

South West Arts
23 Southernhay East, Exeter, Devon.

Stage Management Association
81 St. Mary's Grove, London W4.

Stratford Memorial Theatre
Stratford on Avon, Warwickshire.

T

Tate Gallery
Millbank, London SW1.

Theatre Advisory Council
4 Great Pulteney Street, London W1.

Theatrical Management Association
Bedford Chambers, Covent Garden,
London WC2.

Theatre Writers' Union (TWU)
9 Fitzroy Square, London W1.

Tower of London
London EC3.

Trinity College of Music
Mandeville Place, London W1.

U

United Society of Artists
17 Carlton House Terrace, London
SW1.

V

Victoria & Albert Museum
South Kensington, London SW7.

W

Wallace Collection
Hertford House, Manchester Square,
London W1.

Welsh Arts Council
Holst House, 9 Museum Place, Cardiff.

Welsh College of Music & Drama
Castle Grounds, Cathays Park, Cardiff.

Welsh National Opera
John Street, Cardiff.

West Midlands Arts
Lloyds Bank Chambers, Market Street,
Stafford.

West Wales Association for the Arts
Dark Gate, Carmarthen, Dyfed.

Whitechapel Art Gallery
Whitechapel High Street, London E1.

Winston Curchill Memorial Trust
15 Queen's Gate Terrace, London SW7.

Writers' Guild of Great Britain
430 Edgware Road, London W2.

Y

Yorkshire Arts Association
Glyde House, Glydegate, Bradford,
Yorkshire.

INDEX